THE TRANSFORMATION OF POLITICAL COMMUNICATION IN CHINA

From Propaganda to Hegemony

Series on Contemporary China   (ISSN: 1793-0847)

Series Editors: Joseph Fewsmith *(Boston University)*
                 Zheng Yongnian *(East Asian Institute, National University of Singapore)*

*To view the complete list of the published volumes in the series, please visit:
http://www.worldscibooks.com/series/scc_series.shtml

Series on Contemporary China – Vol. 29

THE TRANSFORMATION OF POLITICAL COMMUNICATION IN CHINA

From Propaganda to Hegemony

Xiaoling Zhang

Nottingham University, UK

World Scientific

NEW JERSEY · LONDON · SINGAPORE · BEIJING · SHANGHAI · HONG KONG · TAIPEI · CHENNAI

Published by

World Scientific Publishing Co. Pte. Ltd.

5 Toh Tuck Link, Singapore 596224

USA office: 27 Warren Street, Suite 401-402, Hackensack, NJ 07601

UK office: 57 Shelton Street, Covent Garden, London WC2H 9HE

Library of Congress Cataloging-in-Publication Data
Zhang, Xiaoling, Dr.
    The transformation of political communication in China : from propaganda to hegemony / by Xiaoling Zhang.
        p. cm. -- (World Scientific series on contemporary China, ISSN 1793-0847 ; vol. 29)
    Includes bibliographical references and index.
    Summary: "This book examines different dynamics such as marketisation, globalisation and new media technologies that have driven the transformation of China's media industry--one of the primary battlegrounds where ideological, social and economic struggles are fought--against the backdrop of the growing tensions between economic growth, globalisation, and political control in China."--Publisher's description.
        ISBN-13: 978-9814340939
        ISBN-10: 9814340936
    1. Mass media policy--China. 2. Communication policy--China. 3. Communication--Political aspects--China. 4. Communication in politics--China. I. Title. II. Series: Series on contemporary China ; v. 29.
        P95.82.C6Z39 2011
        302.230951--dc23

                                                                    2011017555

British Library Cataloguing-in-Publication Data
A catalogue record for this book is available from the British Library.

Typeset by Stallion Press
Email: enquiries@stallionpress.com

Printed in Singapore.

In memory of my father Zhang Fugeng

Contents

Acknowledgements

A number of people have generously contributed to the completion of this book. I would like to thank Yongnian Zheng who has inspired me and greatly influenced my way of thinking and ideas. The discussions we had in the small common room in the China House at the University of Nottingham, very often joined by other colleagues, on the political changes in China and the transformation of the media prompted me to investigate further into the transformation of the media, its rational and the impact.

A profound debt of gratitude is owed to the British Academy, the Research Committee of Nottingham University and the School of Contemporary Chinese Studies which provided funding for me to go to China to conduct field work, without which this book project would not have come into being. I would also like to thank the East Asian Studies Institute, National University of Singapore, which generously took me as a visiting research fellow in 2009 for ten weeks, and not only provided a dynamic research environment with like-minded colleagues but also the necessary working conditions and above all, time, to concentrate on this project.

I am very grateful to Guo Zhenzhi from the School of Journalism, Tsinghua University, China, for her invaluable help in obtaining access for me to materials in Chinese, introducing me to her students who are now working in the media industry, and above all for sharing insights with me.

This study would not have been possible either without the help of the interviewees. For reasons of confidentiality, I have not named them in this book but I am forever thankful to them for their willingness to be interviewed and their generosity in providing me with invaluable materials.

I am also deeply indebted to my family in the UK and China. I would like to thank my mother for understanding why I could not spend more time with her when I was in China. I would also like to thank my life partner Herman who has given me both moral support and practical support, i.e., whenever I am in trouble with my computer, whether it is the computer in my office or the computer at home. My daughter, Linda and my son, Tom have also shown great understanding when I could not spend more time with them. Finally, I would like to dedicate this book to my father who passed away ten years ago.

Xiaoling Zhang
University of Nottingham, UK
August 2010

List of Tables and Figures

List of Tables

List of Figures

Notes on Abbreviations

BBC   British Broadcasting Corporation
CASS   Chinese Academy of Social Sciences
CCP   Chinese Communist Party
CCTV   China Central Television
CNN   Cable News Network
CNNIC   China Internet Network Information Centre
CNR   China National Radio
CPPCC   Chinese People's Political Consultative Conference
DOP   Department of Propaganda
GAPP   General Administration for the Press and Publication
GWTV   The Great Wall TV Platform
MII   Ministry of Information Industry
NPC   National People's Congress
NGOs   Non-governmental Organisations
NCRTS   National Centre for Radio & TV Studies
PRC   People's Republic of China
PRER   Pearl River Economic Radio
RSF   Reporters Sans Frontiers
SARFT   State Administration for Radio, Film and Television
SARS   Severe Acute Respiratory Syndrome
SCIO   State Council Information Office

SMEG	Shanghai Media & Entertainment Group
SMG	Shanghai Media Group
SOE	State-owned Enterprise
SPPA	State Administration of Press and Publishing
UN	United Nations
VOA	Voice of America
WHO	World Health Organisation
WTO	World Trade Organisation

Chapter

I

Introduction

The rise of the People's Republic of China (hereafter China) as a great power has made the country an object of particular fascination: China is the world's largest ongoing experiment in a form of regime — authoritarianism — which is supposed to be in global decline. At the end of the Cold War, Francis Fukuyama famously concluded that the evolution of human societies through different forms of government had culminated in modern liberal democracy. Yet, China has explicitly rejected "Western-style" democracy as a suitable political system. Indeed, in spite of all the debates on the historical and contemporary motives of the leadership of the Chinese Communist Party (CCP), China's developmental path since the late 1970s has aroused the interest of the whole world, especially as the existing economic and political models seem to be pushing against the limits of their ability to cope with the pressures of globalisation and expanding humanity, including those regions currently understood as belonging to the "developed" world. Much has been written in the attempt to answer questions such as the following: How has the Chinese Communist Party-state installed and managed new social relations in a changing socioeconomic system since the economic reform and open-door policy launched by Deng Xiaoping in 1978? How has it managed to survive the legitimacy crisis and stayed ahead of challenges to its authoritarian leadership after its crackdown on the pro-democracy movement in 1989? How sustainable is its reform strategy — pursuing pro-market economic policies under one-party rule? Finally, why has China's transformation not followed the expected trajectory that other former communist countries have taken?

The Chinese phenomenon is being studied by a variety of academic disciplines. However, the role the media plays in the transformation of China is of critical importance. As Sparks and Reading[1] pointed out, each nation's communications infrastructure and philosophy are usually closely in step with the nation's basic political and social systems, and ideology. An examination of the transformation of the media and communications touches on a key issue of contemporary politics in China as the transformation of the media is both a causal factor and a resulting outcome of the whole process of transformation in China. It will deepen our understanding of not only the nature and stability of authoritarian regimes but also the implications for the political systems worldwide and the global flow of information.

During the Maoist period when China was economically autarkic and culturally sealed off from the outside world, the media was a mere propaganda tool to serve the interests of the ruling party. In the last three decades, however, the spectacular economic growth in China has brought about a radically changed communications landscape, shaped by an unprecedented growth in the number of newspapers, TV stations, satellite channels and internet expansion. As a result, the media has become more commercialised, pluralised, and liberalised. Changes in China's media sphere during this period are not the result of a single event, but the consequence of a number of overlapping and interrelated factors and forces, including commercialisation, the new global and regional structure and environment, pluralisation which partly (but not exclusively) results from commercialisation, China's multifaceted interactions with the outside world,

---

[1] Sparks, Colin and Reading, Anna, 'Understanding Media Change in East Central Europe', *Media, Culture and Society*, 16(2), (1994), pp. 243–270.

and the advancement of new information and communication technologies. More importantly, all these changes are happening in the context of the CCP's continuous efforts to stay in power with legitimacy, by struggling to manage the whole process of reform and to stay ahead of the unwanted consequences from reform. These overlapping and interrelated factors and forces constitute the backdrop of the transformation of the media and communications space, although the backdrop itself is in continuous flux.

There have been heated debates in China studies, political science as well as media studies on the implications of the changes taking place in China. However, the focus of the debates has shifted over the past few years. In the 1980s and 1990s, debates were more focused on the possibility of democratisation as China opened itself up to different forces unleashed by economic reforms. For instance, would commercialisation entail an autonomous media that could lead to the emergence of a non-state-interfered public sphere, or would the entrenchment of commercialisation actually become a new form of control in the Chinese media? Would diversification of media play a more independent role in political debates, or would censorship, both political and commercial, and constraints on ownership, prevent the formation of public spheres? Are the technologies underlying new media such as the Internet so inherently liberating that censorship and control would become irrelevant, or does this argument reflect a naïve technological determinism? With China's accession to the World Trade Organisation (WTO) around the turn of the century, observers also started to ask whether transnational media firms would press China to have a more open and free environment, or whether they were compromising with China's leaders to gain market access. All these questions are concerned with the impact of the new forces brought about by the economic reform of the authoritarian system. In the past few years however, the CCP regime has not only been relatively stable since the early 1990s, and very different from other illegitimate regimes that solely depended on harsh suppression of resistances, but also poised itself to be a great player in the world economically and politically. Hence, debates have also emerged on China's influence on the rest of the world. In other words, instead of asking whether the increasing volume of images and ideas crossing China's borders would offer the Chinese people access to new and liberating ideas, observers and analysts have started to wonder if globalisation is offering the Chinese Party-state the opportunity to influence the world with its authoritarian propaganda.

How the above questions are answered not only has an important bearing on our assessments of the CCP's prospects for managing the socio-political changes taking place in China, but more importantly, also impacts our understanding of the nature and prospects of the authoritarian political power in contemporary China.[2] The key to answering these questions, I believe, lies in analysing the CCP's ability to dominate by means of political and ideological leadership — the construction of hegemony — and to create a symbolic environment and meaning system within which the Party-state's performance is framed in ways conducive to positive perceptions of the regime. This framing is imperative "so that the latter is seen as, for example, competent, efficient, fair, committed to the realisation of the common interest while avoiding publicly manifest partiality or bias, aware of social woes and arranging for compensation of the less affluent, capable of selectively embracing the benefits of globalisation while defending national interests on a complex international terrain, and so on".[3] To that end, it is important to examine how the Chinese Communist Party-state uses the much transformed media as one of the most important powers to shape public opinions in a much changed socio-economic environment.

When foreign media watchdogs examine the degree of press freedom in China, they invariably focus on the apparent ubiquitous control that the CCP wields over the media. For instance, according

---

[2] McCormick, Barrat L., 'Recent Trends in Mainland China's Media: Political Implications of Commercialisation', *Issues and Studies,* 39(1)/38(4), (March 2003/December 2002), pp. 175–215.

[3] Holbig, Heike and Gilley, Bruce, 'In Search of Legitimacy in Post-revolutionary China: Bringing Ideology and Governance Back In', German Institute of Global and Area Studies (GIGA) Working Paper 127, (2010), p. 12, from http://www.giga-hamburg.de/dl/download.php?d=/content/publikationen/pdf/wp127_holbig-gilley.pdf, accessed on 29 July 2010.

Table 1.1. Ranking of China from the Worldwide Press Freedom Index by RSF[4]

Year	Number of Countries	Ranking of China
2002	139	138
2003	166	161
2004	167	162
2005	167	159
2006	168	163
2007	169	163
2008	173	167
2009	175	168

to the worldwide press freedom index compiled by Reporters San Frontiers (RSF), China is ranked dismally and consistently at the bottom of the list.

Consistent with Freedom House which considers 58% of the Chinese population to be living under an "unfree regime", the RSF considers China among the "worst predators of press freedom" where journalists continue to risk imprisonment or their lives for keeping others informed. Yet, I argue that such assessments underestimate the complex and dynamic changes that have occurred on China's media scene since 1978. While it is true that the Party's control over the media remains strong, it increasingly has to contend with a proliferation of various media channels driven by market forces and the population's insatiable demand for alternative sources of information. In other words, these assessments do not reflect the balance the Party-state has to find between maintaining control and managing increasing demands by the general public for timely and accurate information, both of which have implications for China's stability, both immediate and long term. They do not reflect the CCP's continuous quest to adjust, change, modify, and sometimes radically alter aspects of public policy and state institutions in order to conform to the perceived demands of legitimacy.

---

[4] Compiled by the author from http://en.rsf.org/.

This book attempts to take a close look at the newly formed intertwining nature of the CCP, the media and various other factors that have driven the transformation of media and communications in China, against the backdrop of China's overall political and social evolution. For this purpose, it does not dwell on the most obvious changes taking place in the media — the relative autonomy gained by the media thus far and the undoubtedly significant resistant and subversive forces, which are fundamental assumptions of this book, and which haven't been amply documented by other researchers. Instead, this book focuses on the political and conceptual transition of China's media industry from propaganda to hegemony, as a result of accelerated commodification, globalisation, intensified ideological and social struggles, and rapid advancement of media technologies, especially the Internet. It argues that the Party-state, beset by the intensifying societal frustrations and pressures of modernisation but focused on the task of staying in power with legitimacy, has been constructing hegemony by continually adapting to new realities, whether political, social or technological. It advances the thesis that the CCP has over the years, developed not only an awareness of the importance of the media as an essential component of its "governing capacity" (*zhizheng nengli* 执政能力) in contemporary China, but also sophisticated strategies to manage the greatly transformed media for consensus and persuasion, so as to retain its legitimacy as the sole ruling organisation. Central to the argument is the idea that the Party-state has been constructing hegemony by a mixture of consensus and coercion, and that the media, which has undergone unprecedented changes since 1978 but is still regarded as one of the most important powers for consensus-building, has gained more bargaining power with the Party-state, thus forming a new force driving the transformation of the Chinese media.

ORGANISATION OF THE BOOK

This first chapter introduces the key concepts and theoretical issues that I have explored in constructing my analytical frameworks, the methodologies adopted, and the theoretical frameworks — mainly Gramsci's hegemony but also Max Weber's legitimacy — for general arguments to be presented in the book. I argue that analytical frameworks based on the state vs. society dichotomy (such as the state vs. the Internet or the state vs. the market) on their own are unable to capture the complexity of what the Chinese media, and indeed China as a whole, is going through. I propose to take the unique relationship of negotiation between the Party-state and media organisations as one of the most important dynamic forces driving the transformation of the Chinese media forward. This chapter also lays out the Chinese political and social context for the application of the theoretical framework.

The first part of Chapter Two offers a brief historical review of the developments in the Chinese communications-state-society nexus since 1949, with a view to present the institutional and ideological legacies Chinese socialism has left behind for the post-socialist era on the one hand and the nature and extent of the transformations that have taken place since 1978 on the other. It then maps some of the key stages of change through the entire Chinese media system since reform, highlighting both the continuities and changes, including its expansion in depth and scope, as well as its growth in sophistication since the early 1990s. In doing so, the struggle between the major forces, political, commercial, global and technological, that have been transforming the practice of communications in China is clearly shown.

The third chapter moves on to the most important controversies in the existing literature on the transformation of Chinese media, namely, debates on the implications of the different forces on the development of the Chinese media (including commercialisation, the extent of diversification, the new media technology development and globalisation) which have great political and social implications on the development of political reform in China.

Chapter Four shows how the Party-state proactively adjusts to the new communication realities created by commercialisation, globalisation and new media technologies, not only through coercion but more importantly, consensus, in order to remain in power with legitimacy. It shows that while repressive measures are still part of the recipe for control, the Party-state has also embraced and promoted the various forces and turned itself into one of the world's most sophisticated in the management of the media.

Chapter Five examines the ongoing tense negotiation and re-negotiation between the central government that tries to control the media and the media that resists the control. The chapter shows that in the ongoing negotiating relationship between the media and the Party-state in China, the media is as much a product of the socio-political transformation as it is an influence on the transformation of China's political system.

Chapter Six demonstrates by providing examples of how the Party-state, in the face of a public transformed by economic reform and globalisation, has actively adjusted to, and sometimes effectively harnessed, powers brought about by commercialisation, globalisation and new media. The first example shows how the current affairs programme "Focus" (Jiaodian Fangtan 焦点访谈) of China Central Television (CCTV), a product of reform, has been used as a far more effective means for the construction of hegemony than crudely made propaganda. The second example shows how the Party-state has embraced the view that apolitical communications loaded with subtle political implications rather than crudely made propaganda may be more effective in transmitting the desired messages, via its colonisation of the popular Spring Festive Gala Party as a vehicle for maintaining its hegemony and promoting its reform agenda. The final example shows not only how the Party-state meets the challenge of new media technologies in order to survive and thrive, but also how it has taken them on board and exploited them to its advantage.

The concluding chapter summarises the major findings and arguments of this study. Based on discussions in previous chapters, an attempt is also made to interpret these transformations and predict new scenarios for the future development of communications, its implications for the political system in China and its impact on the global flow of information.

SEARCHING FOR A NEW ANALYTICAL FRAMEWORK

As many academics and observers of China have found out, what is most interesting, though also certainly most frustrating, is that just like everything else that is undergoing transformation in China, the transformation of the media and communications does not lend itself to analysis by the application of a single theory or model. Indeed, many recognise that China represents one of the most complex and atypical transitions from authoritarianism to a "third way" — neither orthodox Marxism nor liberal democracy. The complexity is compounded by the rapid changes happening in China: whatever is written today may very well be out of date tomorrow. To try to sum up Chinese activities, even in such a limited albeit very dynamic area as media and communications, is a formidable task. For this reason, I draw on China studies, political science, history and media studies for the examination and analysis of the transformation of the media and communications scene in China. It is also important to make explicit at the beginning, some of the theoretical assumptions and normative commitments underpinning this study.

The basic and dominant framework for analysing Chinese media changes heretofore has been a "Party-state vs. society" paradigm, or the modified versions of "Party-state vs. market", "Party-state vs. the Internet", or "Party-state vs. globalisation", all of which assume an inherently antagonistic relationship between the dominant Party-state, the media and the media publics. It has been a very significant context in which the Chinese media system is examined. I argue that none of the approaches on their own is able to capture the growing complexity and dynamics of contemporary China. First of all, we are faced with the obvious difficulty of transferring theoretical commitments first developed in the context of liberal capitalist media (like those in the USA, Canada and Western Europe) to China, which has a completely different political and cultural context.

Secondly, without challenging the importance of these frameworks, I believe any simple juxtaposition of the state and the social forces as inherently hostile is insufficient for the explanation of the social changes and state adaptation that have taken place in China. These analytical frameworks on their own imply that the Chinese Communist Party-state is a dominantly monolithic entity promoting marketisation of the economy, while ignoring the new socio-economic changes that have taken place since reform. Indeed, scholarly and journalistic literature has perpetuated one belief that the media in an authoritarian China is all about control by the ruling party. This belief is oversimplification at best: firstly it ignores the challenges to the control of the ruling party which are coming from the rapid growth of the media as well as social forces, both of which are changing the political process in China. Michael Anti, a former Nieman Fellow using Twitter, the artist and blogger, Ai Weiwei, and Hu Shuli, the founding editor of Caijing magazine, China's leading independent financial news weekly, are some prominent examples. The Chinese media industry has also undergone unprecedented changes. As to be discussed in Chapter Two, it has transformed from being a mere mouthpiece of the Party-state into an entity that performs multiple functions. In the face of a public armed with new information, which in turn creates new demands, especially among the middle class that can afford to have access to alternative sources of information, the Party-state is pressurised to adjust and refine its institutions and methods of governance in order to stay in power with legitimacy. Secondly, this belief ignores the fact that political control over the media has itself become an arena of struggle, with internal divisions and conflicts of interest among different state bureaucracies,[5] including state broadcasting versus telecommunications authorities, broadcasting bureaus and television stations, not to mention those at central, provincial, municipal, and county levels. One major concern for the CCP and the government that will continue to shape China's public policies, particularly media policies, is the survival of the CCP's rule with legitimacy. In its transition from a revolutionary party to a party in power, the CCP has come a long way in learning to stay in power with legitimacy. As Lynn White points out, China's political elite is schizophrenic about "modern" legitimacy.[6] Over the past three decades, the Party-state has derived its legitimacy largely from

---

[5] Zheng, Yongnian, *Technological Empowerment: The Internet, State, and Society in China,* (Palo Alto: Stanford University Press, 2007).

[6] White, Lynn T., 'Introduction — Dimensions of Legitimacy', in Lynn T. White (Ed.), *Legitimacy: Ambiguities of Political Success or Failure in East and Southeast Asia* (Singapore: World Scientific, 2005), pp. 1–28.

its economic performance. The other performance criteria that is better suited to the modern age is international status. Indeed, the Chinese people have waited long enough for a brand new century, a Chinese century, in which China emerges as a benevolent world leader, and China's cultural legacy, particularly its updated Confucian heritage, is to play a large part in pioneering a responsible, egalitarian path towards modernisation and development.[7] It is a broad vision that is also broadly popular as it plays strongly to Chinese (not just mainland) pride. Further commercialisation and globalisation of the media industry is thus expected. However, as Wang rightly argues, today's China is moving in the direction in which the public assessment of the state's performance has shifted from the economic sphere to the political sphere.[8] "Herein lies the dilemma for the Chinese state. Currently, economic performance helps to legitimate the regime. But with economic development comes a public that will question more and more such a performance-based legitimacy. As Huntington has put it, 'The legitimacy of an authoritarian regime was also undermined if it did deliver on its promises. By achieving its purpose, it lost its purpose.'"[9] The tensions between economic growth, globalisation, and political control are reflected in the conflicts of interest among different state bureaucracies and between different interest groups wanting to exert influence on media policies. The Ministry of Information Industry, for instance, has different priorities from the Ministry of Public Security, thus causing tensions and conflicts. Indeed the frequent shift in media policies reflects the divisions at the top. Not surprisingly, the media has become one of the primary battlegrounds where ideological, social and economic struggles are fought, and media policy has become more susceptible than ever to interventions from different forces and agents.

---

[7] Zhu, Ying, *Television in Post-Reform China: Serial Dramas, Confucian Leadership and Global Television Market*, (London: Routledge, 2008), p. 126.

[8] Wang, Zhengxu, 'Political Trust in China: Forms and Causes', in Lynn T. White (Ed.), *Legitimacy*, pp. 113–139.

[9] Huntington, Samuel, *The Third Wave: Democratization in the Late Twentieth Century*, (Oklahoma: University of Oklahoma Press, 1992), pp. 54–55.

Thirdly, I argue that while such frameworks (the liberal democratisation argument) as "Party-state vs. market" hold validity at certain levels of analysis and will continue to serve as powerful analytical tools in furthering the opening of the Chinese media market,[10] it is imperative for us to examine other major dynamics in China's media transformation process, especially the relationship characterised by interaction and negotiation between the state and the media in the current political context. It is true that the Chinese media, like all other social forces in China, "[is] not autonomous in pursuing [its] own development because [it] depends on [its] relations with the government",[11] yet due to its significant role in the attainment and maintenance of consent because of its ability to organise popular world-views, a unique system or relationship "marked by negotiation has developed between state authorities and regulators and media and cultural units".[12] Following Lu[13] who treats autonomy and independence as two analytically distinct concepts in the examination of civil societies in China, I argue that many Chinese media organisations enjoy some autonomy, but remain heavily dependent on the state for their survival, legitimacy and operation. Failing to recognise the interaction and negotiation between the state and other actors, especially media organisations, as one of the major forces in driving media development in China, will have two consequences. On the one hand, it will strengthen the belief in the coming collapse of communist rule in China and on the other, obscure the fact that the interaction and negotiation have affected the development of the media industry and political changes in China.

This leads me to the theoretical framework that I draw on for the understanding and interpretation of the changes that have been a

---

[10] Zhao, Yuezhi, *Communication in China: Political Economy, Power and Conflict*, (Lanham: Rowman & Littlefield Publishers Inc., 2008), p. 145.

[11] Zheng, *Technological Empowerment*, p. xvii.

[12] This relationship of negotiation between the Party-state and media and cultural units is first noticed and mentioned by Rosen, Stanley, in Ying Zhu (Ed.), *Television in Post-reform China*, pp. XIV–XXII. This relationship is not very clearly defined or followed by Stanley.

[13] Lu, Yiyi, *Non-Governmental Organisations in China*, (Oxford: Routledge, 2008).

major challenge confronting China scholars. Needless to say, the interpretation of what has taken place influences our predictions of what will take place in the future. Placing this study in the developing context of commercialisation, diversification, globalisation, new media technologies, and the CCP's construction of hegemony (considered together and understood as both a political and economic process), Gramsci' concept of hegemony is utilised for the understanding and interpretation of the meanings of all the changes that have taken place since reform in China.

THEORETICAL FRAMEWORK FOR THIS STUDY

China scholars are divided in their interpretation of China's approach to development. Some are convinced by China's developmental model that sustained economic development, gradualist economic transition, and a neo-authoritarian developmental state are essential to economic take-off. Some optimistic scholars believe that sustained economic development will make the younger generation of leadership, led by Hu, further downplay the role of ideology and adopt a more liberal and open stance towards both economic and political reform in China.[14] Others, however, are more pessimistic about the future of China because of the failure of the Medicare reform, the occasional strengthening of media control and the ever-increasing social problems prevailing in Chinese society,[15] while still others predict the total collapse of the CCP and even China as a nation-state. For instance, Pei[16] argues that because the Communist Party must retain significant economic control to ensure its political survival, gradualism will ultimately fail. Although Richard Baum argues that

---

[14] Yang, Dali, *Remaking the Chinese Leviathan: Market Transition and the Politics of Governance in China*, (Palo Alto: Stanford University Press, 2004).

[15] E.g., Gilley, Bruce, *China's Democratic Future: How It Will Happen and Where It Will Lead*, (New York: Columbia University, 2004);

Dickson, Bruce, *Red Capitalists in China: The Party, Private Entrepreneurs, and Prospects for Political Change*, (New York: Cambridge University Press, 2003).

[16] Pei, Minxin, *China's Trapped Transition*, (Cambridge, MA: Harvard University Press, 2006).

"consultative Leninism — bolstered by robust economic growth — has arguably extended the lifespan of China's authoritarian regime", he also cautioned that over the longer term, "China's unreconstructed Leninists may already be living on borrowed time."[17] Susan Shirk also indicates such possibilities in her book *China: Fragile Superpower*.[18] The logic for such predictions is simple: the CCP will fall because it cannot meet social demands, as Shambaugh argues: "Leninist systems are not well equipped to respond to the changing demands and needs of society — precisely because they are intrinsically top-down 'mobilisation' regimes [that do not] possess the feedback mechanisms to hear and respond to aggregated social needs and demands".[19] This seems more real than ever as the Party-state today faces more pressing challenges of increasing social stratification and inequality, widespread corruption, pervasive unemployment, rising crime, and rural unrest.[20] China's multifaceted interactions with the outside world and a public having easier access to alternative sources of information have further undermined the Party's control over society.

However, in spite of all the different interpretations, two things are certain: first, the Chinese Party-state has so far been successful in resisting the transformation from authoritarianism to democracy of any western type. In other words, contrary to what the optimistic scholars have hoped, China has not followed, and is not following, the path of political transition that other communist states have taken. Secondly, the pessimistic interpreters of the changes have focused their attention on the authoritarian character of the Party-state governance and ignored the differences between the Maoist

---

[17] Baum, Richard, 'The Limits of Consultative Leninism', in Mark Mohr (Ed.), *China and Democracy: A Contradiction in Terms?* Asia Program, Woodrow Wilson International Center for Scholars, Special Report, No. 131, June 2006, pp. 13–20.

[18] Shirk, Susan L., *China: Fragile Superpower*, (New York: Oxford University Press, 2007).

[19] Shambaugh, David, *China's Communist Party: Atrophy and Adaptation*, (Washington, DC and Berkeley: Woodrow Wilson Center Press and University of California Press, 2008), p. 7.

[20] *Ibid.*, pp. 3–4.

regime and the post-Mao one. It is true that despite its rapid socio-economic transformation in the past three decades, China remains a one-party system with the CCP being the only ruling party in the country. Yet when we delve below the label of authoritarianism, we instantly discover "evidence of an agile, responsive, and creative party effort"[21] in adapting to the new socio-economic situation by introducing changes into the existing political system in order to stay in power with legitimacy. In the words of Yu Keping, Deputy Director of the Central Translation Bureau, the think-tank for the Hu-Wen administration, "[D]emocracy is a good thing. ... In fact, we have already introduced democratic elements and made rapid progress".[22] Democratic elements have thus been introduced to Chinese politics, such as village democracy, township elections and decentralisation of power. These changes have generated tremendous challenges to the CCP but just as Zheng trenchantly argues in his latest book on the CCP,[23] political changes in an authoritarian state like China do not always imply the weakening of party control and the empowering of society, especially if the changes are introduced gradually by the CCP itself.

Many different labels have been used in an attempt to describe and interpret China's new developments[24] such as "post-totalitarianism, post-authoritarianism and soft-authoritarianism", "capitalist-authoritarian hegemony", and "revolutionary or resilient authoritarianism". Shambaugh believes "it is becoming a hybrid party with elements of East Asian neo-authoritarianism, Latin American corporatism and European social democracy all grafted to Confucianist-Leninist roots".[25]

---

[21] Holbig and Gilley, *In Search of Legitimacy in Post*, p. 27.

[22] Yu, Keping, 'Let Democracy Serve China; Economic Crisis can also be Political Opportunities', at http://npc.people.com.cn/GB/28320/160692/166630/9897870.html, accessed on 18 September 2009.

[23] Zheng, Yongnian, *The Chinese Communist Party as Organisational Emperor: Culture, Reproduction and Transformation*, (Oxford, New York: Routledge, 2010).

[24] *Ibid.*, p. xii.

[25] Shambaugh, David, 'The Road to Prosperity', *Time*, 28 September 2009, at http://www.time.com/time/magazine/article/0,9171,1924366-3,00.html, accessed on 22 October 2009.

In spite of all the different labels, the Chinese official line has remained rather consistent: China is firmly on the path of building "socialism with Chinese characteristics" or developing a "socialist market economy", whatever definitions these may have. What is more important, beyond the business of labelling, is "a broad consensus that the current regime in China enjoys relatively robust legitimacy across the population".[26] It is often believed that totalitarian regimes are indifferent to public opinions. The logic is that if the state possesses a strong repressive capacity — comprising 1.9 million policemen and a 660,000-member specialised internal security force as in the case of China[27] — that has proved capable of containing large-scale local disturbances in the past, dissatisfaction among the populace does not matter. However, any leadership needs to determine if policies work and are popular and, if not, why. Leaders of a Leninist regime are especially sensitive to the extent and nature of grassroots grumbling precisely because such dissatisfaction finds no stable institutional outlets. The modern state cannot rely solely on instructions, commands and punishment. It educates, informs, persuades, and discourages. In the past three decades, in responding to the changes brought about by unprecedented, rapid socio-economic transformation, the CCP has attempted to bring to perfection, its machinery for governing an increasingly complex Chinese society. Holbig and Gilley identify a clear shift in emphasis from an earlier economic-nationalistic approach to a more ideological-institutional approach in the CCP's quest for legitimacy.[28] The CCP's willingness to learn from public opinion at home and abroad, and the application of these lessons have been stunning to witness. So far, the effort has been successful: according to a study on governance by the World Bank, using subjective perception-based data taken over the period from 1996 to

---

[26] Holbig and Gilley, *In Search of Legitimacy in Post,* p. 6.

[27] Pei, M., 'The Political Impact of the Economic Crisis on China', at http://www.carnegieendowment.org/publications/index.cfm?fa=view&id=23185, accessed on 14 July 2010.

[28] Holbig and Gilley, *In Search of Legitimacy in Post,* p. 6.

2006: China ranks seventh out of the world's twenty most-populous countries in terms of political stability.[29]

The most important source and channel for the CCP to determine the will of the masses, whether with the aim of fulfilling or thwarting it, is arguably the Chinese media. During the pre-reform period, journalists in China had the dual responsibility of writing propagandist material for public consumption and writing "internal reference materials" for restricted circulation within the Party leadership. Through their internal reporting, journalists identified flaws in policies and social problems, and highlighted the need for specific reforms and disciplinary actions against delinquent officials. Obviously, in its heightened attention to the Party's morality over society, or its struggle to maintain its ideological domination over the state and society in the reform period, the CCP has continued to use the media to play the pivotal role of not only "the mouth and tongue" of the Party, but also its "eyes and ears". In November 1989, shortly after the June Fourth Incident, the then Propaganda Chief, Li Ruihuan, re-emphasised at a journalism "seminar" a seldom publicised function of the media. "News units should reflect problems to the highest authorities", he told the assembled editors and journalists, by "means of reference materials and briefings for internal use. They should make every effort to ensure the accuracy of the materials and not adulterate them, lest they provide erroneous information".[30] The question to ask then is, how is the media made to continue to perform the same role in the much changed socio-economic circumstances, since it has undergone unprecedented transformation?

The exploration of the transformation of the media and communications and its role in the reproduction of the CCP's domination in China should be placed in the context of the CCP's struggle for

---

[29] Kaufmann, Daniel, Kraay, Aart and Mastruzzi, Massimo, 'Governance Matters VI: Governance Indicators for 1996–2006', *World Bank Policy Research Working Paper* 4280 (July 2007), at http://ssrn.com/abstract=999979, accessed on 20 February 2009.

[30] Hood, Marlow, 'The Use and Abuse of Mass Media by Chinese Leaders during the 1980s', in Chin-Chuan Lee (Ed.), *China's Media, Media's China*, (Boulder, Colo: Westview Press, 1994), pp. 37–57.

hegemonic rule and its interest in maintaining power with legitimacy. To that end, this study draws on Italian Marxist Antonio Gramsci's concept of hegemony.[31] Focusing on the hegemonic nature of state-society relations, the Gramscian paradigm can help us understand why the CCP leadership has been successful so far in resisting the transformation from authoritarianism to democracy of any Western type, and how and why China maintains a one-party domination while accommodating democratic elements. Gramsci's concept of hegemony also provides us with a powerful tool to examine the new relationship between the CCP in its construction of hegemony and the transformed and transforming media organisations, as well as the implications of this relationship.

Gramsci's Concept of Hegemony

Gramsci made a clear distinction between "hegemonic" and "coercive" forms of rule in human history: hegemony means the supremacy of one group or class over other classes or groups, by means other than reliance on violence or coercion. These means include coercion, bargaining and reciprocity.[32] According to Gramsci, hegemony is achieved through a combination of the three, with different mixtures of the components at different times. Gramsci believed that compared with coercion, which is exercised as a way to force people to do what you want them to do against their will, bargaining and reciprocity are often more effective forms of domination. To him, hegemony is "a relation, not of domination by means of force, but of consent by means of political and ideological leadership. It is the organisation of consent".[33]

In Gramsci, developed capitalist polities whose legitimacy rests on a fairly stable "equilibrium of hegemonic and coercive institutions"

---

[31] Gramsci, Antonio, *Selections from the Prison Notebooks*, Q. Hoare and G. Nowell Smith (Eds. and trans.) (New York: International Publishers, 1971).

[32] Zheng, *The Chinese Communist Party as Organisational Emperor*, p. 33.

[33] Simon, Roger, *Gramsci's Political Thought: An Introduction*, (London: Lawrence & Wishart Ltd., 1991), p. 2.

are directly contrasted with an older type of state that lacks this vital reciprocity with civil society.[34] Though he took careful note of direct interventions by the state against society to suppress opposition, to contain dissent, and to manipulate educational, religious, media and other ideological apparatuses for the production of popular compliance, Gramsci expressly linked hegemony to a domain of public life (e.g., "civil society" or "public sphere") that is relatively independent of such controls and hence makes its achievement a far more contingent process. Notably, Gramsci's view of civil society differs from the liberal-democratic model in the assumption that civil society is not separate from the state. What Gramsci has accomplished is a broadening of the notion of the state: to Gramsci, the state is seen as the ensemble of socio-economic and political-cultural relations. Thus the state becomes the integral state, where the latter is defined as "dictatorship + hegemony", and as "political society + civil society". In this way the state is not separate from society and market but is fundamentally shaped by the latter. Because states are parts of societies, during the process of interacting with each other, they affect each other and transform each other. In the absence of civil societies, the state needs to create one (alternative voices) to maintain equilibrium and stay in power with legitimacy. By creating "civil society" and a "public sphere", the bourgeois class is able to maintain its hegemonic position and reproduce its power domination over other social classes.

Gramsci advocated that a culturally diverse society can be dominated by one class that has a monopoly over the mass media and popular culture. Indeed, to establish its supremacy, a dominant class must not only impose its rule via the state, it must also demonstrate its claims to "intellectual and moral leadership", and this requires the arts of persuasion, a continuous labour of creative ideological intervention. The capacity "to articulate different visions of the world in such a way that their potential antagonism is neutralised", rather than simply suppressing those visions beneath "a uniform concept of the

---

[34] Gramsci, *Selections from the Prison Notebooks*, p. 54.

world", is the essence of hegemony.[35] Furthermore, Gramsci carefully distinguished elements of pluralism and competition, as well as persuasion and consent, from the more repressive and coercive forms of rule and the conventional process of governing in the administrative sense.

Gramsci's hegemony is susceptible to change and negotiation not just because it involves the pursuit of consent under conditions of pluralism but also because this process operates through social relations of dominance and subordination structured by class inequality and therefore involves contradictory and opposing interests. To Gramsci, hegemony is characterised by uncertainty, impermanence, and contradiction. As Geoff Eley and Keith Nield point out, hegemony "is not a fixed and immutable condition, more or less permanent until totally displaced by determined revolutionary action, but is an institutionally negotiable process in which the social and political forces of contest, breakdown and transformation are constantly in play".[36] In this sense, hegemony is always in the process of construction; it is always open to modification, and under specific circumstances, may be more radically transformed or even broken down altogether. In other words, the dominance of a given social group has to be continually re-negotiated in accordance with the fluctuating economic, cultural, and political strengths of the subordinate classes.

Applying Gramsci's Concept to the Chinese Context

Writing at the beginning of the process of globalisation with all his concerns set within the global perspective of the 1930s, Gramsci famously claimed that while in the West, rule was already hegemonic, in the East, rule was still more by naked force of the state.[37] Today,

---

[35] Laclau, Ernesto, *Politics and Ideology in Marxist Theory*, (London: New Left Books, 1977), p. 161.

[36] Eley, Geoff and Nield, Keith, 'Why Does Social History Ignore Politics?', *Social History*, 5(2), (1980), pp. 249–271.

[37] Davidson, Alastair, 'Hegemony, Language and Popular Wisdom in the Asia Pacific', in Richard Howson and Kylie Smith, (Eds.), *Hegemony: Studies in Consensus and Coercion*, (New York: Routledge, 2008), pp. 63–79.

however, "under global capitalism, in all cases, at all times, and in all places, all rule combine[s] both force and consensus, or hegemony, whatever the practical mix of force and consensus".[38] Although Gramsci developed the concept of hegemony as a means to capture the power dynamics and power differences and to show the ways and means by which power persists and endures over time within modern bourgeois society,[39] it is of particular relevance and has great explanatory value to the understanding and explanation of the strength and the resilience of the political power structure in contemporary China.

First of all, Gramsci's hegemony provides researchers with a powerful framework for the examination of the Party-state, not as a monolithic entity but as an organisation that has transformed to lead and direct the country's development through its continuous institutional adjustments and adaptations, in accordance with the changing socio-economic environments. Indeed, economically, China is pulling off one of the most successful economic transitions in history, and yet it maintains the core political status quo of one-party rule. This political power structure has proven relatively strong and has provided a basis for some resistance to pressure for neoliberal reform. It is therefore logical to argue that the political system has not remained static: what is obvious is that China is moving away from totalitarianism towards hegemonic rule, which, according to Gramsci, is characterised by a combination of coercion and consensus, with the latter as the driving force in social and political relations.[40] White points out, "Most contemporary Asian regimes act, most of the time, as if they accepted that open violence cannot for long procure compliance".[41] In the contemporary world where debates about the role of the state now centre on good governance, ideology, civil society, the rule of

---

[38] *Ibid.*

[39] Fontana, Benedetto, 'Hegemony and Power in Gramsci', in Richard Howson and Kylie Smith, (Eds.), *Hegemony: Studies in Consensus and Coercion*, (New York: Routledge, 2008), pp. 81–105.

[40] Harada, Yoko, 'Hegemony, Japan, and the Victor's Memory of War', in Richard Howson and Kylie Smith, (Eds.), *Hegemony: Studies in Consensus and Coercion*, (New York: Routledge, 2008), pp. 219–236.

[41] White, 'Introduction', p. 23.

law and the importance of institutions in the creation of viable states,[42] those states that lack these characteristics are believed to have "failed", or at least be failing.[43] While the Chinese Party-state is determined to sustain this regime at all costs and by all means, China as a new member of the international community does care about its image. Therefore although much of the structure and essential nature of the political system has remained largely the same, the CCP, obsessed not only with staying in power but also doing so with legitimacy, has been constantly revamping and perfecting this regime, and progressively undergoing amplification and modernisation since the early 1990s.[44] It is true that in maintaining its domination, the CCP has often resorted to coercive measures to stop popular demonstrations and to suppress political organisations threatening its authority. However, coercion alone cannot explain the Party's hold on power. After thirty years of reform, Chinese society has developed a momentum of its own and the Party-state has had to rely on measures other than coercion to stay ahead of challenges to its hold on power. Bruce Dickson argued that the CCP was in a phase of what Samuel Huntington called "adaption". However, Dickson did not believe that, like the KMT in Taiwan, the CCP would follow the path to democratisation.[45] In his more recent work, Dickson contends that the initiative of the CCP to recruit private-sector entrepreneurs is consistent with the evolution of other East Asian ruling parties. That

---

[42] Fukuyama, Francis, *State Building: Governance and World Order in the Twenty First Century*, (London: Profile Books, 2004).

[43] E.g., Gros, Jean-Germain, 'Toward a Taxonomy of Failed States in the New World Order: Decaying Somalia, Liberia, Rwanda and Haiti', *Third World Quarterly*, 17(3), (1996), pp. 458–461;

Kaplan, Robert, 'The Coming Anarchy', in Phil Williams, Donald M. Goldstein and Jay M. Shafritz, (Eds.), *Class Readings and Contemporary Debates in International Relations*, 3rd Edition, (Belmont, California: Thomson Wadsworth, 2006);

Rotberg, Robert I., 'Failed States, Civil Wars and Nation Building', in Robert J. Art and Robert Jarvis, (Eds.), *International Politics: Enduring Concepts and Contemporary Issues*, 7th Edition, (New York: Pearson Longman, 2005).

[44] Zhao, *Communication in China*, p. 61.

[45] Dickson, Bruce, *Democratization in China and Taiwan: The Adaptability of Leninist Parties*, (Oxford: Clarendon, 1997).

is, this initiative is an effort to "adapt" itself in order to save itself. In other words, the Party-state has to meet the challenge or face the risk of obsolescence. It has to be adaptable and open to embracing elements from different countries and political systems, especially Western democratic countries. In solving the problem of governance in transitional periods, the Party-state tries to develop a form of leadership, which helps to legitimise its authority and rule over the society. The neo-Gramscian approach or "hegemonisation" as Zheng calls it,[46] captures the essence of how the CCP has so far sustained itself: The CCP has selectively adopted democratic elements and neoliberal logic as a strategic calculation to strengthen its dominance without changing the character of the state apparatus. The recruitment of private entrepreneurs into the Party is one of the examples of the CCP adjusting itself to suit China's changing political reality: the CCP used to regard itself as a proletariat party representing the interests of workers, peasants, soldiers and government officials. Now, party membership has opened up to other social groups, especially the newly arising social groups such as private entrepreneurs who used to be regarded as the Party's enemies. To a great extent, whether the party can maintain its domination depends on whether and how it responds to growing social complexity and value shifts, and coordinates the different and often conflicting interests. To maintain its domination over capitalists, the CCP has to represent the interests of this newly arising social force and allocate certain space for them within the regime.

For the same reason, grassroots democracy has also been introduced and well established. In addition to the wellknown and widely established semi-competitive elections at the village level, a variety of direct-election experiments on the part of People's Congresses, leadership committees, and the leaders of both government and party at the township and county (or district and city) have taken place. Non-governmental organisations (NGOs) have been encouraged to develop and are invited to help formulate public policies. The anti-corruption stance at all levels of the government and efforts to make

---

[46] Zheng, *The Chinese Communist Party as Organisational Emperor.*

the state more responsive to public opinions are some other examples. Finally, the refinement of media management techniques,[47] including opening part of the media sector to private and foreign investment to reproduce its power domination over social classes, is another attempt. From Deng Xiaoping and more so under Jiang Zemin and Hu Jintao, great importance is placed, at the rhetorical level at least, on strengthening the relationship between the Party-state and the people, some more successful than others. The emphasis is on building trust and confidence between the ruler and the ruled.

Zheng has argued forcefully that it is important to situate hege-monisation in the context of China's development as directed by the CCP.[48] The fact that the CCP has initiated and directed China's development means that staying in control of the process and main-taining its domination over social forces is an integral part of this development. It also means that in order to guarantee economic reforms and political and social stability, the CCP not only needs to respond pro-actively to the changing political, social and economic circumstances by continuously adjusting its institutional framework but also interact with the society. Zheng[49] calls the interaction between the Party-state and society a dual process of domination and legitimation: the Party/state struggles for its continuous domination over society, especially vis-à-vis newly rising social forces. Effective domination, however, is also a process of legitimation. That is, while the political system of one-party rule is non-negotiable, political changes have been gradually introduced to increase the country's productivity and efficiency, in order to strengthen the regime. It has appropriated the concept of democracy as a strategy to cope with drastic socio-economic changes. Therefore, political changes are not intended to suddenly open up the political process to the general public, but are a part of a managed process of institutional adjustment on the part of the CCP to ensure further economic growth and new

---

[47] Brady, Anne-Marie, 'The Beijing Olympics as a Campaign of Mass Distraction', *The China Quarterly*, 197, (2009), pp. 1–24.
[48] Zheng, *The Chinese Communist Party as Organisational Emperor*, p. 139
[49] *Ibid.*, p. 148.

bases for legitimacy of authority. When socio-economic changes result in unintended consequences — for instance, the opening up of the path for the subordinates to the higher authority, the nation, to resist the state — they have often been met with coercive measures as the existing institutions were no longer able to accommodate them. The crackdown on the pro-democracy movement in 1989 is such an example. However, compliance from coercion provides little legitimacy and low legitimacy tends to create pressures for changes to the state itself. So using brutal forces to ensure authority does not mean that the CCP has refused to make adjustments to meet the new socio-political and economic situations. Rather, it means that the CCP wants to lead and manage the process of China's political development at its own pace to make sure that it remains in power.

As hegemony is dynamic, a process rather than a fixed state of domination, and as hegemony is in nature not given but has to be sustained and reproduced, "it constantly has to be made and unmade".[50] So the same applies to political legitimacy. Weber's conception of legitimacy was derived from his conception of power as being relational. That is, actors did not possess power *per se* but rather their power stemmed from others' belief in that actor's rightfulness to exercise power.[51] Legitimacy rested upon this notion of belief, so that "the basis of every system of authority, and correspondingly of every kind of willingness to obey, is a belief, a belief by virtue of which persons exercising authority are lent prestige".[52] Moreover, the effect of this belief in the legitimacy of the ruler(s) converts the exercise of power into that of authority. According to Muthiah Alagappa, legitimation is "an interactive and…dynamic process among the government, the elite groups, and the politically significant public: those in power seek to legitimate their control and exercise their power; the subjects seek to define their subordination in acceptable

---

[50] Comaroff, Jean and Comaroff, John, *Ethnography and the Historical Imagination*, (Boulder: Westview Press, 1992), pp. 28–29.
[51] Weber, Max, *The Theory of Social and Economic Organization*, Talcott Parsons (Ed.), (New York: The Free Press, 1964).
[52] *Ibid.*, p. 382.

terms".[53] After a certain type of legitimacy is established, new challenges will exert pressure on political leaders to search for new sources of legitimacy. From the 1980s, the CCP has been able to remain in power due to the sustained economic development which has been providing employment and material benefits to the people. However, China's remarkable economic growth has unwittingly led to the emergence of other challenges such as deepening social division, which are not easily resolved through economic measures alone. The early 2000s therefore saw public sentiments become more sceptical about the growth-oriented market economy, especially with the rising social tensions caused by a significant increase in unemployment, serious corruption of party cadres and government officials, widespread materialism, growing inequality and increasing labour unrest triggered by unemployment. Mainstream political thought has thus moved from how to build a prosperous China in the 1980s and 1990s to how to regulate economic growth for a more egalitarian outcome in the 2000s, while public assessment of the state's performance has shifted from the economic sphere alone to the political sphere as well. To reclaim the Party's political legitimacy, the country's economic success alone is no longer a sufficient condition.[54] Therefore, while it forcefully represses efforts to challenge its authority and monopoly on political power and organisation, it has also pursued a variety of political reforms that are intended to enhance the capacity of the state to govern effectively. Tsang has observed that the CCP has undergone continuous governance reform in order to pre-empt public demands for democratisation. It has used a mix of measures to shore up popular support, resolve local protests, and incorporate the beneficiaries of economic reform into the political system to broaden its base for

---

[53] Alagappa, Muthiah, 'Part I. Legitimacy: Explanation and Elaboration', in Muthiah Alagappa (Ed.), *Political Legitimacy in Southeast Asia: The Quest for Moral Authority*, (Stanford: Stanford University Press, 1995), pp. 1, 58.

[54] Shue, Vivienne, 'Legitimacy Crisis in China?' in Peter Hays, Gries and Stanley Rosen, (Eds.), *State and Society in 21st-Century China: Crisis, Contention, and Legitimation*, (New York: RoutledgeCurzon, 2004), pp. 24–49.

hegemony.[55] Since coming into power in late 2002, the Hu-Wen leadership has tried to address the excesses of capitalistic development in the 1990s through a combination of social policy and ideological initiatives. These include the launch of redistributive policies — such as abolishing the agricultural taxes to relieve the burden for farmers and expanding social security but also, perhaps more importantly, articulation of a whole series of new political doctrines and the launch of a massive ideological education campaign that aims to build up a "harmonious society", and the popularly invigorating spectacle of China's rapidly increasing global prominence (e.g., the hosting of the Olympics in 2008, the 2010 Shanghai Expo). In 2003, the so-called scientific concept of "sustainable development" in the language of "scientific socialism" was propagated to correct the single-minded pursuit of neoliberal economic growth at the cost of social development and environmental sustainability. This construction of a "harmonious society" led by the Hu-Wen leadership has almost everyone on board, earning their loyalty and the party, legitimacy.

While it has great explanatory power to the understanding and explanation of the strength and the resilience of the Party-state in contemporary China, Gramsci's hegemony, as the word "hegemony" suggests, also reminds us that there are counter-hegemonic forces from grassroots forces. This means that while the state is trying to construct hegemony, there is in the Gramscian sense, resistance to state attempts to impose hegemony. It means resistance, defiance and counter-official ideologies are integral parts of the production and reproduction of hegemony. Hence, at its core, hegemony does not mean the absence of resistance, but formulation of certain modes of resistance. Hegemony is, therefore, a power in the process of formulating both domination and resistance. Gramsci's concept of hegemony thus allows researchers to go beyond the control argument and focus on the newly formed relationship between the

---

[55] Tsang, Steve, 'Consultative Leninism: China's New Political Framework?' The China Policy Discussion Paper 58, 2010, School of Contemporary Chinese Studies, University of Nottingham, at http://nottingham.ac.uk/cpi/documents/discussion-papers/discussion-paper-58-consultative-leninism.pdf, accessed 10 April 2010.

Party-state and social forces, which is not only mutually transformative but opens up different possibilities for political development in China.

The Role of the Media in the Construction of Hegemony

In this book, "the media" is used to refer to the four major conventional print and electronic media (newspaper, magazine, radio, and television), and the latest technological innovation, the Internet. "Media publics" is used to refer to the readers, listeners, audiences and netizens that get information from any form of the media mentioned here.

In the construction of hegemony, the manufacture of consent is as important as coercive measures, if not more. Since China started its economic reform, its sustained efforts to enhance the party's capacity to elicit, respond and guide public opinion has been impressive[56] and the media has played a pivotal role in China's transition from totalitarianism to hegemony.

The Chinese media has gone through a zigzagging path of reform and change. Within the broader context of political, economic and social transformations in China, the relationship between the media and the Party-state is also undergoing changes. The CCP's move from totalitarianism towards hegemony not only sets a new context for but also redefines the nature of media reform. It means that the party would base its legitimacy not only on economic growth but also a renewed emphasis on ideological work. That gives rise to a unique relationship between the Party-state and the media: on the one hand, the media, like other social forces in China, depends on its relationship with the government in pursuing its development; however, as society gets increasingly more complex and more empowered, a more innovative, sophisticated and credible media is needed to

---

[56] Tsang, 'Consultative Leninism: China's New Political Framework?' at http://nottingham.ac.uk/cpi/documents/discussion-papers/discussion-paper-58-consultative-leninism.pdf, accessed 10 April 2010.

justify the political legitimacy of the CCP government, and to manufacture consent for its continuing rule. In other words, the Chinese media needs more autonomy from politics in order to play a convincing role. This kind of mutual need has given a certain amount of bargaining power to the media for more autonomy from the Party-state.

From this perspective, the transformation of the media is not just the result of tense adversarial struggles between a control-freak Party-state and freedom-seeking media workers. Rather, it is that of a far more complex and diverse process during which the state needs the media to "educate" the people to accept the changing economic, social and political order from which consensus is built,[57] while the media has over the years evolved from being solely the mouthpiece of the CCP subsidised by the state into a group in which the majority has gained financial independence although still owned by the government. In other words, the commercialised media has the potential to contest as well as help secure the legitimacy of the Party.

METHODOLOGIES

The book is based on research conducted both inside and outside China between 2003 and 2009, including documentary research, media content analysis, field trips which involved formal and informal interviews with media workers, policy makers, and academics. The importance of these interviews may not be immediately evident in the text, because I do not often quote from them directly. But they form an extremely important source of "deep background".

SUMMARY

In seeking to show the marked changes that have accelerated in the last decade as the Party-state has had to confront a rapidly changing society and a more ubiquitous media, an effort is made to cross

---

[57] Davidson, 'Hegemony, Language and Popular Wisdom in the Asia Pacific', pp. 63–79.

disciplinary boundaries between media studies, China studies, history, and political science. I propose to consider the relationship characterised by negotiation between the state and the media in the current political context as one of the major dynamics in China's media transformation process. This approach, while avoiding the exaggeration of the role of the Party-state and the underestimation of the media organisations, places the changes in the context of the struggles the CCP has placed upon itself — in managing the forces that were unleashed by itself, and in managing the processes, the interactions and negotiations between the Party-state and other social forces, especially the media organisations. It reflects and captures the new conditions of complexity, with mutual influences among multiple actors to keep the equilibrium. It recognises that states are embedded in societies and interact with them constantly in a process of mutual transformation.

A number of questions need to be answered before we examine how the Party-state has formed a new relationship with the media and how the media has increased its negotiating power over the years. For instance, how has it changed from the pre-reform era to the more recent stage? What are the continuities and changes over time? What are the key stages of changes through the entire Chinese media system since reform? The next chapter attempts to answer these questions.

The Chinese Media in Historical Context

All those who want to topple a regime must first do ideological work and mold public opinion.

—Mao Zedong[1]

Propaganda is imperative for all revolutionary work.

—Deng Xiaoping[2]

The press must be the mouthpiece of the Party.

—Jiang Zemin[3]

---

[1] Jiang, Jianguo *et al.*, 2008 "Cadres Must Enhance the Capacity to Work with the Media", in *Forum for Chinese Party and Government Cadres*, 17 November 2008, at http://theory.people.com.cn/GB/49150/49152/8352146.html, accessed on 20 July 2009.

[2] *Ibid.*

[3] 'Jiang Zemin Talks with Wallace', in *CBS News*, 31 August 2000, at http://www.cbsnews.com/stories/2000/08/31/60minutes/main229663.shtml, accessed on 15 January 2010.

Correct guidance of public opinion is beneficial to the Party, the country and the people; wrong guidance of public opinion misleads the Party, the country and the people.

—Hu Jintao[4]

When they conducted their study of media change in the former East European Communist countries, Sparks and Reading (1994) believed that any concrete study of the restructuring of media must perforce start with a clear picture of the initial state of affairs from which any changes are departures.[5] Following Sparks and Reading, this chapter starts with a brief review of the history of China's Communist communication, highlighting its communication philosophy and theory in Mao's era, which serves to provide the context within which the country's media reform and the fast-moving social transitions in the post-Mao era have been occurring. It will also serve to improve our understanding of not only the continuities and changes in communication but also the changing relationship between the Party, citizens and information in the last three decades.

LEGACIES FROM MAO'S ERA

China's philosophy of media and communication was derived from the Marxist theory central theme that the media and communication is an ideological state apparatus, and that its first and foremost function is to reflect the regime's point of view on ideological issues. As a party that came to power through the power of the pen as much as through the barrel of the gun, the Chinese Communist leaders knew all too well the importance of ideological domination and the use of the media as part of the Party's ideological apparatus for social mobilisation. Indeed, the Chinese Communist Party and government have evolved a very large and complex communication system over the

---

[4] See Note 1.

[5] Sparks and Reading, 'Understanding Media Change in East Central Europe', pp. 243–270.

years, just as Yuezhi Zhao has observed, "China's elaborate regime of Party-state power in public communication has few parallels in the contemporary world".[6]

Communication in CCP history before 1978 can be divided into three periods. The first period began in 1921 when the CCP was founded and ended in 1949 when the CCP, under the leadership of Mao Zedong, founded the People's Republic of China (PRC). The CCP leaders from the very start, had been highly sensitive and attentive to the political role of the media. Therefore ever since 1921, the media had been integral components in the Party's management system, playing an important role in communicating to the Chinese people, the ideas and values that the party believed to be crucial to their revolutionary objectives. Many newspapers and periodicals were developed, including the influential Labour Weekly in Shanghai, Worker's Weekly in Beijing, Vanguard Weekly and New Youth,[7] to make ideological preparations for the founding of the new China by promoting Marxism and the views of the Communist Party. During the Anti-Japanese war and the Civil War in the 1930s and 1940s, the CCP also developed its own journalistic institutions, both in the base areas and in other parts of the country, effectively gaining a dominant voice, influencing public opinion, winning people over for revolution, and successfully organising and mobilising the people. The Red China News Press, which formally changed its name to Xinhua News Agency in 1937, Liberation Daily, Popular Daily, Resistance Daily, Central China Daily, China National Radio and China Radio International are some of the institutions developed during this period. With increasingly rich experience of using the media to promulgate the Party's guidelines and arouse people's political awareness, the CCP gradually developed its own theory of journalism that emphasised the Party principle. This theory had three components: (i) the news media must accept the Party's guiding ideology as their own; (ii) they must propagate the Party's programmes, policies, and

---

[6] Zhao, *Communication in China*, p. 61.

[7] Chang, Won Ho, *Mass Media in China: The History and the Future*, (Ames: Iowa State University Press, 1989), p. 13.

directives; and (iii) they must accept the Party's leadership and stick to the Party's organisational policies and the press policies. This is the so-called "Party Journalism".[8]

The second period ran from 1949 to 1965, seventeen years after the founding of the PRC. Although various forms of the media had been used extensively throughout the early history of the CCP, the mass media system was not formally established until the founding of the new China in 1949. After it assumed power, the CCP quickly took over the entire mass media. In the wake of the establishment of the PRC, the CCP inherited around 400 functioning newspapers and 49 radio stations from both the revolutionary base areas of the CCP and the areas formally controlled by the National Government throughout the country, which were the foundations of the media system in the early history of the PRC.[9] Mao is reputed to have the best understanding of the importance of mass media and public opinion of any twentieth-century world leaders. By the early 1950s, the government had turned all the private newspapers, radio stations, and publishers into state-owned institutions. The mass media system was thus integrated fully into the CCP and the government, and it became focused on contributing to system maintenance by teaching the attitudes, values, aspirations, and behaviours the nation's leaders considered desirable.[10] Since the media system was largely built out of the Soviet model, the media was considered to be the vehicle for social and political control, based on the Soviet media theory. The Soviet interpretation of the mass media as propagandists, agitators and revolutionists rendered the media to be very little more than the

---

[8] Zhao, Yuezhi, *Media, Market, and Democracy in China: Between the Party Line and the Bottom Line*, (Champaign: University of Illinois Press, 1998), p. 19.

[9] Womack, Brantly, 'Editor's Introduction: Media and the Chinese Public', *Chinese Sociology and Anthropology*, 18, (1986), pp. 6–53.

[10] Schramm, W., *Men, Messages, and Media: A Look at Human Communication*, (New York: Harper and Row, 1973);

Chu, Leonard, 'Press Criticism and Self-Criticism in Communist China: An Analysis of Its Ideology, Structure, and Operation', *Gazette*, 31(1), (1983), pp. 47–61.

mouthpiece of the socialist state and the Party.[11] Mao assigned to the media the role of "bringing the Party programme, the Party line, the Party's general and specific policies, its tasks and methods of work before the masses in the quickest and most extensive way"[12] for the realisation of the socialist cause as envisioned by the leaders. To achieve these missions, the mass media had to be run by the Party and become the Party's "loyal eyes, ears, and tongue".[13] Therefore, high-level Party organisations were responsible for directing, supervising and managing them. In other words, in order to make the communication process function highly effectively, a tight and rigid control system was maintained. Because of its important role, the media in the early years of the People's Republic of China grew rapidly.

In the 1950s, Mao tried to encourage academic and press freedom within the limits set by the Party and started a campaign to "let a hundred flowers blossom and a hundred schools of thought contend". However, the campaign was finally seen as a threat to the Party's control and sparked an "anti-rightist movement" which led to the political persecution of hundreds and thousands. In the late 1950s came the Great Leap Forward, a campaign through which Mao hoped to rapidly develop China's agricultural and industrial sectors in parallel. The media played a notorious role during this period: it exaggerated production figures and concealed famines and crop failures. Ironically, those who invented this news fabricating machine started to believe in the reports themselves. Famine and disaster followed as a result of miscalculation and the blind pursuit of industrialisation. During the last few years of this period, a view emerged in

---

[11] Chen, Xi, 'Dynamics of News Media Regulations in China: Explanations and Implications', *The Journal of Comparative Asian Development*, 5(1), (Fall 2006) 199, at https://louisville.edu/asiandemocracy/conferences/links-and-images/dynamics-of-news-media-regulations-in-china.html, accessed on 14 July 2010.

[12] Chen, M. and Chu, J., 'People's Republic of China', in G. Kurian (Ed.), *World Express Encyclopaedia*, (New York: Facts on File, 1982), pp. 219–231.

[13] Chang, *Mass Media in China*, p. 163.

the top leadership that a general cleansing and a restoration of the revolutionary spirit were essential.[14] The reawakening was the Cultural Revolution, which started the third period of the media industry in Mao's era.

The media during the Cultural Revolution from 1966 to 1976 was characterised by complete control of the Party, single-minded expressions of opinion, politicisation to the extreme and personal cultism of Mao Zedong.[15] The People's Daily, for instance, was under direct control of the Party's top leadership. It was used against Mao's enemies and copied verbatim by every other newspaper in the country. An editorial in the People's Daily would be considered an authoritative statement of government policy and was studied across the nation. The radicals used the media as an instrument for extreme political indoctrination and persecution. By the end of the Cultural Revolution, the media had lost much of its credibility.[16]

When Mao died in 1976, the media institutions he left behind had served as the collective propagandist, agitator and organiser. It was taken as part of the ideology and superstructure of China's socialist economy. It was the mouthpiece of the leadership, designated to define the objectives and philosophy of the Party and the government. The media was also regarded as weapons in class struggles against the Party's enemies.[17] News values were based on "how an event embodies the Party's political line and whether it serves to promote the political life and social progress".[18] Consequently, the

---

[14] Starck, Kenneth and Xu, Yu, 'Loud Thunder, Small Raindrops: The Reform Movement and the Press in China', *International Communication Gazette* 42, (December 1988), pp. 143–159.

[15] *Ibid.*

[16] Fang, Hanqi, Chen, Yeshao and Zhang, Zihua, *A Brief History of Chinese Journalism*, (Beijing: People's University Press, 1982).

[17] White, Lynn T., 'All the News: Structure and Politics in Shanghai's Reform Media', in Chin-Chuan Lee, (Ed.), *Voices of China: The Interplay of Politics and Journalism*, (New York: The Guildford Press, 1990), pp. 88–110; Chu, Leonard, 'Continuity and Change in China's Media Reform', *Journal of Communication*, 44 (3) (Summer 1994), pp. 4–21.

[18] Lent, John, 'First the Cultural Revolution, Now the Media Revolution', *Media Development*, 1, (1986), pp. 23–25.

media had generally focused on the communication of goals rather than reality.[19] As a rule, the ideals that the leaders wanted to achieve were given conspicuous and ample attention in the media, while any reality that ran counter to the fulfilment of the ideals was left unreported. The CCP believed then that without such a service by mass media, their leadership could not take any effective action and would be toppled inevitably by "counterrevolutionaries".[20] The media in China "[was] turned into political bulletin boards, propaganda trumpets, and announcers of CCP combat orders".[21] Inevitably, the flow of information during Mao's time was decidedly top-down and vertical. Emphasis was placed on constructing a mass-media and telecommunications system that could relay orders hierarchically from the central government in Beijing to the People's Communes in every corner of the country, from the state to society. The media was used, to the greatest possible extent, by the Party and the state to create a "total institution" and to impose ideological hegemony on the society.[22]

THE MEDIA IN POST-MAO CHINA — CONTINUITIES AND CHANGES

What the subsequent generations of Communist Party leaders have inherited from Mao is a clear understanding of the importance of the mass media in dominating a culturally diverse society. They know that if a state can control a society's communication processes, it can structure the symbolic environment in such a way that citizens are more likely to accept the state's political order as legitimate and less

---

[19] Chu, Leonard, 'Mass Communication Theory: The Chinese Perspective', *Media Asia*, 13(1), (1986), pp. 14–19.

[20] Chen, Chu, 'People's Republic of China', pp. 219–231.

[21] Lu, Keng, 'Press Control in "New China" and "Old China"', in Lee, Chin-Chuan, (Ed.), *China's Media, Media's China*, (Boulder, Colorado: Westview Press, 1994), pp. 147–161.

[22] Lee, Chin-Chuan, 'Mass Media: Of China, About China', in Chin-Chuan, Lee, (Ed.), *Voices of China, the Interplay of Politics and Journalism*, (New York: The Guildford Press, 1990), pp. 3–29.

likely to challenge the state's rule; citizens might even be encouraged to identify affirmatively and enthusiastically with state goals. Conversely, states that are perceived as illegitimate have to increasingly rely on physical coercion and the satisfaction of material wants to maintain control. It is therefore not surprising that as the CCP struggles to manage all aspects of the reform during the past three decades, especially since the mid 1990s, it has vested high stakes in communication, accelerating and strengthening its efforts to occupy what Zhao calls the "commanding heights".[23]

Communication in China after 1978 can also be divided into three stages known as marketisation, conglomeration and capitalisation. Each of the stages reflects the Chinese media's progress by trial and error, an unchartered process, or, in Deng Xiaoping's words, "feeling the stone while crossing the river", as well as the Party-state's efforts at maintaining control of the reform process and dealing proactively with unintended consequences. In fact, while various reform measures have been implemented in accordance with changing economic, social, and political circumstances, one major theme has stood out and remained unchanged — all reforms have to enable the CCP and the state to increase or strengthen their political legitimacy.

Stage One: Marketisation

The first period started in the late 1970s when Deng launched sweeping reforms covering the country's economy, politics, ideology, culture, and mass media. Three critical policies marked this period. The first one was in 1978, when the government issued a policy removing the rein on media advertising. Under the pre-reform framework, the government owned, controlled and financed all the newspapers, journals, radio stations and TV stations as bureaucratic agencies. In 1978, however, the financially stressed state started to progressively withdraw direct subsidies from media organisations, particularly those at local levels, while giving them financially favourable policies such as tax breaks, performance linked financial

---

[23] Zhao, *Communication in China*, p. 101.

rewards, and operational freedoms. This policy of allowing the media to carry advertisements marked the beginning of the whole process of marketisation. Since then, advertising has become an increasingly important source of income for all kinds of media. This is even true of the most mainstream media outfits. For instance, CCTV used to be fully funded by the central government. But since reform, it has become dependent on advertising for almost all of its revenues. In 2000, CCTV raised 5.5 billion Yuan through advertising, while the government only allocated 30 million Yuan to it or a mere 0.5% of its total funds.[24]

The second important policy in this period is Document No. 37, issued in 1983 by the Chinese Ministry of Radio, Film and Television (the predecessor of the State Administration of Radio, Film and Television, or SARFT), which formally articulated that the media system henceforward would have four levels, namely, central, provincial and autonomous regions, prefectural cities and county-level cities. It allowed governments at different levels to establish, finance and operate their own media outlets, including newspapers, radio stations, and TV stations. Although the primary purpose of this policy was to improve the effectiveness of the media as a medium for the dissemination of Party-state policy initiatives and as its "eyes and ears", it also resulted in the four-tier media structure.

With two-thirds of the 1,750 registered newspapers still reliant on state support at the end of 1992, in late 1992, the State Administration of Press and Publishing (SPPA, the predecessor of the General Administration of Press and Publication, or GAPP) issued another important policy as part of a concerted plan to dislodge inefficient state enterprises. It required all newspapers to be financially independent by 1994 except a few major party organs such as the People's Daily, the Economic Daily and Qiushi (求实 or Seeking Truth). This was an obvious effort from the Party-state to regulate the rest of the market even though some of the presses were

---

[24] Li, Xiaoping, '"Focus" (Jiaodian Fangtan 焦点访谈) and the Changes in the Chinese Television Industry', *Journal of Contemporary China*, 11(30), (February 2002), pp. 17–34.

established as market-oriented in the 1980s. Meanwhile, the state acknowledged the economic significance of non-political coverage by no longer requiring afternoon and evening publications, news digests, culture and lifestyle papers and trade journals to carry ideological propaganda.[25]

These three policies resulted in an unprecedented proliferation of media outlets, which met the demands of a population — whose living standards and education level were greatly improved — for a much greater range of information and points of view. At the beginning of the reform period, China only had a handful of newspapers, magazines, radio stations and TV stations. In the 1980s, newspaper titles multiplied at a great speed, with one new title published every 11/2 days.[26] At the same time, general and interest papers also increased in length. TV stations increased rapidly from 47 in 1982 to 366 in 1987.[27] By the end of the 1980s, China had developed a rather elaborate media network. According to Chen,[28] Xinhua was the largest news organisation with "three major departments: domestic department with bureaus in all provinces; international department with more than ninety foreign bureaus; and translation department, providing reports from foreign countries for restricted distribution among Party and government bureaucracies".[29] The People's Daily was the organ of the Party Central Committee; the China National Radio and China Central Television were the

---

[25] Lee, Chin-Chuan, 'Ambiguities and Contradictions: Issues in China's Changing Political Communication', in Chin-Chuan, Lee (Ed.), *China's Media, Media's China*, pp. 3–20.

[26] Chang, *Mass Media in China*, p. ix.

[27] Zhu, Hong, 'Experiences from the 30 Years of Reform in TV Industry', in Cui, Baoguo, (Ed.), *Blue Book of China's Media*, (China: Social Sciences Academic Press, 2009), pp. 203–207.

[28] Chen, 'Dynamics of News Media Regulations in China: Explanations and Implications', at https://louisville.edu/asiandemocracy/conferences/links-and-images/dynamics-of-news-media-regulations-in-china.html, accessed on 14 July 2010.

[29] Zhao, *Media, Market, and Democracy in China: Between the Party Line and the Bottom Line*, p. 18.

broadcasting monopolies. The CNR's morning news and CCTV's evening news were transmitted nationwide on a daily basis, making them the most authoritative news programmes in the country. These four outlets were at the very top of the Chinese news hierarchy. The media landscape in Deng's era was also coloured by the emergence of a number of important special interests national newspapers such as the Guangming Daily, Reference News, People's Liberation Army, China Youth News, Farmers News and China Woman's News. This media structure was more or less replicated at the provincial and municipal levels.

While the crackdown on the democracy movement in 1989 suppressed democratic discourses and re-imposed tight political control on the media, market forces gained momentum after Deng Xiaoping used his "southern tour" to give his personal approval to more aggressive economic reform in 1992. Media organisations, like much of the rest of China, responded to the opportunity by embracing the market economy in an unreserved way to make money with vigour and enthusiasm. As a result of further development in China's economic and political system, the Chinese media expanded enormously in the 1990s. According to Todd Hazelbarth, during the 1980s and 1990s, the number of newspapers increased from 332 to 2,200; there were more than 7,000 magazines and journals in the country by 1997. It was also estimated that there were approximately 700 conventional television stations — in addition to some 3,000 cables channels and 1,000 radio stations then.[30]

The proliferation of media outlets also led to the diversification of media products. In sharp contrast to the pre-reform media landscape that was dominated by a few central-government-published newspapers and journals, such as People's Daily and Guangming Daily, a myriad of new types of newspapers, journals, magazines, radio and TV programmes/channels burst onto the media scene. Amongst them were the journal, Red Flag, a network of central, provincial and

---

[30] Hazelbarth, Todd, *The Chinese Media: More Autonomous and Diverse — Within Limits: An Intelligence Monograph*, (Central Intelligence Agency: Center for the Study of Intelligence, 1997), p. 1.

municipal "People's Radio Stations" and TV stations which carried more or less the same ideologically charged reports and commentaries about national and international events. They varied widely in content and style, catering to different interests such as economics, sports, health, culture, and the environment, and served specific groups of people, such as business people, legal professionals, youths, retirees, and women. In addition, the Internet since 1994 has introduced to the Chinese public even greater varieties of information and entertainment. By the end of the 20th century, the communication system in China included all forms of modern advanced media.

During this period of marketisation, the organisation and operation of media organisations have also changed. They have been called "administrative units with enterprise management". What it means is that they were still structured as Chinese government organs but started to operate like companies. In other words, they were still state-owned organisations that needed to fulfil political tasks, but at the same time they were largely financed by advertising rather than subsidies from the government. It also means that government and party organs still maintained various forms of administrative oversight, including, for example, appointing leading personnel, but they had become increasingly more like market-based enterprises rather than bureaucracies. As early as 1978, the Ministry of Finance approved the introduction of business-style (rather than bureaucratic-style) management to the People's Daily and several other newspapers published in Beijing. They hired and fired professional employees on their ability to generate profits. They also contracted programmes out to independent producers and sold pages and blocks of time to business interests.

An obvious accompanying change with marketisation was a redefinition of the political role of the media. The CCP, while retaining ultimate control over politically sensitive information, also wanted the media to play a major role in the promotion of a market economy, consumerism, and the nationalistic project of building a "wealthy and powerful" nation. Its primary function thus shifted radically away from serving merely politics to a combination of promoting a market economy, public relations for the Party, information and knowledge sharing, and making commercial profits. Another equally important new role taken up by the media was to act as the channels through which the Party-state reinvented and reconnected itself with the people, by expressing people's desires and grievances, especially after the 1989 Tiananmen Incident, which caused a crisis of legitimacy for the CCP. In fact, since as early as the Thirteenth Party Congress in 1987, the CCP has routinely called for media oversight of the government. The call has led to an increasing amount of investigative journalism since the mid-1990s, represented by the prime-time programme "Focus" on CCTV and the weekly newspaper Southern Weekend. They broke the norm of positive reporting by exposing the wrongdoings of government agencies and officials.

Needless to say, while marketisation of the media launched by the Party-state led to the transformation of the whole media landscape, it also brought unintended consequences for the Party. Take the press for example. First of all, marketisation gave rise to an unprecedented expanding array of Chinese media outlets, which threatened to dominant position of the central and provincial party organs, both in terms of number and overall circulation. That is to say, with the intensification of market reforms, the central and provincial party organs, which had relied on office subscription, started to lose to those run by municipal Party (such as evening and metro papers), governments and professional papers. The latter had been so successful in their expansion that they started to undermine the circulation and advertising bases of the papers run by central and provincial party organs. For one thing, party organs had mandatory propaganda topics to cover and had to reach Party functionaries at the village level, while market-oriented mass appeal papers had much fewer requirements of this kind. They targeted urban consumers, which rendered them far more attractive as advertisement vehicles. Taking the top national Chinese Communist Party papers (People's Daily, Guangming Daily, and Economic Daily) as examples: they mostly featured Party speeches, announcements, propaganda, and policy viewpoints, and were steadily losing circulation and much-sought-after advertising revenues to evening municipal papers that had far more diverse content. The circulation of People's Daily, whose subscriptions were overwhelmingly mandatory for Party and government organisations, fell from 3.1 million copies a day in 1990 to 2.2 million in 1995; the paper's 1994 advertising revenues decreased as well. Similarly, the Liberation Army Daily became almost entirely dependent on state subsidies. Its circulation fell from 1.7 million in 1981 to fewer than 500,000 in 1995. By contrast, the circulation of the Xinmin Evening News, operated by the Shanghai Municipal Government, had risen from 1.3 million to 1.7 million over the same time period. The Guangzhou Daily, owned by the Guangzhou Municipal Government, doubled its circulation in six years to 600,000 in 1994, and its advertisement revenues also increased.[31]

Secondly, commercialisation also transformed political restrictions into economic assets, thus weakening the Party-state's control of media content. The most obvious was the persistent traditional ownership patterns that were once a means of guaranteeing supervision over the media. With commercialisation, it became a method of regulating access to lucrative economic opportunities. For instance, in book publishing, only officially approved publishers had the right to grant the license to publish a book. These licenses became valuable commodities that could be bought and sold; similarly, no newspapers were to be set up as independent businesses — all had to be assigned an official rank and registered under a recognised institutional publisher or sponsor; the license to publish a periodical was also valuable, and organisations that lacked the capital or know-how required to publish a profitable periodical could lease their license to commercial interests; similarly, television stations and film studios could also contract out production work to independent or semi-independent producers. Obviously, the financial interests of media organisations and the government, as well as the Party organisations that owned them, were often best served by collaborating with anyone who could provide marketable content and effective distribution. However, this

---

[31] Chen, 'Dynamics of News Media Regulations in China: Explanations and Implications', at https://louisville.edu/asiandemocracy/conferences/links-and-images/dynamics-of-news-media-regulations-in-china.html, accessed on 14 July 2010.

licensing system had its flaws: not all sponsoring institutions were keen on the ideology of the papers, books or TV programmes. Instead, they were more interested in getting some financial benefits in return. In their ruthless pursuit of commercial profits, they became innovative and went beyond their areas of specialisation, frequently breaking the Party's political and moral codes by contracting out publishing rights, and selling licenses to unauthorised organisations or individuals.

Third, the policy on setting up the four-tiered media structure led to the rapid growth of local media. In the broadcasting sector, for instance, TV stations mushroomed, especially at the county level, the numbers increased dramatically from hardly any in 1980 to 60 in 1985, and then to 1,262 in 2001, accounting for nearly 80% of the total number of TV stations in China.[32] With the decentralisation of television operations from the national and provincial levels, municipal and county governments were able to mobilise local resources to launch their own television stations, in part to transmit central and provincial programming, but more importantly, to broadcast local programmes for local government publicity and commercial interests. As a result, these television stations morphed from what were meant to be relay stations into fully operational TV stations, creating tensions between local and central interests: the SARFT insists that local stations transmit CCTV's national news as a "political task", after all, it is the Party-state's main means by which to broadcast its propaganda and ideology to the vast region and diverse ethnic groups of the country, to shape public discourse or, as the official term has it, "correctly guide public opinion". However, local stations, while relaying the national news as a political mission, also created more commercial channels which broadcasted other programmes. These channels attracted audiences away from CCTV with local news, since they were better positioned to cover local problems in their proper specificity, and entertainment programmes or "soft" news. For

---

[32] Yuan, Yan, 'Dilemma and the Way Out for County-level TV Stations during the Reform Era', *Journalism University*, 80(2), (2004), pp. 56–62.

instance, since 2004, the Sea County TV Station[33] has developed another two channels for exclusively commercial purposes: a "song and music channel", where the audience pays to get a song played, and an "advertisements channel", composed of advertisements with pictures and words only. Both of these do not cost much to maintain but nonetheless generate revenues for the station, and also distract audiences, especially the young ones, from the relayed CCTV National News at 7:00 pm.

As a result, by the mid-1990s, the media structure appeared to be fragmented, bureaucratised, overextended, and lacking in economics of scale.[34]

However, media marketisation initiated from the top means that the Party would not allow itself to lose control of the changes. Castells argued that China's modernisation and international opening up is, and was, a deliberate state policy, designed and controlled so far, by the leadership of the Communist Party.[35] As a consequence, reform in the media industry has been like reform in other areas throughout China — although it involves "feeling the stone while crossing the river", media reform initiated from the top means that the Party is in a position to adapt its system and management to the changing circumstances to retain its dominant position. What is more important, media reform from the very start has been meant to be part of the economic reform rather than a key component of reform in the political system. As early as in 1987, the State Science and Technology Commission listed newspaper publishing and broadcasting as "information commodification industries". This was repeated and emphasised at later stages of the reform. In the 1980s, there were those who suggested that the Party-controlled and state-owned media institutions become independent like other

---

[33] From the author's field work in the Sea County, Zhejiang Province, in 2006.

[34] Liu, Bo, 'An Overview of Chinese Press Development in 1996', in *China Journalism Yearbook 1997*, (Beijing: China Journalism Yearbook Press, 1997), pp. 37–40.

[35] Castells, Manuel, *End of Millennium*, (Malden, MA: Blackwell, 1998), p. 289.

enterprises. There was also a suggestion for the Chinese media, especially television, to take a central stage in Chinese politics and culture during this period when political mobilisation and ideological ferment sought reform that would bring both economic prosperity and democratic political transformation.[36] The practice of applying economic reform to the media sector, however, was discouraged as it threatened to challenge the Party's monopolistic control. Hu Yaobang, then General Secretary of the CCP, was quoted as saying that although journalistic institutions were managed as a kind of enterprise, they were above all mass media organisations: "No matter how many reforms are introduced, the nature of the Party's journalism cannot be changed".[37] The lesson the CCP learned from the 1989 Tiananmen Incident, in the words of the former General Party Secretary Jiang Zemin, is: "The Party and its journalism stand together through ups and downs. Journalism is part of the Party's life. Working with public opinion means working with the political and ideological. It is linked to the fate and future of the Party and the government".[38] The collapse of the former Soviet Union in 1991 also served as a shocking lesson for the CCP, which believed that the political liberalisation of the media was a major contributing factor. As a result, the CCP reasserted media control and upgraded its ruling technologies in the post-1989 era. It fortified the state's entire propaganda apparatus and elevated the propaganda and ideology portfolio within the Party leadership.

In 1992, Deng Xiaoping reignited domestic economic reforms, after which the media went on a different course from the 1980s. Communication in this period seemed to have never been so central

---

[36] Zhao, Yuezhi and Guo, Zhenzhi, 'Television in China: History, Political Economy, and Ideology', in Janet Wasco, (Ed.), *A Companion to Television*, (Blackwell, 2005), pp. 521–539.

[37] Hu, Yaobang, 'On the Party's Journalism Work', speech delivered to the CCP Central Committee Secretariat, 8 February 1985, published in the People's Daily on 14 April 1985.

[38] Zhang, Zhixin, 'Reflections on Comrade Jiang Zemin's Work on Journalism', *TV Research*, (5), (2001), p. 20.

to the reproduction of political legitimation, the re-establishment of ideological hegemony, the re-installation of new social relations, capital accumulation, cultural transformation and the projection of a good image of China to the international publics.

Stage Two: Conglomeration

The second stage saw the Party-state not only deepening the market logic, but also determined to maintain and secure the "commanding heights" of the commercialised media industry. If the first stage was marked by decentralisation as a result of marketisation, the second stage from the mid-1990s to 2002 was characterised by re-centralisation and rationalisation, especially the consolidation of diverse media through the creation of conglomerates, to achieve the optimal integration of political control and market efficiency.

In the mid-1990s, the SPPA started to curb the proliferation of media outlets by tightening the issuing of licenses. In the second half of 1995, it stopped issuing new licenses completely. Further to the control on the expansion of media outlets, the authorities also started to work on the integration of effective propaganda and efficient business. In 1996, the Central Party Committee and the State Council jointly issued a critical policy named "Circular on the Administration of Press, Publication, Radio and Television Industries". The policy was to encourage the formation of media groups which were seen by the Party and government as ideal organisational forms for optimal integration between control and business, by the matching of enterprising media outlets with its own regulating organs. It was also seen as an effective way to induce profitable papers to cross-subsidise the unprofitable, but socially and culturally important, papers. Not surprisingly, only those centrally approved media papers that met a series of operational criteria could take other papers.

The first media group in China — Guangzhou Daily Group — was established that year. Guangzhou Daily, as the most commercially successful Party paper, was selected by the central authorities to establish the first press group as a pilot project. The group streamlined its organisational structure, strengthened editorial control, upgraded facilities, and built an extensive distribution system both inside and outside the Guangzhou area. The success of the group in terms of commercial profits (the group became one of Guangzhou's top 10 state enterprises and a major economic powerhouse), influence as well as editorial control[39] led to the process of consolidation in the Chinese media circle in the next two years. By July 1998, China had officially set up six national and regional press groups. As a result, instead of replacing the party organs, mass appeal papers acted as cash cows that cross-subsidised the party organs, thus securing the financial basis of traditional party organs.

In August 2001, the Propaganda Department, the State Administration of Radio, Film and Television and the General Administration of Press and Publication jointly issued Document No. 17, reaffirming the idea of allowing cultural institutions to form business groups. It further encouraged the cross-region and cross-sector consolidation of the media and started to allow media conglomerates to collect capital within the press, publishing, radio, film and TV system by exercising financing, bank loans, and share holding. This reaffirmation policy had three purposes: firstly, it was to promote further marketisation. Secondly, it was to further prepare itself to face the challenge of international media companies coming into China after China's accession to the WTO in 2001, and thirdly it was to build up the capacity to compete on the international stage. In 2001, the People's Daily took the lead in implementing the Party's newly formulated capital-friendly policy in the media by raising 50 million Yuan in investment capital from Beida Qingniao, a state-owned online education provider, to launch its subsidiary Jinghua Time for the Beijing market, which rendered the central party organ the first truly commercialised mass appeal media platform.

Many media outlets, in response, have developed into business conglomerates that comprise a variety of news, entertainment, educational and other seemingly unrelated business activities (e.g., car

---

[39] Zhao, Yuezhi, 'From Commercialisation to Conglomeration: The Transformation of the Chinese Press within the Orbit of the Party State', *Journal of Communication*, 50(2), (Spring 2000), pp. 3–26.

repairs). For example, the Shanghai Media Group (SMG), the predecessor of Radio and Television Shanghai under the Shanghai Media & Entertainment Group (SMEG), was formed in 2001, as the result of a merger between the People's Radio Station of Shanghai, East Radio Shanghai, Shanghai Television Station and Oriental Television Station. It was a multimedia television and radio broadcasting, news and internet company, boasting of 5,200 employees, with capital assets totalling RMB 11.7 billion. SMG's core business was television broadcasting and related media entertainment services including sports, showbiz, performance arts, science and technology, and finance. The television broadcasting media consisted of eleven analogue TV channels, ninety digital paid cable TV channels, a full broadcasting internet TV service, along with ten analogue and nineteen digital radio services. The group also operated and owned five sports centers and fourteen cultural art centers. Other areas of operation included newspapers, magazines, news websites, and audio-visual publishing.

Today, there are a total of 40 press groups in China, a blend of media outlets and government regulators.[40] Document No. 17 is also important in showing that the function of the government has shifted from a market player *per se* to a policy maker, regulator and supervisor, wielding ideological, personnel and policy control. At the same time, media outlets have shifted their status from affiliated organisations to direct market players and started to enjoy relative autonomy in economic activities such as capital management and structural adjustment.

For better usage of resources and control, in 2001 the central government also ordered all TV stations below the provincial level to stop all channels broadcasting self-made programmes. Many magazines and newspapers were also closed down due to a government restructuring regulation requiring the closure of newspapers.[41]

---

[40] The Blue Book Project Team, 'Survey of the Development of Press in China', in Cui, Baoguo, (Ed.), *Blue Book of China's Media*, pp. 089–096.

[41] That is, if the population of a county is below 500,000. Yang, Fei, "China Readjusts the Press Market; Many Papers are to be Stopped", 2003, at http://www.people. com.cn/GB/14677/14737/22036/1997395.html, accessed on 15 March 2008.

However, media conglomerates have not been as commercially successful as the Party and the state policy-makers have wished. After some
years of development, for instance, the whole broadcasting media in
China gained a total annual income of about 82.5 billion RMB Yuan
(app. $10 billion) in 2004, while Time Warner on its own made an
annual income of nearly $41.1 billion in the same year. The commercial
failure is largely due to the nature of the media groups which decide
that they are more for the maximisation of ideological control over
media for political stability than the maximisation of profits. Although
they are financially independent and are expected to rationalise production and take advantage of economies of scale, the groups are not
officially incorporated as independent businesses, nor are they registered with the government's industry and trade bureau. Rather, they
are affiliated with the Party's Propaganda Departments at different
levels, and their publishers and editors-in-chief are appointed by and
accountable to their affiliated Party committees. At the Guangzhou
Daily Group, for instance, the editor-in-chief is also the head of
Guangzhou city's Propaganda Department. Media groups are thus pre-
vented from deepening the market logic by conducting property
rights-based business transactions such as mergers and takeovers.

Stage Three: Capitalisation

Some scholars have argued that China's model is one of "economic
reform without political reform", or one with "development first and
democracy later".[42] Whether one agrees with these views or not,
China is obviously following the pattern of "economic development
first, social/cultural development later". After nearly three decades of
high economic growth, cultural development finally came to the fore.
The third stage thus saw the new generation of the Party and state
launch a new reform programme for the Chinese culture sector with the
promulgation of Document No. 21 in July, 2003. With this document,

---

[42] Zheng, Yongnian and Lye, Liang Fook, 'Political Legitimacy in Reform China', in
Lynn T. White (Ed.), *Legitimacy: Ambiguities of Political Success or Failure in East
and Southeast Asia*, pp. 183–214.

the CCP shifted the culture sector, including the media, from the periphery of policy-making to the core. Although the idea of culture as an industry and as an official discourse can be traced back to 2001 when it was first given a visible place at the Tenth Five Year Plan since the reform began, it was not until the Sixteenth Party Congress in 2002 that the state propaganda machine officially and substantively differentiated the concept of "public cultural institutions" (*wenhua shiye* 文化事业) from "commercial cultural enterprises" (*wenhua chanye* 文化产业), attributing to each clear-cut missions, different means and ends of development.

What is significant about Document No. 21 is that it provides the new conceptual and policy framework for accelerating the restructuring and development of the culture sector. There are many reasons for this move. First, in line with Hu-Wen's policy adjustment towards a more balanced development and social harmony, cultural development in this way entails equalising cultural opportunities for the masses and increasing accessibility of public cultural facilities and services to the economically and socially disadvantaged. The "cultural system" reform is thus to sustain the economic reforms and forge a new hegemony over a fractured Chinese society. It is to keep a balance between all fragments of the society, as one media analyst in Shanghai has observed, "advertisers want to advertise on programmes that would be popular among young and affluent audiences, but the Government doesn't want to run programmes that would be offensive to older people or too controversial for a mass audience".[43] Secondly, it re-conceptualises culture as a commercial industry, thus making culture, including the media, a new site of economic growth and a strategic site for the development of "comprehensive national power" — that is, both economic power and cultural or "soft" power in a competitive global context. This new concept of a "cultural industry" marked a break with the past: previously, culture was largely seen

---

[43] Li, Benjamin, 'Shanghai Media Group Restructure Puts Focus on Content Production', 23 October 2009, at http://www.media.asia/newsarticle/2009_10/Shanghai-Media-Group-restructure-puts-focus-on-content-production/37638?src=mostpop, accessed on 10 January 2010.

as a sector in the service of politics, insulated from commercial interests. Now for the first time in PRC history, the connection between culture and economy was officially recognised. Last but not least, this concept effectively displaces media reform as a key component of political reform within the broad agenda of cultural system reform, making the reform of this sector a continuation of the Party's economic reform.

Following this new reform policy, different organisations in the media sector have been separated into two sub-sectors: the public service sector and the commercial sector. According to the policy, all of the mainstream state-owned media entities like the party organs, be they press groups, broadcasting groups or publishers, are public service units in nature. They are the ones to provide political information including news and current affairs. Other entities such as advertising, printing, distribution and transmission are business units in nature and therefore are open to non-state investment and ownership. Evidently, this is a result of the Party-state recognising the limits on its ability to maintain tight control over an industry that has been expanding rapidly on the one hand and making an effort to further economic development on the other. In other words, this document shows the state's determination to maintain control over political information, but at the same time allow the commercial sector to flourish. After the promulgation of the document in 2003, nine provinces and municipal cities carried out the reform on an experimental basis, including Beijing, Chongqing, Guangdong, Shanghai, Zhejiang, and Lijiang, a tourist destination in southwest China.

This important document also authorised state capital to monopolise media heavyweights, leaving medium and small media organisations to non-state enterprises, or leaving them to the jungle law of the survival of the fittest. This practice of *zhua da fang xiao* (抓大放小 "grasping the big and letting go of the small") is similar to the deregulatory moves that had already taken place in other State-Owned-Enterprises (SOEs). It means that state capital is to exit gradually from these medium and small firms through asset sales and transfers, mergers, and bankruptcy. However, these medium or small media companies would in no way have complete autonomy. To ensure that they keep their "socialist" nature, they are not fully left to private capital, domestic or foreign. A clear distinction is made between editorial and business operations of these organisations: for the operational sectors, they may be split off from the editorial sectors and restructured into commercial companies, which can open up the service-related value chains such as printing and publishing, retail, information transmission and distribution to investment from non-media SOEs by organising shareholding or limited companies.[44] Thus even though they are shareholders in name, domestic investors from non-media sectors are barred from intervening in content delivery and asset management of the company. The same holds true for foreign investors whose sphere of influence is for the time being contained within the publishing sector only. The editorial sectors, on the other hand, must remain state-monopolised and no overseas and private investment would be allowed. It is the government that still takes full responsibility for their functioning. For instance, it took Beijing a whole year to expand this "dual-track" policy to private and foreign investors in 2004 — allowing private and foreign investors access to the commercial sectors of state-controlled media outlets, a force harnessed to strengthen the national economy in general and the media and cultural sector in particular.

Similarly, although the production of TV programmes and the distribution of publications can absorb overseas and private sources, the state must be the dominant shareholder in order to stay in the dominant position. Zhao gives an excellent example of such an arrangement: in 2004, the Zhejiang Film and Television (Group) Ltd., a joint venture between the provincial broadcast conglomerate and the country's largest private construction company, was established. While the Zhejiang state sector contributed broadcast license "resources" and personnel, and the private sector provided capital and "superior" institutional mechanisms, Zhejiang broadcast group's

---

[44] 'Chinese News Media Will Not Accept Foreign and Private Investment', in *News Front*, No. 2 (2002), at http://peopledaily.com.cn/GB/paper79/5498/566029. html, accessed 20 July 2010.

51% ownership and its control of the final editorial rights clearly show who the dominant owner in this state-private partnership is.

In January 2006, the Central Committee and the State Council sent out "Opinions on Further Reform of the Cultural Industry" to deepen the reform of China's cultural sector. It re-emphasised that reform in different sub-sectors within the cultural industry should be carried out in line with their different natures. That means that news media is to follow the principle of correct guidance of public opinion, maintain the role of the mouthpiece of the Party and people, adjust the structure, integrate resources, and improve management, while the non-news units are now in a position to seek outside capital and become more market-driven in operation. In September in the same year, the General Office of the Communist Party of China Central Committee and the General Office of the State Council jointly issued "The National Programme on Cultural Development for the 11th Five-Year Period (2006–2010)", the first such programme since the founding of the People's Republic of China in 1949.

In response to the SARFT's calling for a nationwide separation of production and broadcasting functions, Shanghai Media Group, for instance, announced in 2009 that it would split into two company units: one non-profit division that would deal with news operations; the other unit, named Shanghai Oriental Media Group, would cover advertising, distribution and content development. The former would remain controlled by the Shanghai authorities, and the latter would now be in a position to seek outside capital and become a more market-driven operation.

CONCLUSION

After examining the ongoing media reform that started three decades ago, we can find the Chinese way of transition distinct from other transitional countries. The Chinese reform journey has been gradual and selective, following its own roadmap and timetable: it first started in the rural area in a radical way, and was followed by a quick opening of the economy to trade, and only gradual reform of the state-owned enterprises. As the existing political system became more adaptable to the changing circumstances, and thus more resilient, it started the reform of the cultural sector in 2003 in an experimental way but more substantially from 2006. It is obvious that the media reform has taken a bold but cautious way, avoiding any threat to the dominant political ideology and the ruling power of the Party and State.

Consistent with the pace of reform that started from the countryside, moved to the SOEs and then to the cultural Industry and education, there are different stages within the media sector itself. Take the reform of press as an example. What distinguishes it from the reform of other SOEs is that it needs to keep its function as "the mouthpiece" of the Party. In other words, it needs to maximise its social and political function while also maximising its economic function. This dual task that the press faces makes the reform unique and more challenging. The reform first started with the state-owned non-current affairs press. It then continued with the non-political press of different associations and societies, and finally newspapers and magazines by different government ministries. The reform of commercial newspapers and magazines followed. The focus is on the distribution of Party-owned newspapers and magazines, so that they enter the market and run as commercial ones. The aim of the restructuring was to separate institutional functions from business enterprise functions and to consolidate and strengthen the control over core media institutions.

The development of the three different stages shows that as the Party introduces reform to the media sector, gradualism has been the key which enables the Party and the political system to evolve and to adapt to new political and social realities. So far, the Party has stayed in control of the reform. With a much more sophisticated view of the media, it has begun to redefine the role of the state in the media sector. What is obvious is that the Party is moving away from complete control over the whole media sector towards complete control over the core part, which is political information, while partially deregulating the other business in the media sector, giving more space to the commercial sector to pursue economic interests. If state-engineered recentralisation and conglomeration did not quite achieve the goals of deepening market relations and accelerating commodification, the new project of "cultural system reform" aimed to achieve them through divestment, that is, by spinning off market-oriented operations from existing Party-state media conglomerates and turning these operations into relatively autonomous market entities that are free to absorb outside capital and pursue market-oriented expansion. Although market principles present challenges and transform the Chinese media, they do not function outside, or without constant reference to, the Chinese political culture and existing institutional structures. On the contrary, the Party has proven to be able and willing to appropriate them and turn them to its own advantage. Consequently, though the Party organs in the competition may appear to be losers, because of the institutional relationships between mass appeal papers and Party organs, the former are under the control of the latter, especially in terms of institutional and editorial autonomy, while the latter are cross-subsidised by the former.

Chapter

Unleashed Forces at Work

Chapter Two has given a brief introduction to the development of the media since the founding of the CCP, highlighting the continuities and changes in the post-Mao period and the three different stages of media development initiated by the Party-state. This chapter will focus on the academic debates on the implications of the different forces released by the reform, which in turn robustly contest the system, namely, marketisation, globalisation, and the development of the new media technologies, especially that of the Internet.

MARKETISATION

The CCP launched the economic reform which, pragmatic as it seems, was necessary to salvage the CCP from the brink of losing its legitimacy after the Cultural Revolution. Chinese economy has grown dramatically, since then with the growth by liberalisation, privatisation and marketisation. These transitions have brought about increasing marketisation of the Chinese media, which, as discussed in the previous chapter, has changed the Chinese media landscape forever. Questions asked by many scholars and observers have been: Has increasing economic liberalisation of the Chinese media resulted in proportional political liberalisation? Has the commercial imperative accommodated or challenged the Party's control? To what extent does the market present a democratising alternative to the Party's control?

Answers to these questions have been divided, all supported by empirical evidence. Many hold the view that marketisation has turned media organisations into self-interested economic entities, which in turn has motivated the media to challenge the Party's control. Zha, for instance, believes that marketisation can solve the problems raised in 1989 without confrontation with the Central government.[1] Zhao finds that market-oriented competition has led to significant journalist innovations such as investigative reporting,[2] which pose a threat to the one-party political system. Zhang's study in 2008 also shows that most Chinese media scholars and professionals consider marketisation to be the leading force that drives the Chinese media to privilege "media logic" as much as "Party logic", if not more.[3] Zhang concludes that media organisations are taking more risks, including breaking regulations in pursuit of commercial profits. The logic is simple. Severance of the state subsidies to the media unleash media workers' energy to meet intense market competition, stimulating them to cater to the growing needs and tastes of an increasingly diverse and demanding audience. To satisfy the preference, of an ever more demanding public and compete with one another to win sizable market shares, newspapers, magazines, radios, TV stations and internet service providers have had to distribute content that attract the media publics that advertisers want. For instance, the need to deliver media publics to the advertisers leads them, as Li writes, to offer more investigative reports and longer stories such as corruption scandals.[4]

---

[1] McCormick, 'Recent Trends in Mainland China's Media', p. 179.

[2] Zhao, 'From Commercialisation to Conglomeration', pp. 3–26.

[3] Zhang, Xiaoling 'From Totalitarianism to Hegemony: The Reconfiguration of the Party-State and the Transform of Chinese Communication', *Journal of Contemporary China*, 20(68), (2011), pp. 103–115.

[4] Li, Xiaoping, '"Focus" (Jiaodian Fangtan 焦点访谈) and Changes in the Chinese Television Industry', pp. 17–34.

As a result, in contrast to the pre-reform era when the content of the media was almost exclusively political sloganeering, content today has become increasingly apolitical and lively. While the headlines may still be dominated by Party content, a substantial portion of the content now focuses on social problems that used to be taboo subjects, such as poverty, unemployment, crime, corruption. Mundane issues that used to be unworthy of news reporting, such as traffic congestion, family relationships, consumer information, and entertainment programmes of various shades as well as celebrity gossip which used to be viewed as a manifestation of unhealthy bourgeois taste and sentiment, are also daily offerings. As Chinese media organisations enjoy greater financial autonomy, they are able to hire and retain more and better journalists, further boosting their capacity to compete. Ratings and circulations have become the basic concern of all media outlets in China now, though they still have to obey the bottom line set by the Party and have to complete the political propaganda tasks ordered by the Party. Commercialisation has therefore been considered a major liberating force in China. Those who believe in the liberating force of the market hold that the regime is far less able than before to wield financial leverage over the media, which has increasingly become self-supporting through advertising revenues and circulation.

However, not everybody subscribes to this view. Many have also illustrated that marketisation works as a double-edged sword. That is, it may give media organisations incentives to challenge Party control in order to pursue commercial profits, but it can also lead to the reorientation of the content provided by the media on the one hand, and self-censorship on the other. In his summary of the literature on Chinese media, McCormick[5] pointed out that while those who apply the framework of market vs. state accept the market as a necessary means of providing autonomy from the state on the one hand, they also express reservations about media monopolies and the displacement of meaningful political discourse by entertainment and tabloid journalism. For instance, Yuezhi Zhao in 2000 carefully cultivated an

---

[5] McCormick, 'Recent Trends in Mainland China's Media: Political Implications of Commercialisation', p. 181.

awareness of problems arising from the commercialisation of Western media and made this commitment even more explicit in subsequent articles. Chin-Chuan Lee also allows that "the market may betray the ideals of democracy".[6] Therefore, although it is true that marketisation has provided the necessary institutional imperatives for the media to pursue innovations, sometimes even offering challenging content (e.g., investigative reporting), advertising-based financing and accelerated commercialisation have led to a drastic reorientation in the content of Chinese media, with profound political and ideological implications. Zhao gave a convincing example of how Wang Changtian, a leader of China's fledgling private media and entertainment industry, abandoned his initial content plans to find a politically safe and commercially attractive market niche: news reporting in the realm of entertainment, or infotainment.[7] The success of Hunan Satellite television as a leading provincial satellite channel also confirms that for the Chinese television sector, light entertainment is the safest and fastest means to popularity and commercial success. This fusion of Party-state control and market power has fuelled concerns by many academics who believe that the reform of the Chinese media only means the transformation from a strong political propaganda and educational orientation to a stronger entertainment orientation.

Some even believe that marketisation has resulted in a paradoxical situation, in which marketisation has helped the government reach the people faster and in greater numbers and also offers the CCP ways to improve its propaganda. Indeed, in its efforts to deliver the largest number of media publics to advertisers, it is believed that the media has not only gone from mass propaganda to mass entertainment but has also moderated the radicalism of previously dissident media by consolidating their position on the middle ground. Many therefore believe that although the media now enjoys relatively greater editorial independence, media organisations continue to operate within the orbit of the Party-state for two reasons: first, they

---

[6] *Ibid.*, p. 182.

[7] Zhao, *Communication in China: Political Economy, Power and Conflict*, p. 220.

are still owned by or affiliated to Party and government organs who have given them enough interest to stay within the Party-line. As a result, most of the time media organisations and the majority of journalists discipline themselves in order to avoid any open break with higher levels. That is to say, media organisations and media managers have developed a vested interest in sustaining the current political economic order by following the Party line while pursuing financial gains. As Li has observed, "The people working in companies like SMG (Shanghai Media Group) are civil servants. They move up the career ladder and get promoted when they follow the Government's policies and do not focus on market needs".[8] Zhang's interviews with county-level journalists also show that keeping the job by staying in the red line is the priority for many.[9] Fierce competition for advertising revenue and media publics has forced media organisations to converge on the middle ground. Media firms, in short, trade political obedience for the state's sustenance of their monopolistic operations.

Consequently, these observers believe, the role of censor is now played by the market as well as the government. As is discussed in the previous chapter, commercialisation has changed the management and internal organisations of the media. In addition to ideological guidelines, most media organisations have to face targets regarding how much revenue they generate. It has prompted many media organisations to establish target or quota systems in which journalists' compensation, or even their job security, depends on their steady production of content meeting specified standards. Wang from China Youth Daily has compared Chinese journalists to "migrant workers on the assembly line in the media industry" — meaning journalists are paid like workers in a shoe factory, with payment calculated on

---

[8] Li, 'Shanghai Media Group restructure puts focus on content production', 23-Oct-09, 12:09, at http://www.media.asia/newsarticle/2009_10/Shanghai-Media-Group-restructure-puts-focus-on-content-production/37638?src=mostpop, accessed on 10 January 2010.

[9] Zhang, Xiaoling, 'Seeking Effective Public Space: Chinese Media at the Local Level', *China: An International Journal*, 5(1), (2007), pp. 55–77.

how many words they have produced.[10] Therefore those who are not strong believers in the liberating effect of marketisation argue that although there are exceptions and some liberal-minded elite journalists continue to challenge the kind of clientism and collusion between the state and the media organisations, by and large, media commercialisation has contributed to the entrenchment of state control in the media.

GLOBALISATION

Globalisation of the Chinese media from the early 1980s is characterised by two different trends. The period from 1980 to the late 1990s is particularly noted by Chinese media firms searching for content, and by transnational firms seeking to enter China's potentially lucrative media markets, especially the advertising market. Because of the proliferation of media outlets as a result of commercialisation, there was a severe shortage of domestic content provision. In 1999, for instance, China's television broadcasting capacity (of CCTV, provincial and other local stations combined) reached five million hours annually — a market demand of eight thousand drama series alone per year. As a result, CCTV alone imported thirty percent of its programmes from abroad, and one fourth of the TV dramas throughout the nation were imports. For transnational media companies, as China's economic growth remains strong, every major international media player wants a toehold in the Chinese market because "the point is, China is the green field".[11]

Globalisation in this sense is a variation of commercialisation, and many observers have speculated its impact on China. Some claim that Beijing's domination of the circulation of political information is eroding as it cannot prevent the broadcasts of such western

---

[10] 'Appendix 1: Journalist Fellows 2007–2008', in *Annual Report 2007–08*, Reuters Institute for the Study of Journalism, (University of Oxford, 2009), p. 31.

[11] Leow, Jason, 'China's Media Shake-up', *The Straits Times* (Reprinted in *Asia Pacific Media: The Asia Pacific Media Network*), at http://www.asiamedia.ucla.edu/article.asp?parentid=10080, accessed on 14 June 2009.

broadcasters as Voice of America (VOA), Radio Free Asia and British Broadcasting Corporation (BBC) from entering the country's communications networks. In the southern province of Guangdong, 97% of the households have television sets, and all — except those in a few parts of the city of Guangzhou where reception is poor — have access to Hong Kong television through cable networks. Some local stations even intercept the signals and insert their own commercials. These claimers believe that Beijing is unable to effectively monitor, let alone control, the illicit cable operators who have sprung up since the early 1990s: as of 1995, about 1,000 of the 3,000 cable stations in China, linked to perhaps 50 million homes, were unlicensed.[12] At the same time, transnational satellite television, such as the Chinese language services of Cable News Network (CNN), Star TV, and another jointly owned by Time Warner, has significantly expanded its reach in China. Satellite dishes in mainland China that are used to receive programmes from Hong Kong, Taiwan, and other places are regulated, but government entities such as the Ministry of Machinery Industry and the military services produce such dishes outside allowable quotas and guidelines and then sell them illicitly to eager customers. According to the Central Intelligence Agency,[13] efforts to halt this practice have been ineffective, mostly because of the large profits involved — up to 50% per dish. Indeed, the government has backtracked in its efforts to stop these practices — moving from an outright ban on satellite dishes in 1993 to requiring that they be licensed in 1994, to specifying allowable programmes and viewing hours in 1995.[14] Phoenix, a Hong Kong-based television broadcaster, is considered to be "the channel of choice for much of China's new elite and perhaps does more to shape its political views

---

[12] 'The Chinese Media: More Autonomous and Diverse — Within Limits', from the website of the Central Intelligence Agency, USA, at https://www.cia.gov/library/center-for-the-study-of-intelligence/csi-publications/books-and-monographs/the-chinese-media-more-autonomous-and-diverse-within-limits/copy_of_1.htm#rft21, accessed on 15 July 2010.

[13] *Ibid.*

[14] *Ibid.*

than the neither Party's media outlets".[15] The government can easily block the borderless Internet transmissions from introducing a liberalising political force. Some observers believe that the dramatic increase and "improvement" in the Chinese media coverage of the Severe Acute Respiratory Syndrome (SARS) epidemic, following an initial cryptic, sketchy or even non-existent one, is due to the mounting demand from the public who have easier access to international information sources.

Competition from outside mainland China has also impelled domestic media organisations to improve their attractiveness to the publics by providing content that is more diversified and critical. For example, in order to compete against Hong Kong radio stations that can be received in Guangdong Province, Guangdong radio managers created the Pearl River Economic Radio (PRER) in 1986. PRER, copying Hong Kong radio's approach, began to emphasise daily life, entertainment, "celebrity" deejays, and caller phone-in segments, while eliminating ideological, preachy formats that included little information beyond what was provided by government sources. By 1987, PRER had obtained 55% of the Guangdong market; previously, Hong Kong radio stations had held 90% of this market. Local Party cadre in southern China were reportedly unhappy about PRER, mainly because some of the station's commentators as well as its talk radio programmes highlighted Party failures and the misdeeds of individual Party members in the region.[16]

Globalisation is therefore taken as a strong force that would inevitably increase pressures for political reform. This group of viewers also holds that although the requirement to join the WTO may not have directly affected China's media at first, it does prompt the government to take concrete measures to industrialise the media

---

[15] Pan, Philip P., 'Making Waves, Carefully, on the Air in China', *Washington Post*, 19 September, 2005, A01.

[16] 'The Chinese Media: More Autonomous and Diverse — Within Limits', at https://www.cia.gov/library/center-for-the-study-of-intelligence/csi-publications/books-and-monographs/the-chinese-media-more-autonomous-and-diverse-within-limits/copy_of_1.htm#rft21.

industry so that Chinese media can compete with the international media equally in the global market. They therefore firmly believe that China's membership in the WTO has added a strong force for further liberalisation of the media market. They point out the fact that under the WTO agreement, China agreed to allow foreign investment in China's advertising market. China also agreed to allow foreign companies in the printing and packaging of publications. In 2002, the Chinese government approved 202 foreign-invested printers, followed by an additional 84 in 2003. In addition, as China's commitment included permitting foreign participation in the retail and wholesale of books, magazines, and newspapers, by August 2004, China had approved more than ten foreign companies' applications to enter the retail business.[17] Finally, China also agreed to import a growing number of foreign films each year. Financially, considering the increasingly expanding media sector's urgent need to access the international capital market and foreign investors' growing interest in the Chinese media market's huge potential in the post-WTO context, the government faced growing pressure to have a clear and positive policy response.

Even if the introduction of transnational capital into the previously state monopolised media sector has little impact on the country's media democratisation course, it is argued, it may however help establish a more financially rational and professionally constructive media system. The reason is that, logically, even media globalisation in a non-Western local context such as the Chinese one implies the need of a structural change toward a more independent (at least in terms of greater financial freedom and editorial autonomy), more competitive and law-ruled (as required by the modern capitalist corporation system), and therefore more professional and less corrupt media system. China will simply need more efficient and more rule-based governmental behaviour in order to compete internationally.

As China further opens up to the world, especially via the hosting of the Olympic Games in 2008 and the 2010 Expo in Shanghai, freer

---

[17] Wang, Lianhe, 'The Logic of Publication Regulations under Authoritarianism', *Research on Publication and Distribution*, (3), (2005).

policies, albeit being ad hoc in nature, such as the Regulations on Reporting Activities in China by Foreign Journalists during the Beijing Olympic Games and the Preparatory Period, guarantee foreign journalists wider freedom to conduct their work in China. Prior to the bid to host the 2008 Olympic Games in Beijing, foreign correspondents had to first get permission before making reporting trips within the country and reporters often faced harassment if they covered delicate issues. As part of its bid to host the 2008 Olympics, China promised to relax constraints and "be open in every aspect to the rest of the country and the whole world". In January 2007, Chinese Premier Wen Jiabao signed a decree that allowed foreign journalists to report without permits before and during the Beijing Games. The decree also allowed foreign journalists to interview any individual or organisation as long as the interviewee consented. The new guidelines came into effect on January 1, 2007, and lasted through to October 27, 2008.

Many observers believe that the large numbers of foreign journalists who have benefitted from the freer policy and the foreign-invested and foreign-owned advertising companies, along with their clients will have an impact on Chinese media and media publics. Indeed, Chinese citizens who now have access to alternative meaning systems will use them to challenge the domestically prevalent meaning systems that the Party-state seeks to promote. Not surprisingly, books written more than a decade ago on the effects of globalisation on China's political, cultural and economic reform implied that in the years to come, China would inescapably face pressure to conform to certain global norms. Although they did not conclude that the pressures of globalisation would overwhelm the authoritarian state and finally bring sweeping political reform and the rule of law to China, the strong collective implication was that some kind of important breaking point was in the making and that globalised media markets would contribute heavily. The new attitude in the handling of the press during the Xinjiang riots in June 2009, where an international press centre was established in Urumqi (site of the clashes between ethnic Uighur and Han) with daily briefings and access to the streets for foreign reporters further encouraged observers to believe that even if news is managed, competition and the greater openness of the country has produced some positive results for foreign reporters: in stark contrast to the Tibetan riots a year earlier, the Ministry of Information was intent on giving at least the impression of unfettered access.

Again, not all observers hold the same view. Many have aired concerns over the considerable degree of ideological convergence between global capitalism and "socialism with Chinese characteristics". Although nearly all foreign media investors currently "are losing money in China", according to Vivek Couto, executive director of a Hong Kong-based media consultancy, very few Western capitalists can resist the temptation of the Chinese media market's huge potential. As Lyric Hughes, publisher and CEO of China Online Inc., a U.S.-based media company, said at a public hearing on WTO Compliance and Sectoral Issues: "Why are foreign media giants so focused on China? In a word, advertising".[18] This mutual need paves the foundation of Chinese-foreign co-operation. "Transnational media corporations and the Chinese authorities work in tandem to produce a state-global media complex".[19] This is particularly the case in entertainment and popular culture production. For instance, foreign magazine publishers enjoy a slightly modified rule from other media sectors — they can compete for government permission to license their brand names and contents for publication in the Chinese mainland. Yet not surprisingly, foreign magazines published or distributed in China are non-political titles and "censor themselves or steer clear of controversy".[20]

Corporatism is typically reflected in the reciprocal landing rights and programme exchanges, under which the Chinese media outlets and their foreign partners agree to exchange programmes

---

[18] Hughes, Lyric, 'Written Testimony of China Online', Public Hearings on WTO Compliance and Sectional Issues before the U.S.-China Economic & Security Review Commission, 18 January 2002, at http://www.uscc.gov/textonly/transcriptstx/teshug.htm, accessed on 15 July 2010.

[19] Zhao, *Communication in China: Political Economy, Power and Conflict*, p. 147.

[20] 'Foreign Magazines Facing China's Newsstand Fever', *Business Week*, 5 November 2003, reprinted at http://www.chinadaily.com.cn/en/doc/2003-11/05/content_278774.htm, accessed on 25 June 2010.

for use over each other's channels. As Chin observed,[21] China has opened up some of the TV markets in Guangdong to a number of foreign media on a "reciprocal and mutually beneficial exchange of knowledge and expertise". As a result, "in exchange for being allowed cable access, News Corp agreed that its United States network, Fox, would carry the English-language channel of Chinese state broadcaster, CCTV-9", according to a report on BBC website (BBC News, 23 October 2001). According to another report from BBC, AOL Time Warner "agreed to broadcast the Chinese state-owned English-language channel, CCTV-9, in the U.S." (BBC News, 6 September 2001). Another example was the deal in 2003 with the MTV Musical owned by Viacom, which enabled CCTV-9 to broadcast to hotels in the US.[22] The remark of the spokeswoman for the SARFT is self-revealing: "Americans want to come in. We of course want to go there too. It should be mutually beneficial".

Observers argue that it is also clear China has adopted a pragmatic, partial opening up policy, aiming at absorbing Western capital and know-how on the one hand and losing no ownership and political control of the media sector on the other. "While Beijing has thrown open sectors such as manufacturing and retail, it has, over the past decade, granted the likes of News Corp, Viacom and AOL Time Warner only limited scope to enter what is the world's largest untapped media market."[23] In the final negotiations over China's entry into the WTO in 2001, the Chinese government only committed itself to opening up certain sectors of its audio-visual market to foreign investment, but the broadcasting market was

---

[21] Chin, Yik-chan, *From the Local to the Global: Chinese Television from 1996 to 2003*, PhD thesis, (London, University of Westminster, 2005), p. 191.

[22] Fung, Anthony, 'Think Globally, Act Locally: China's rendezvous with MTV', *Global Media and Communication*, 2(1), (2006), pp. 71–88.

[23] Hu, Zhengrong, 'Towards the Public? The Dilemma in Chinese Media Policy Change and Its Influential Factors', Joan Shorenstein Center on the Press, Politics and Public Policy: Harvard University (2005), p. 3, at http://www.global.asc. upenn.edu/docs/anox06/secure/july21/zhengrong/21_zhengrong_reading1.pdf, accessed on 25 June 2009.

excluded. In other words, under the terms of China's membership into the WTO, the media sector was not required to open to foreign investors.[24] Neither do China's WTO agreements bind it to content liberalisation. The partial opening of the media sector should be therefore considered an initiative from China to absorb capital and advanced technology. Meanwhile, Beijing has tried to apply some carefully planned devices to accommodate and localise transnational capital for its own purposes.

First, as far as content provision is concerned, a "no news, sex, violence" policy is imposed to monitor Chinese-foreign media cooperation. In addition, all foreign content is subject to rigorous censorship prior to distribution. Rupert Murdoch's success in China so far has a lot to do with the limited censorship of content on topics such as science and technology, finance and economy, leisure and lifestyle, and ideologically neutral mass-market fare, such as game and talk shows, sports and drama. Such a policy is considered beneficial to the growth of China's domestic TV content industry, currently a weak value chain in the cultural sector, but also ensures its own economic and political control of the media.

Secondly, China's decision to partially open the media sector to foreign investors also reflects its strategic intentions to learn from Western know-how of modern media corporation management and to establish its own national and global media networks by co-operating with transnational media corporations. Therefore, joint production of entertainment programmes with transnational heavy-weights such as News Corporation's new deal with the Hunan Radio, Film and TV Groups is welcome. However, in the joint venture the majority-shareholder must be the Chinese state-owned media company who can get a license to sell their products in China because only domestic companies are entitled to hold licenses to carry media products.

---

[24] Dudek, Mitch and Xu, L. Lucy, 'Market Access Report: Media & Publishing', *China Law & Practice*, May 2002, at http://www.chinalawandpractice.com/Article/1693674/Channel/7576/Market-Access-Report-Media-and-Publishing.html, accessed on 25 June 2010.

Thirdly, as is illustrated above, reciprocal landing rights and programme exchanges with foreign broadcasters are China's real goals and gains — the bargaining chips that foreign conglomerates are required to bring to the negotiating table to gain access to some Chinese market. With China's rise as not only an economic power but also a political power, some observers believe that another trend is setting in, albeit being very recent. Namely, debates have emerged on China's influence on the rest of the world, especially with China's determination to project its soft power. In recent years, China has greatly increased its investment in the media to air its views, break the Anglo–American monopoly, enhance China's international influence, and showcase its rise as a great power in a non–threatening and non–confrontational manner. Organisations such as China Central Television, Xinhua News Agency and People's Daily could reportedly receive up to RMB 15 billion (U.S. $2.19 billion) respectively for ambitious schemes geared toward enhancing China's international influence.[25] In order to help the English Channel CCTV News (also known as CCTV-9 and CCTV International)[26] that targets a global audience, China has opened up some southern Chinese TV markets to foreign media in exchange for cable access in the United States.

Because of the recent communications expansion initiatives, while some are still arguing that the increasing volume of images and ideas crossing China's borders would offer the Chinese people access to new and liberating ideas, others are starting to wonder if globalisation is offering China the opportunity to influence the world with its authoritarian propaganda. As David Bandursky, a professor of journalism at Hong Kong University recently told the China Economic Quarterly, China's international media push amounts to

---

[25] Lam, Willy, 'Chinese State Media Goes Global: A Great Leap Outward for Chinese Soft Power?' *China Brief*, 9(2), (2009) at http://www.jamestown. org/single/?no_cache=1&tx_ttnews%5Btt_news%5D=34387, accessed on 18 March 2010.

[26] According to Global Times, CCTV 9, China Central Television's (CCTV) English-language channel, switched to CCTV News, an English-language news channel with 19 hours of news broadcasts every day in April, 2010.

the "commercialisation of propaganda" for an overseas audience.[27] In other words, people outside China can now easily access official Chinese websites and are thus subject to the state's version of the world view.

ADVANCES IN NEW MEDIA TECHNOLOGIES

Marketisation has also stimulated other important changes to the field of communications, such as the rapid development of technical advances which are believed to be undercutting the Party-state's efforts to control media content — including the popularity of television and recorded movies in the 1980s, and the Internet from 1994. Although all are considered to pose some potential as a "technology of freedom" in autocratic governments intent on controlling the information their citizens can receive, from the very beginning there have been higher expectations of the Internet in China to play an even greater role in the future because of its nature.

According to the China Internet Network Information Centre (CNNIC), the number of internet users in China has been growing at an exponential rate. Within a matter of 15 years, the number of users has expanded almost 150 times from a mere 2.1 million in 1998 to 384 million by the end of 2009, and the Internet penetration rate has reached 28.9%.[28]

Remarkably, the number of rural internet users has reached 106.81 millions, accounting for 27.8% of all internet users, according to the China Internet Network Information Centre. The number of internet bloggers in China has also expanded from 26.9 million in 2005 to 78.3 million in 2008, growing at an annual rate of 42.8%.

---

[27] Mott, Glenn, 'A New Media in China: More Information, More Control', *The American Society of News Editors*, (2010), at http://asne.org/article_view/articleid/779/a-new-media-in-china-more-information-more-control.aspx, accessed on 21 July 2010.

[28] At http://www.cnnic.cn/uploadfiles/pdf/2010/3/15/142705.pdf, accessed on 10 July 2010.

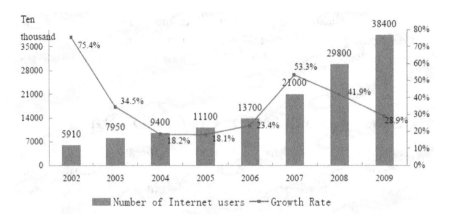

Figure 3.1. Number of Internet Users and Growth Rate in China[29]

The ratio of bloggers to non-bloggers is 1: 2.8.[30] This means that for roughly every three individuals who use the Internet, one of them is a blogger and blogging is becoming an increasingly important means of online expression for a growing number of netizens. By the end of 2009, the number of blog users reached 221 million, and the utilisation rate was 57.7%, an increase of 59.40 million users and 3.4% in utilisation rate, compared to the end of 2008. The proportion of active blog users continues to grow, and the number of users who update their blog within six months has increased to 145 millions, an increase of 37.9%.

The growing popularity of blogs/personal online spaces demonstrates an emerging trend in internet applications, that is, the rise of social internet applications in China. Numerous netizens, the urban youth in particular, prefer to express opinions, exchange ideas and share information with their peers via the Internet. In addition, a

---

[29] From http://www.cnnic.cn/uploadfiles/pdf/2010/3/15/142705.pdf, accessed on 22 August 2010.

[30] '2007 Market Research Report on China's Blog Development', from the website of the China Internet Network Information Centre (CNNIC), at http://www.cnnic.cn/uploadfiles/doc/2007/12/26/113707.doc.

series of big events in the past few years, such as natural disasters including the earthquake in 2008 and the 2008 Olympics Games, have enhanced the popularity of online news.

Many observers of China, especially those in the early phase of the development of the Internet in China, believe that the Internet has created a technological condition for the transition of an authoritarian country to a democratic one. They argue that internet technology, with its uniquely decentralised structure and absence of hierarchy, would overcome authoritarian restrictions on the flow of information and pose an insurmountable threat to the regime. Such a threat may arise from internet use by the masses, civil society, the economy, and the international community, as such usage could provide new channels for political participation from below and thus effect political changes. They also argue that the mounting numbers of netizens will require far more transparency and accountability on the part of the Party and government, and may even hasten the process of political reform in China, transforming China into not only an open society but also an open and democratic regime. That is because in the face of a public having easier access to alternative sources of information, the Party-state would have to adjust and refine its institutions and methods of governance to remain in the dominant position. Some even believe that the new media such as the "blogosphere" makes the debate over state control or interference irrelevant as bloggers can find other ways to get their news and information. Being interactive and reciprocal in its nature of communication, the Internet is also believed to be able to constrain negative consequences resulting from the old format of one-way communication between the state and the citizens. Northeast Asia media expert Ashley W. Esarey believes that it is likely that the Internet will play a role in Chinese media reform, because its "absolute control has proven difficult, if not impossible".[31]

---

[31] Quoted in Bhattacharji, Preeti, Zissis, Carin and Baldwin, Corinne, *Media Censorship in China* from Council on Foreign Relations, New York, 2010, at http://www.cfr.org/about/, accessed 15 July 2010.

Indeed, it is hard to imagine that advances in information and communication technology (ICT) will not bring more possibilities of access and options for Chinese users, especially the Internet, which challenges current media policy that is still control-oriented. It is even harder not to compare new ICT with more traditional media such as newspapers, television and broadcasting, which opens possibilities for Chinese users to communicate among themselves and to form networks on a scale and with a speed that is beyond the government's ability to control. Indeed individuals in Chinese society no longer need to accept the state's definition of reality. ICT has also made it possible for social groups to initiate novel forms of collective action. The questionable religious group, Falungong, has perhaps made the most effective use of the Internet, both through pro-Falungong web pages and by using e-mail for internal group communication. The Internet in China has also become an important forum for public opinion. When major events occur, very intensive and extensive discussions suddenly emerge on websites, placing high political pressure on the authorities and pushing the latter to change existing policy practices. The clear impact of comments and actions of bloggers and participants in internet BBS forums on the handling of specific cases and incidents, as well as the influence on the Chinese media's coverage of these incidents are encouraging many to think that such opinions on the Internet are having a growing influence on sectors including government organs and China's mainstream media. These cases range from the high profile case involving a hotel worker named Deng Yujiao who killed an official she said tried to rape her — in which the intervention of a blogger led to a nationwide outcry, and arguably saved her from a heavy sentence, to more mundane cases where official utterances have been challenged by internet users, resulting in public debate which would have been unlikely a few years ago.

The abortive introduction of the controversial Green Dam software to block violence and pornographic contents on the Internet has also been hailed as a victory, in the Gramscian sense, of the public resisting the state's attempts to impose hegemony, empowered by the Internet itself. China's Ministry of Industry and Information

Technology announced that all computers produced or sold in China would have to be installed with some filtering software (known as Green Dam) from 1 July 2009. The purported intent of the Green Dam software was to filter violence and pornographic contents on the Internet. Critics, however, have condemned the move as a means for the government to keep tabs on internet users who visit politically sensitive websites. The installation of the software would make it easier for the authorities to clamp down on its critics. In the face of intense public opposition, much of it online, the authorities have postponed the installation of this controversial software.[32]

Of course, opposing views are as strong. The establishment and growth of the political control regime has especially led to various pessimistic conclusions regarding the impact of the Internet on political changes in China. They argue that as is so often encountered by researchers on contemporary Chinese politics, the prediction that the almost unlimited potential of the technology would promote democratic development in China is just another case of wishful thinking: the Internet is not as powerful or omnipotent as commonly thought of, merely a force that by itself alone cannot topple or even change the current Chinese regime. They point out that there is only minimal evidence that dissidents have been able to make effective use of the Internet. Neither is there evidence that any dissident group is using the Internet to mount a credible threat to the Chinese government. Furthermore, similar to incidents of social protest such as riots and demonstrations that happen in the real world, protests on the web typically have no leaders or political objectives, characterised by un-institutionalised and chaotic patterns of political participation. The staged demonstrations may be violent, but seldom sustainable beyond a few days. On the contrary, they believe the institutionalisation of government transparency and citizen participation lag far behind government efforts to strengthen and refine methods of control and governance on the one hand and on the other, government

---

[32] 'China Postpones Mandatory Installation of Controversial Filtering Software', *Xinhuawang*, 30 June 2009 at http://news.xinhuanet.com/english/2009-06/30/content_11628335.htm, accessed on 8 August 2009.

strategies — including distributing false and misleading information via the Internet, sowing discord among dissident groups — all of which have been effective. Since 2003, the Ministry of Public Security has led the operation of the so-called "Golden Shield Project", more commonly known as the Great Firewall of China, with 30,000 employees screening out information sent from specific Internet addresses. They argue that China has experienced phenomenal Internet growth without the government losing much control. Although the countervailing strategies of internet users are outstanding in China, the regulators appear to have the upper hand so far.

Some also argue that in the long-run, the Internet may hasten the process of democratisation in China by exposing users to alternative ideas and views. Yet, the democratising effect of the Internet should not be exaggerated, given the dominant role the Party plays in Chinese politics, its determination to remain in control and the fact that there are still many in China who have no access to the Internet. Though the penetration rate is rising continuously, compared with developed countries, China's internet penetration rate is still low. As of December 2009, the penetration rate for USA, Japan and Korea was 74.1%, 75.5% and 77.3%, respectively. In addition, the growth rate of internet users in China was gradually slowing down. It decreased from 41.9% in 2008 to 28.9% in 2009.

Most importantly, they point out the fact that although western attention still seems to focus predominantly on the control role of the state and often depicts it as a monster intent on destroying the Internet in China, the Chinese decision-makers have not treated the Internet as an evil monster but rather as an engine for economic and social growth and have even adopted a proactive policy to develop the Internet. Undoubtedly, the Chinese leadership needs to simultaneously develop the information technology and maintain its control of the development. In other words, it has to implement effective policies to promote rapid development on the one hand and on the other, it has to control, manage, and minimise political risks brought about by the very same technology. While development requires decentralisation, with market principles and policies that are not guided by political ideology, political control requires centralisation, with political

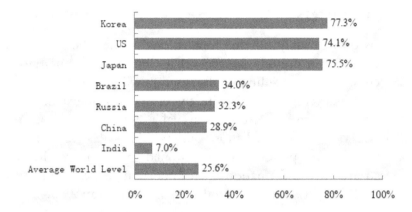

Figure 3.2. Internet Penetration Rate of Countries in December 2009[33]

priorities and policies that conform to political ideology. In their study, Shanthi Kalathil and Taylor Boas conclude that "the authoritarian state is hardly obsolete in the era of the Internet".[34] This is so because the authoritarian state plays a crucial role in charting the development of the Internet and in conditioning the ways in which it is used by societal, economic, and political actors. The very fact that the Chinese state acts as the designer of the Internet development makes it less likely that non-state actors will exert political impact because Internet users "may back away from politically sensitive materials on the web, and entrepreneurs may find it more profitable to cooperate with authorities than to challenge their censorship policies. The government's monitoring structure also promotes an atmosphere of self-censorship. They believe that in the short term, the Internet will continue to be used as a tool by the Chinese leadership as a means to reinforce the image of a caring Party and government, and a channel for promoting and publicising its ideologies and policies.

---

[33] From http://www.cnnic.cn/uploadfiles/pdf/2010/3/15/142705.pdf, which sourced the information from http://www.internetworldstats.com/, accessed on 22 August 2010.

[34] Kalathil, Shanthi, 'China's New Media Sector: Keeping the State In', *The Pacific Review*, 16(4), (2003), pp. 489–501.

CONCLUSION

Opinions differ widely on the implications of the changes in the Chinese media but nobody disagrees that China's economic reform and opening up have resulted in pluralisation within the media environment — a development that directly results from an expansion in the number of both media outlets available within society and the sources of content that feed those outlets. Many observers of contemporary Chinese politics have mentioned that Chinese citizens' increased access to information is an important source of pressure for political reform. Indeed, thanks to the proliferation of media outlets, advances in communication technologies and globalisation, Chinese citizens are much less dependent on official sources for information as they were before 1978. Today, the people of China have a much wider variety of information sources from which to choose, whether in broadcasting, print or telecommunications. This proliferation has changed Chinese citizens' consumption patterns forever: individual freedom of choice is promoted. It implies that even if the diversity is not directly political, it greatly reduces the direct influence of the state over the private spheres of social life. It implies that Chinese citizens no longer need consume the offerings of the central media outlets and also implies the drowning out of messages the central Party-state seeks to impart. The symbolic environment that is created and managed by the Party-state alone is changed forever.

However, the widely different views also indicate that the link between changes in contemporary Chinese media and political reform is complex and therefore there is no simple answer. In the case of the Internet, for example, on the one hand, the Internet may well have an enormous impact on how and what information circulates through Chinese society and may eventually require profound adjustments in the way the state regulates information and legitimates itself; yet on the other hand, the balance of evidence and opinion indicates that no new technology will create an ideal public sphere. Guobin Yang's analysis over online activism in China shows neither the triumph of total control on the part of the Internet-control regime nor of resistance from internet users and activists.[35] Both the state and individual users bring old habits and practices with them when they move to new media and then struggle to define how that media will be used, perhaps only gradually finding its most strategic uses. Technology matters but so do institutional and individual interests. What matters most is that "information and communication technologies have become central means, stakes, and arenas of political struggle".[36]

As the next chapter will show, commercialisation, globalisation and new media technologies notwithstanding, letting market and other forces into the Chinese communication system does not mean taking the state out. On the contrary, the Party-state has tried hard to create and regulate commercial media in a manner that supplies more information, but still legitimates the Party's privileged position in Chinese politics. As will be shown in Chapter 6, an expanded realm of commoditised media and popular culture — from watchdog journalism to popular television gala — has provided a much-needed buffer zone for the Party-state to redefine and establish hegemony over a deeply fractured and rapidly globalising Chinese society. The Party has embraced the marketised provision of media and culture consciously and proactively.

---

[35] Yang, Guobin, *The Power of the Internet in China: Citizen Activism Online*, (New York: Columbia University, 2009), p. 62.
[36] *Ibid.*

IV

Managing the Forces to Stay in Power with Legitimacy

While regime changes in general mean a transition from authoritarian to democracy, the Chinese leadership has managed to stay in control of the process of such a transition. Chapters Two and Three have shown how the Party-state had launched the media reform and how a combination of the unleashed forces from commercialisation, globalisation and technological advances has brought changes to the media sector, with both desired and undesired consequences for the Party-state. Undoubtedly, the leadership has amplified coercive state power to deal with the unwanted consequences, including the closure and major reorganisation of a number of outspoken publications, the removal of editors, and even the arrest and prosecution of journalists. However, the Party-state does not rely exclusively on coercive state powers to control the flow of information. This chapter attempts to reveal how, contrary to the belief that combined forces will produce a serious reduction in the Chinese Party-state's ability to control public communication flows, the CCP has dealt with challenges presented by each of the different forces to maintain its dominant position. It shows that in order to lead and direct the development of communications, there has been a managed process of institutional adjustments to make the political order in which citizens live more appealing. These adjustments are deliberately designed to enable the CCP to provide order for economic growth and new bases for legitimacy of authority in general, and significant expansion of the role of the government in macro-managing media structure and disciplining the media in particular. In other words, while continuing to exercise tight control, the Department of Propaganda and relevant bodies in charge of the media have constantly devised new strategies and policies for regulating media management, practices and content in order to stay relevant to the ever-changing socio-economic environment. It means that as it reconsiders its regime of control in the communications system, the Party-state has not only been reactive but has also progressively embraced and promoted the various forces and transformed the economic basis of the media, while turning and elevating it into a new site of market expansion.

STRUCTURE STRENGTHENING TO ENHANCE REGULATION CAPACITIES

Many have wondered about the mechanism of media policy-making in China. There is certainly a lack of analysis in literature on the mechanism of media policy-making. One obvious reason is that just as China's political system is characterised by its non-transparency, the process of media policy-making is similarly not transparent. Media policies are thus often seen to be uncertain, easy-to-change, and unpredictable.

For a long time, the CCP, "to use Curry's terminology, has preferred a broad and implicit 'directive mode' of media supervision rather than specific, explicit methods such as pre-publication censorship",[1] and media workers are to figure out what should or should not be done. Judy Polumbaum also points out that the operation of

---

[1] Polumbaum, Judy, 'Striving for Predictability: The Bureaucratization of Media Management in China', in Chin-Chuan Lee (Ed.), *China's Media, Media's China*, (Boulder: Westview Press, 1994), pp. 113–128.

the media is governed by a combination of the Party's implicit and explicit policy statements and instructions.[2] One important channel is the annual conferences on propaganda, often presided over by the head of the Central Propaganda Department and attended by heads of the Propaganda Departments at the provincial level. These conferences serve to review the media sector's work in the previous year and provide detailed instructions for the coming year. In addition to the annual conferences at different levels, there are also long-established rules and periodic propaganda guidelines that can come from the CCP Central Committee, the State Council, the Department of Propaganda in the form of "red headed" documents such as speeches by leaders, "urgent announcements", "minutes" of conferences, "opinions", (e.g., on January 12, 2006, the CCP Central Committee and the State Council issued the "Several Opinions on Deepening Cultural System Reform" document, officially launching the wholesale programme for restructuring the media and cultural sector), "circulars" (e.g., "Circular on the Administration of Press, Publication, Radio and Television Industries"), or even the wording for use on a particular issue. Finally, there is also the face-to-face briefing, during which key media gatekeepers are summoned to the Party's Propaganda Department to receive instructions. During these meetings, "the officials tell [the gatekeepers] what they think has gone bad in the coverage, but usually place more emphasis upon the kind of topics they want to see covered in the weeks ahead. They also discuss the work of particular reporters".[3] That policies come in such a great variety of forms may seem to be messy to not only an outsider but also a media worker, who may find the practice of following the various forms of instructions difficult. My interviews with officials working for the Propaganda Department in Sea County in 2006 and 2007 confirm that as in other places at all levels, the Communist Party's Propaganda Department at county level — which has general oversight of all local media content, especially the political correctness,

---

[2] *Ibid.*

[3] Gu, Xuebin, as quoted in De Burgh, Hugo, *The Chinese Journalist: Mediating Information in the World's Most Populous Country*, (London: RoutledgeCurzon, 2003), p. 21.

and manages all the local broadcasting networks — is responsible for ensuring that policies in different forms and from different channels are interpreted and implemented in accordance with the central authorities. The local Propaganda Department considers the local features and then interprets the policies so that they fit with the locality.

While the practice of issuing directives on media operations through a variety of channels has in no way stopped, the past few years has witnessed a clear shift from more fluid and personal oversight toward administrative and legal regulation of the media. This shift is consistent with the Party's shift: from the economic-nationalistic approach of the early reform period to the ideological-institutional approach of recent years. Holbig and Giley argue that it is little surprise as "Party building", which includes both ideological and institutional dimensions, is a central aspect of legitimation strategies.[4]

In coping with the rapid expansion of the media industry, especially with the non-Party entities in media production and distribution, the rapid development of new media technologies, and globalisation which gives rise to pressure from transnational capital entering the Chinese market, the Party and the government have been pressurised to do two things: first, restructure and refine the institutional system that governs China's media industry. Specialised government agencies have been set up by establishing micro-management and micro-operational systems that not only promote a market environment that facilitates the better allocation of resources, competition and order, but more importantly ensure Party leadership and "correct" opinion orientation. Second, starting in the late 1990s but especially in the early 2000s with the start of the reform of the cultural industry, Chinese leaders have embarked on a new strategy for controlling the media which represented a marked departure from the approach to media management in the past. The new approach involves a shift from informal to formal regulatory mechanisms. This can be seen from the amount of information that is provided on relevant websites serving as rules and guidelines. This

---

[4] Holbig and Gilley, 'In Search of Legitimacy in Post-Revolutionary China', p. 6.

new approach makes the system of inspection more transparent on the one hand, and makes predictability paramount in certain realms, notably political coverage, while allowing for flexibility in certain realms of information, such as "service", entertainment, and economic coverage.

The institutional communications system extends from Beijing to the lower administrative levels and can be largely divided into two broad categories, namely government agencies and Party organisations. For both categories, there is the horizontal sector coordinating system, and the vertical four-tier (national, provincial, pre-fectural and county) linkage. At the horizontal government level, the key government organisations under the State Council enforcing laws related to information flowing within, into, and from China include the State Administration for Radio, Film and Television (SARFT), the General Administration for the Press and Publication (GAPP), the Ministry of Culture, the Ministry of Information Industry (MII), and the State Council Information Office (SCIO), each responsible for the regulations of certain sectors in the media industry. The following figure is an illustration of the government regulatory organs for the media in China, some evolved from existing bodies and some recently created:

Table 4.1. Media Regulatory Organs in China

State Council				
State Administration of Radio, Film and TV (SARFT)	General Administration of Press and Publication (GAPP)	Ministry of Culture	Ministry of Information Industry	State Council's Information Office
Radio, TV, Film, Animation (including those on the Internet)	Newspaper Magazine Publication	Art Entertainment	Telecom Wireless Service Broadband	Online Media Internet

For the vertical linkage, each media sector at different tiers are owned, regulated and operated by the corresponding level of government. So coordination is needed not only among the different media sectors but also from the centre to the local. On some occasions, these state organisations may collaborate or work with other government departments to mount national campaigns. For instance, when the campaign against pornographic websites in the summer of 2004 was launched, as many as 14 Party-state agencies were mobilised.

However, all these government agencies are subject to the directives of the Department of Propaganda (DOP). The DOP reports directly to the Standing Committee of the Political Bureau of the CCP's Central Committee, the most powerful decision-making body in China. It answers for the information and cultural networks of institutions, and coordinates with different government agencies to make sure content promotes and remains consistent with Party doctrine. It is therefore the DOP that wields real control of the media under the rule known as the "Party Principle", according to which the media must adhere ideologically to the Party line, propagate the Party message, and obey its policies. The head of the DOP usually holds a concurrent appointment in other Party institutions, such as the Politburo. At the moment the DOP is headed by Liu Yunshan, concurrently a member of the Politburo. Parallel to the state media institutions, the DOP also has the four-tier local units. Thus activities in the lower level media organisations are circumscribed by the local Propaganda Departments, answerable to the Central Propaganda Department in Beijing.

This division between the Party and government agencies ensures that the Party can legitimate its will through laws and regulations and employ state apparatuses to implement its policies. So, as the Party takes care of the media, state agencies expand their role in managing communication structures and policing communication flows, serving as the judicial and executive arms of the Party. Take the SARFT as an example. Unlike any other government departments, this agency is regarded as both a news organisation and a broadcasting administrative bureaucracy. This means that it is also subject to the leadership of both the Party and the government. Three national broadcast networks — China Central Television, China National Radio and

China Radio International — are all under the direct control of the SARFT. The editorial board of the SARFT, under the leadership of the Party committee, is composed of deputy ministers, heads of the three radio and television networks, leaders of other departments such as the Film Bureau, the Broadcast Publishing House, and the Television Arts Committee. According to Zhao, it is directly "in charge of the news, features and programming of the three stations and its detailed duties include delivering Party and government directives to the news outlets, drafting strategies for carrying out these directives, organising and coordinating large-scale media campaigns, approving major media activities, propaganda plans and programme change initiated by the broadcast network, and exercising editorial control of important news items and programmes".[5] The organisation is also a "huge government bureaucracy in charge of every aspect of the country's broadcast operations — issuing regulations, setting technical standards, training personnel, and coordinating research".[6]

The SARFT is also a good example of further expansion and strengthening of government agencies responsible for both communication content and the structure of the rapidly expanding information, media, and cultural systems in the 1990s. The predecessor of the SARFT, known as the China Broadcasting Affairs Management Division and formed in June 1949, became an organisation directly under the State Council in March 1998. As its name suggests, the SARFT oversees matters related to broadcasting, film and television. Another example is the upgrading of the Foreign Propaganda Office, more commonly known as the State Council Information Office overseas. As the central component of China's overall foreign strategy was to improve its infrastructure and capacities for building a favourable image of China overseas throughout the 1990s,[7] the Central Foreign Propaganda Group, established in 1980

---

[5] Zhao, *Media, Market, and Democracy in China,* p. 23.

[6] *Ibid.*

[7] This was to address negative foreign perceptions after the June 4th crackdown on the pro-democracy movement in 1989, when China was bombarded with international criticism for its lack of human rights and democracy.

but dismissed in 1988, was revitalised in March 1990 and in 1993, it was renamed the Central Foreign Propaganda Office in China. The same office at the provincial, municipal and city levels was also established.[8] The Central Foreign Propaganda Office, or the State Council Information Office, has thus become China's international public relations department[9] projecting China to the world in a positive light.

Indeed, what set the year 1998 was that during that year apart, the government initiated massive efforts to reorganise the whole bureaucratic system under the State Council, to form the foundation of its regulatory state in order to meet the requirements for China's entry to the WTO. However, in the midst of major bureaucratic streamlining that witnessed the reduction in the number of government ministries from 40 to 29, the government not only established the Culture Bureau under the Ministry of Culture and added personnel to strengthen the State Administration of Press and Publishing (SPPA), which was set up to tighten up administrative supervision of the press in 1987 by drafting and enforcing press regulations, licensing publications, and monitoring text, but also established the Ministry of Information Industry to regulate both the technological and industrial structures of China's Internet system. In 2000, the SPPA was renamed the General Agency of Press and Publication (GAPP), and its status was upgraded from a deputy ministry-level agency to a full ministry level one, indicating the importance attached to this body in the regularisation process, with corresponding agencies at lower levels. While this government agency has no authority over central Party newspapers, it is in charge of all the publication agencies at provincial and county level. According to statistics published by GAPP in July 2009, the GAPP currently oversees 1,943 newspapers, 9,549 magazines, 579 publishing houses, 378 audio-visual publishing houses, 240 electronic publishing houses, 161,256

---

[8] Zeng, Jianhui, *Melting the Ice, Building a Bridge and Breaking through,* (Beijing: Wuzhou Publishing House, 2006), p. 2.

[9] Shirk, *China, Fragile Superpower,* p. 95.

distribution outlets, and 6,290 printing companies in China.[10] An important reason for this upgrade was the agency's added responsibility for approving web-based publishing applications and monitoring web-publishing content, while strengthening its capacities to combat illegal and pornographic publications and expanding its regulative capacities in publication and copyright-related issues.

Perhaps the evolution of China's control regime in dealing with the fluid and multi-faceted nature of the Internet is most revealing of the Chinese state's determination to ensure a thriving and yet controlled internet: Chinese authorities at different levels have been promoting the development of information technology by using a similar approach — focusing on the technological and commercial applications while keeping an eye on the political and social implications. From the way the Chinese leaders initially dealt with the Internet, it was clear that they first saw the information and communication technologies industry primarily as a new economic sector, not as an arena of political contention. They developed the industry out of the conviction that China lagged behind the West by one century in Industrialisation; however, in the history of information technology, especially the Internet, China was only 10 years behind. So China could catch up with western developed powers. They considered this new industry as a core industry in the national economy and national security, a driving force for innovation and growth in other industry sectors, and fundamental for informatising Chinese society. In fact, as the size of users at the beginning was very small, the state was dubious of its political and social implications, and it therefore managed the Internet in the same way as it did for the conventional media. Policy-makers did not think it was fundamentally different from newspapers or radio and TV stations, each of which had been transformed in the reform era while remaining under the firm control of the Party-state.

---

[10] From the website of the General Administration of Press and Publication of the People's Republic of China, at http://www.gapp.gov.cn/cms/html/21/464/List-1.html, accessed on 8 August 2010.

However, the authorities soon recognised the differences between the conventional media and this highly dispersed and versatile new media. Like all authoritarian states, China moved quickly to come up with a variety of more refined and flexible strategies, ensuring that the development of this new domain promotes their own interests and priorities. When the MII, created through a merger of the Ministry of Post and Telecommunications and the Ministry of Electronic Industry, proved to be inadequate and ineffectual in macro-managing a rapidly converging and globalising information and communication sector, a new unit, the Internet Information Management Bureau, was quickly added to the State Council Information Office in 2000. This unit is responsible for the monitoring of internet news and Bulletin Board Services (BBS) and for directing Party-state propaganda on the Internet. Other state agencies, from the Ministry of Culture, the State Industry and Commerce Administration to the Ministry of Public Security and the Chinese Military, all have jurisdiction over the Internet. In August 2001, the Chinese Leadership Group in Information was established, with the then Premier Zhu Rongji as its leader. Since 2006, this supra-ministerial body has been headed by Premier Wen Jiaobao, with Huang Ju, Politburo Standing Committee member and Deputy Premier, Liu Yunshan, head of the Party's Propaganda Department, Zeng Peiyan, head of the State Development and Reform Commission, and Zhou Yongkang, Minister of Public Security, as the group's deputy leaders. Its members comprise the heads of other relevant state commissions, ministries, Party departments, and government agencies responsible for various sectors of the communications and information industries. The establishment of this de facto "information cabinet" above the State Council has multi-fold objectives: "to further strengthen leadership over the promotion of our country's information build-up and over the maintenance of the state's information security". It is to ensure the highest and broadest possible state stewardship over China's rapidly expanding information and communication fields. It is true that most states are attempting to regulate the Internet to benefit from this new technology and reduce its undesirable consequences, but what sets China apart is that the Chinese government has become one of the most sophisticated political organisation of today's world in regulating the role of the Internet, even though it is almost impossible for the Chinese state to "eliminate" all undesirable political consequences. Still, with the strengthened government agencies, administrative and technical personnel, rules and laws, a cyber police force, as well as increasing sophistication of firewalls and filtering software, the authorities seem to be confident that the positive aspects of the Internet outweigh the negatives. This is revealed in China's general principle regarding the Internet, which prescribes "developing it actively, strengthening its management, seeking advantages and avoiding harmfulness, making it serve our purpose". The rhetoric of high-level leaders like Wen Jiabao and more importantly, enormous investments in telecommunications infrastructure by state-owned firms show that the Chinese state does not stand in opposition to the Internet but, for economic and ideological reasons, has enthusiastically promoted this new technology. According to the China Network Information Centre, the government has been increasing expenditure in infrastructure. In order to promote economic recovery, the state invested 4 trillion in funds, mainly focusing on infrastructure construction, which promoted steady growth in telecommunications network development. Data from the Ministry of Industry and Information Technology show that, as of November 2009, the telecommunications investment in fixed assets was $277.34 billion, an accumulated increase of 28.5% from the same period in 2008.[11] The application of standard restrictions on internet media organisations, the state's willingness to devote considerable resources to its development, and the adoption of countervailing technologies have so far worked for the Chinese government in using the Internet to advance its own agenda rather than seeing the Internet as a threat.

To conclude, after decades of experience in using mass media as instruments for social and political control, the Chinese government

---

[11] From the website of the China Internet Network Information Centre, at http://www.cnnic.cn/uploadfiles/pdf/2010/3/15/142705.pdf, accessed on 8 August 2010.

and the CCP have strengthened the structure for regulating media management, practice and content.

HEIGHTENED ATTENTION FROM TOP LEADERS TO THE MOST POPULAR AND INNOVATIVE FORMS

Improving regulatory mechanisms is certainly an important aspect of controlling the media industry. Regular attention from top leaders to important media outlets also indicates the leaders' determination to keep them under the leadership of the Party. The special attention from the Party-state on the 24-hour news channel launched in May 2003 as a symbol of reform in the Chinese media by CCTV, the only national level television station, exemplifies the unwillingness of the Party-state to loosen its control over CCTV news content. In February 2003, CCTV submitted to the Politburo a proposal for the launch of a news channel, which had already been checked many times by the SARFT's Party Committee and its director Xu Guangchun, who was also deputy head of the Propaganda Department.[12] According to Zhao Huayong, then president of CCTV, Party Secretary Hu Jintao and all Politburo members gave written instructions on the proposal.[13] A special mobilisation meeting was held on April 9. The words of Zhao Huayong at the mobilisation meeting reveal both the anxiety and determination of the Party-state in its control of the news channel[14]:

> CCTV has started other channels without a mobilisation meeting. But this time Director Xu Guangchun ordered for a mobilisation meeting. This shows the great attention from the State Administration of Radio, Film and Television.

---

[12] Zhao Huayong, 'Stick to the Right Orientation and Go All out to Ensure High Quality in News Channel', *TV Research*, 5, (2003), pp. 9–10.

[13] *Ibid.*, p. 9

[14] *Ibid.*

On April 30, the day before the launch, Li Changchun, member of the Politburo in charge of propaganda, and Liu Yunshan, head of the Propaganda Department, went to CCTV and gave specific requirements for the news channel, namely, "correct guidance of public opinion, unity, stability and the cultivation of propaganda art".[15]

Likewise, every term of top leaders chooses a special occasion to go and inspect the People's Daily, one of the most important national level media outlets of the Party. On such occasions, they would call for continued ideological vigilance and loyalty to Party dictums. On the 60th anniversary of the founding of the People's Daily in 2008, General Party Secretary Hu Jintao went to meet the editorial board, chiefs of all departments and some journalists; his speech once again reasserted the leadership of the CCP.

The top leaders' high-profile visits to important media outlets also indicate the leaders' determination to stay in control of any innovative development in the media, be they results of journalistic innovations or technological advances. The visits from the three generations of premiers to the crew of the current affairs programme "Focus" by CCTV, a product of media reform, demonstrates the continuous attention from Chinese top leaders to the most popular media of the time and their determination to shape public discourse. Indeed, among all the changes and developments in the media in the early 1990s, the rise of the CCTV's current affairs programme "Focus" — with a special in-depth or investigative aspect and the format of discussion on topical issues rather than merely echoing official political slogans — became the most noticeable. With over 300 million people watching this programme every night in the mid-1990s, its impact was unprecedented. Premiers Li Peng, Zhu Rongji and Wen Jiabao all visited the crew and conferred epigraphs to the programme, a typical Chinese way of great attention from high-level officials.

As will be shown in Chapter Six, the Party-state also utilised the popular Spring Festival TV Gala, watched by over 1 billion people on

---

[15] See the articles by Wang, Ping and Shen Zhi Rui 'Comrade Li Changchun Visited CCTV Staff', *TV Research*, 5, (2003), p. 4, and Liu Yunshan's 'Talk on the Visit to CCTV Staff', *TV Research*, 5, (2003), p. 6.

every Chinese New Year's Eve since 1983, as a source of re-establishing and maintaining its political legitimacy for its leadership after the 1989 Incident. In 1990, a few months after the Tiananmen incident, a specially made video clip was played at the Spring Festival TV Gala Party, with the then General Party Secretary Jiang Zemin and Premier Li Peng wishing the whole nation "stability and unity". Their appearance at the Gala reflected the Party-state's better understanding of the use to which the media, especially television, may be put to increase their popularity.

When the Party-state realised the importance of the Internet, they did not hesitate to occupy the commanding heights. Indeed, as the social contradictions of China's capitalistic development become more acute, the Party has been compelled to elaborate its ruling ideology in a way that may still have some appeal to the vast majority of the population. Thanks to its nature of two-way traffic communication, the Internet provides a relatively more direct channel for the leadership to engage with members of society. In June 2008, Hu Jintao visited the headquarters of the People's Daily and chatted online with netizens via the "Strong China Forum". During the dialogue, Hu Jintao expressed his concern over the well-being of netizens at various social levels. He disclosed to the netizens that he always read domestic and foreign news online. This was apparently the first time a top leader of China had openly conveyed his well-wishes to netizens. Just before his online debut, Hu said in a speech delivered at the People's Daily headquarters that the Internet had become the catalyst for promoting the Party's ideology and culture, and an amplifier of public opinion, from which the voice of the masses could be accumulated and augmented easily. He concluded that the social influence of the new media should be fully recognised, and that government leaders and Party cadres should attach great importance to the construction, implementation and management of the Internet.[16]

Nine months later, in March 2009, Premier Wen Jiabao made his online chat debut a week prior to the opening of the annual National

---

[16] 'Speech Delivered While on a Visit to the People's Daily', *People's Daily*, dated June 2009 at http://media.people.com.cn/GB/40606/7409348.html, accessed on 3 July 2009.

People's Congress (NPC) and Chinese People's Political Consultative Conference (CPPCC) sessions.[17] Going beyond Hu's earlier 20 minutes showcase chat, Wen's dialogue with netizens lasted almost two hours. He was deluged with about 90,000 questions on various subjects ranging from the shoe-throwing incident in Cambridge,[18] his income level, and the economic crisis, to healthcare reform and corruption among officials.[19] This dialogue can be seen to be a reflection of the Chinese leaders' more open and confident style of governance in the information age on the one hand and on the other, a further attempt to be closer to the people during a time of economic hardship, in order to prevent social grievances from getting out of hand.

TAKING ADVANTAGE OF NEW MEDIA TECHNOLOGIES

As discussed above, both the Party and government have given their imprimatur to capitalise on the Internet's potential. As many have observed, through a combination of reactive and proactive strategies, an authoritarian regime can effectively counter the challenges posed by internet use and even utilise the Internet to extend its reach and authority. In other words, while NGOs and dissidents from within and without China have utilised the Internet to expand their political influence, the Chinese state has also used the Internet for various purposes, some of which are listed below.

Channel for Accessing Public Opinion

Obviously the Internet is an effective channel for the Party-state to explain its policies and positions on various issues to the public, and

---

[17] 'China's Wen makes Internet debut', section of 'Breaking news technology' of *The Sunday Age*, 1 March 2009, at http://news.theage.com.au/breaking-news-technology/chinas-wen-makes-internet-debut-20090301-8l5r.html.

[18] A protester threw a shoe at the Chinese Premier as he was delivering a speech at Cambridge University, 2 February 2009. Information can be found at http://www.timesonline.co.uk/tol/news/uk/article5643558.ece, accessed on 5 June 2009.

[19] 'Premier Wen Talks Online with the Public', *China Daily*, 20 February 2009.

in turn, receive public feedback. In a society where there are few feedback mechanisms, the online comments and opinions from the public are becoming a valuable source for the Party and government to gauge public reactions to policies and their implementation.

At the 38th regular study session of the Politburo in 2007, Hu Jintao called on government officials to "actively and creatively nurture a healthy online culture" that meets public demand. What it means is that he expects officials at all levels to facilitate the development of the Internet while improving the administration of web technologies, content and network security.[20] He urged senior officials to improve their internet literacy and use the Internet well, so as to improve the art of leadership.[21] It is therefore expected that Chinese leaders and officials pay increasing attention to citizens' online views as a way to better understand their preoccupations and concerns.

Such a feedback channel also serves to give the public some assurance that their views can be heard, thereby enabling the authorities to nib any grievances in the bud before they snowball into a bigger problem. Acutely aware of the function, Wen Jiabao, for instance, on hearing complaints about the differences between the Government report and the report from the Chinese Academy of Social Sciences (CASS) on the unemployment rate in China in 2009, reportedly instructed that all ministries should respond immediately to queries on the Internet rather than wait for his approval.[22] It is unsurprising then that when Madam Fu Ying, then Ambassador to the Chinese Embassy in London, had a meeting with students and

---

[20] 'President Hu Jintao Asks Officials to Better Cope with the Internet', *Xinhuawang*, 24 January 2007, at http://news.xinhuanet.com/english/2007-01/24/content_5648674.htm, accessed on 20 July 2010.

[21] See 'Chinese Premier to Talk Online with the Public', *Xinhuawang*, 28 February 2009 at http://news.xinhuanet.com/english/2009-02/28/content_10916529.htm, accessed on 20 July 2010.

[22] Cao, Jianwen, 'The Significance of Premier Wen's "Do not Wait for My Approval"', at http://politics.people.com.cn/GB/30178/9038416.html, accessed on 10 July 2010.

members of staff in the University of Nottingham in the UK in 2008, she opened her speech by saying that she went online every day, indicating that she paid great attention to what was said on the Internet.

In addition to using the Internet as a barometer of public mood, the leadership has also ascribed to the public a role, albeit within limits, in using the Internet to supervise the conduct of Party and government officials. Netizens are encouraged to help the Party and government identify and report on official malpractice and abuse of power to improve governance and strengthen the Party and government's legitimacy. 2008 was known as the "Year of Internet Supervision in China".[23] In that year, netizens demonstrated their power by helping to disclose a number of high-profile incidents ranging from a corrupt city official in Jiangsu Province[24] to ostentatious spending and abuse of public power.[25] From the list of incidents, compiled by Lye and Yi, that first gained prominence on the Internet, as shown in Table 4.2 below, we can see that such disclosures had not been met with the usual news blackout. Instead, the relevant authorities had taken quick and decisive actions to punish officials identified by the anonymous online postings.

The ability of the Internet to generate instant and huge public opinion empowers the society to protest against government misbehaviour. Meanwhile, it also empowers the state to gauge public opinion and make proper policy adjustments. Effective government reactions to the problems exposed by public opinions on the Internet help to maintain stability that the regime deems so dear.

---

[23] 'Online Supervision Offers Fresh Dynamic Mechanism for the Fight against Corruption and the Construction of Social Harmony', *People's Daily*, 3 February 2009.

[24] 'Official Sacked for Costly Lifestyle', *China Daily*, 21 January 2009. (A picture of the official, Zhou Jiugeng, was posted on the web showing him with a pack of Nanjing 95 Imperial cigarettes, which cost about 150 *Yuan* and wearing a Swiss-made Vacheron Constantin watch, retailing at about 100,000 *Yuan* in China).

[25] 'Online Video Exposes Corrupt Officials', *Straits Times*, 24 February 2009, and 'For China, A Costly Lesson in Engaging Its Netizens', *Straits Times*, 2 March 2009.

Table 4.2. Major Incidents that First Gained Prominence on the Internet in 2008[26]

Locations	Incidents	Outcomes
Chongqing	Homeowners refused to move, apparently due to insufficient compensation	1. Greater awareness of the rights of individual home owners under the Property Law passed in 2007. 2. The local officials, construction companies and the nail families[27] eventually worked out a compromise.
Shanxi	Child labour in coal mines	1. Shanxi government took tough actions against child labour. 2. Governor made a public apology.
Shaanxi	False sighting of rare South China tigers	1. Zhou Zhenglong who fabricated the sightings was arrested and sentenced to two and half years of imprisonment, but given a three years reprieve. 2. Launch of an educational campaign against fabricating false information for three months. 3. The deputy director of the Shaanxi Provincial Forestry Department and 12 other relevant local officials were suspended.
Wenzhou	Local officials' extravagant spending on overseas travel at public expense	Officials concerned were sacked or required to report their movements to the proper authorities within a prescribed time and at a prescribed place (双规).
Jiangsu	An official with a luxurious lifestyle	1. The official, Zhou Jiugeng was sacked when his extravagant lifestyle was made public. 2. The provincial civil service launched a public education campaign against such practices.

---

[26] Complied by Lye, Liang Fook and Yang, Yi, 'The Chinese Leadership and the Internet', *EAI Background Brief No. 467*, (2009), at http://www.eai.nus.edu.sg/BB467.pdf, accessed on 20 July 2010.

[27] The nail families or nail houses are the last ones left standing in areas slated for clearance, so called because they stick out when all around them have been demolished.

IMPROVING GOVERNANCE

To a great degree, modern governance is a matter of information. ICT in China has become crucial in helping the government build a modern system of governance. With the online presence of government portals, information is believed to be more available for the public, and citizens are believed to be more informed.

Many observers agree that China has never had a routinised system of institutional censorship. The decisive factors in whether information or ideas are released or suppressed, and where and how they are presented, tend to be situational rather than fixed.[28] However, the move from the Party and government to rely more on regulations rather than whim in order to better manage the media is clearly shown in all government portals providing information that serve as regulations for the media industry. For instance, the information provided on the website of the SARFT, while serving as rules and guidelines, also helps administrative departments, broadcasting, circulation and production organisations, and other related bodies, producers and investors to make more effective decisions. The "Announcement of TV Shooting and Production Registration" on the SARFT website, for instance, may help them pursue, purchase, cooperate, inspect and make requests to relevant programmes, to more effectively handle all manners of market actions, including topic selection competition, rights disputation, topic overlap and duplicate shooting and production.

Interestingly, the Central Department of Propaganda that has always been considered an invisible actor in the control of media content has also set up its website called "China Civilisation Website" (中国文明网), jointly with the Spiritual Civilisation Office of the Central Committee.[29] It is intriguing that the Party has framed its ideological hegemony in terms of "civilisation". In addition to staging top leaders' activities in relation to propaganda work, this website provides

---

[28] See Polumbaum, Judy, 'The Tribulations of China's Journalists after a Decade of Reform', in Chin-Chuan Lee (Ed.), *Voices of China*, pp. 33–68.

[29] The website of the Central Department of Propaganda: http://www.wenming.cn/.

policies, speeches from top leaders on propaganda work, and directives on national ideological campaigns. Local DOPs have their own "Civilisation Websites". These websites provide more direct guidance and efficient management.

At the government level, almost every provincial government in China has launched its own website to promote e-government.

Table 4.3. Online Channels to Facilitate Public and Provincial Government Communication[30]

Province/Municipality/ Autonomous Region	Channel for Online Communication
Beijing Municipality	http://szxx.beijing.gov.cn/webmayorbox
Tianjin Municipality	http://szmail.tj.gov.cn/szf/newmail.nsf/first?openform
Hebei Province	http://www.hebei.gov.cn/interaction/mail
	http://hudong.sjzchina.com/mailbox
Shanxi Province	http://www.shanxigov.cn/structure/hdjl/hdjl.htm
Inner Mongolia Autonomous Region	http://www.nmg.gov.cn/zx
Liaoning Province	http://www.ln.gov.cn/html/ldxx.html
Jilin Province	http://www.jl.gov.cn/zt/jlsszrx
Heilongjiang Province	http://www.hljxf.gov.cn
Shanghai Municipality	http://wsxf.sh.gov.cn/wsxf/zgsh/login.asp?Addressee= E99 7636B
	http://www.shanghai.gov.cn/shanghai/node2314/ node19802/index.html
Jiangsu Province	http://www.jiangsu.gov.cn/tmzf/zfld/lzjdsz/
Zhejiang Province	http://www.zj.gov.cn/gb/zjnew/node3/node22/ node165/node1749/index.html
Anhui Province	http://www.ah.gov.cn/szzc/szxx.asp
Fujian Province	http://www.fz12345.gov.cn
Jiangxi Province	http://www.jiangxi.gov.cn/gtzf/szxx
Shandong Province	http://www.shandong.gov.cn/col/col142/index.html

(*Continued*)

---

[30] Complied by Lye, Liang Fook and Yang, Yi, based on findings by People's Daily dated 5 January 2009, from Lye Liang Fook and Yang Yi, 'The Chinese Leadership and the Internet'.

Table 4.3. (*Continued*)

Province/Municipality/ Autonomous Region	Channel for Online Communication
Henan Province	http://www.hnxf.gov.cn
Hubei Province	http://www.hubei.gov.cn/hdjl/index.shtml
Hunan Province	http://www.hunan.gov.cn/hdjl/szxx
Guangdong Province	http://www.gd.gov.cn/gzhd/szxx/
Guangxi Province	http://xinfang.nanning.gov.cn
Hainan Province	http://www.hainan.gov.cn/code/V3/leader.php governors@hainan.gov.cn
Chongqing Municipality	http://www.cq.gov.cn/publicmail/citizen/ writemail.aspx
Sichuan Province	http://www.sc.gov.cn/hdjl/gmxf/szxx/index.shtml
Guizhou Province	http://www.gzgov.gov.cn/pages/zfjg/pages/szf_ly.asp
Yunnan Province	http://xfservice.yn.gov.cn/xinfang/xfjcx.jsp
Xizang Autonomous Region	http://www.xizang.gov.cn/mailBoxForm.do
Shaanxi Province	http://www.shaanxi.gov.cn/IssuedContentAction.do? dispatch=vContForXFMain&colid=643
Gansu Province	http://www.gansu.gov.cn/Szxx.asp
Qinghai Province	http://www.qh.gov.cn/qzlx
Ningxia Autonomous Region	http://www.nx.gov.cn/structure/myhd/wyxx.htm
Xinjiang Autonomous Region	Unable to access website at time of entry in July 2009 (due to riots by Uyghurs against Han Chinese on 5 July 2009)

Almost every county in China has also launched its own website. *Gateway to Sea County,* run by the local government from 8th December 2004, is such an example. Located in the northern part of Zhejiang Province, 118 kilometres away from Shanghai, Sea County is economically developed, ranking 32nd among the nationally awarded "One Hundred All-round Strong Counties" (百强县). A visit to the website brings up the following set of items:

- Introduction to Sea County
  — *Sea County on video* (four video clips, each lasting 15 minutes)

- News from Sea County
  — *Sea County Today* (Internet version of the newspaper)
- Organisation of the county government
  — Administrative departments
  — Service departments
  — Supervision
  — Policies and guidelines
  — New documents
- Chinese Communist Party and Youth league construction
- Investment in Sea County
- Foreign finance and trade
- Education
- Information
  — Sightseeing in Sea County (a 15-minutes' video clip)
  — Housing
  — Jobs
- Surveys, invitation for suggestions, criticism and comments

A close examination of the website in 2006 suggests that it is more of a gateway to Sea County for the outside world than a service window for the locals. In other words, local people do not seem to be the audience of the electronic government services. Instead, Sea County has taken advantage of the latest technologies to raise its profile and to reach an overseas audience. The topics the website covers and the language used both deliver the message to the user that Sea County has a transparent government, and that it has a very good environment for investment. The website uses both simplified and the traditional Chinese characters, and the video clips introducing the history and the recent development of the county have two versions, one in Mandarin Chinese and the other in English. Interviews with the manager confirm that the Chinese characters target investors from Taiwan, Hong Kong and Asian countries, while the English language text is meant for possible international investors. It seems that the intention for the website is to help the country gain more recognition and to invite investment from the whole world rather than to be a platform for local citizens to engage in discussion and participation. An examination of the site also makes it obvious that in addition to its existing mouthpieces such as the TV and radio stations, the local government has developed another important platform to make announcements on policies, regulations and documents to provide it with as well as political publicity. It is another means of expression for the local community at best, rather than of the community.

However, more recent visits show that although the above mentioned functions still remain, the local government is also using the Internet to conduct some surveys and for some charity work, which opens up a channel for interaction between ordinary people and the government, albeit to a limited degree. In the months of August and September 2008, for instance, the website was used to invite comments on the adjustment of taxi prices in the county. The County's Women's Federation is also using the Internet as a platform for raising donations for people in need. These observations lead to the argument that compared with other traditional media forms, the website run by the county government, while having its own limitations, may have the greatest potential to facilitate critical deliberation and the formation of public opinion, which may increase the prospects of having some effect on policy formulation.

It is no coincidence that Chinese leaders are looking to the Internet as a tool to extend their reach. Needless to say, the two-way communication that characterises the Internet is more favourable for the strengthening of government legitimacy than one-way propaganda. The government has not only reacted to online public opinions quickly, but also started to take initiatives to utilise the Internet as a platform to communicate with the society.

Construction of a Favourable Image

Given the Internet's relative ease of use and increasing appeal to an expanding pool of Chinese youth, the CCP has been quick to capitalise on it for both e-government and for the promotion of a pro-people image. Hu and Wen's online chat with netizens have set a good example for other leaders at the lower levels. For instance, the governor of

Guangdong Province issued New Year greetings by using Internet jargon to convey his well-wishes to the people. Such greetings were apparently better received by the public. The governor of Qinghai Province also thanked netizens in 2009 for making useful suggestions that helped improve local governance.[31] Many other officials have set up personal blogs to further engage netizens.[32] In fact, since September 2008, The People's Daily has sanctioned an official fan club webpage for top leaders in the central government[33] By the beginning of 2009, 17 provincial governors and general secretaries have established the practice of personally responding to letters from netizens.[34] This approach has been highly commended by netizens who view it as a practice in line with the Party's good tradition and as a hallmark of good leaders genuinely concerned about the people.

Sometime around 2005, Party leaders had already started becoming more creative about how to influence public opinion on the Internet.[35] A number of public relations blunders taught the Party and government the painful but important lesson of putting out timely and accurate information. For instance, in 2003, China's public image, both domestically and externally, was battered by its initial slow reaction to the outbreak of SARS in the country. Other subsequent major events such as the bird flu, the Olympic Torch Relay and the Earthquake in 2008 further underscored the value of seizing "the right to speak" through various channels including the Internet. They learnt that releasing information first, even when it is incomplete, may not necessarily lead to instability; instead they can take the

---

[31] 'Governor of Qinghai Song Xiuyan Answered Messages Delivered by Netizens', *People's Daily*, 11 February 2009.

[32] These include Zhu Yongxin (Vice Mayor of Suzhou), Li Chao (Director of Shenyang Bureau of Environmental Protection) and Chen Junan (Director of Zhengzhou Pricing Bureau).

[33] For instance, the fan club of Hu-Wen can be accessed via http://shijinbabaofan. g.ifensi.com/main/show. As of 31 July 2010, there are over 9,400 members.

[34] 'Wang Yang and Huang Huahua again Send Their Wishes to Netizens', *Southern Metropolitan Daily*, 20 January 2009.

[35] Bandurski, David, 'China's Guerrilla War for the Web', *Far East Economic Review*, 7 July 2008.

wind out of the sails of critics that they are mounting a cover-up. This marks an important departure from the past image of the Party-state covering up negative news.[36] In addition, the strong views articulated by netizens on Tibet's Independence, the Olympic Torch Relay outside China, and during the earthquake in 2008 made the Party-state realize the Internet's potential for mobilising social forces to support it.

Even more important for the leadership is that the majority of the Internet users are between 18 and 35, well-educated, and at a young and malleable age. Many of them use the Internet to express their opinions, exchange ideas and share information. For this group of people, they may not find the traditional media channels such as the print media, broadcasting and books as appealing. The Internet, however, allows the leadership to identify more easily with this group of people, as well as to portray itself as forward-looking and dynamic, and as making an effort to better understand the concerns and preoccupations of the younger generation.

BOLSTERING THE CAPACITY TO WORK WITH THE MEDIA

The Chinese media has been undisputably growing in size, autonomy and diversity in recent years. Although the government wants to maintain considerable control over the media, there are nevertheless incentives for the government to push forward media reforms which will not only enable it to contribute to economic growth but also to gain credibility and creativity for better guidance of public opinion, which could only come from more autonomy. What is imperative for the Party and government in the context of a more autonomous media is then the enhancement of its ability to work with the media. Indeed, the Party-state has issued many calls to officials at all levels to enhance working capacity with the media. In 2004, the "Decision of

---

[36] For instance, in the Tangshan earthquake of 1976, no official information about what actually happened or the number of casualties was made available. This was done in the interest of protecting state secrets.

the CCP Central Committee on the Enhancement of the Party's Governance Capability" passed at the 4th Plenum of the 16th Party Congress explicitly states the need to "strengthen the abilities to guide public opinion and assume pre-emptive power in public opinion work". In January 2010, at the national conference on propaganda work, the propaganda chief, Li Changchun, re-emphasised the importance for the Party's Propaganda Departments at all levels to improve their capability to recognise the media's role in pooling strength to carry out certain tasks. At the conference, he praised highly the proactive efforts that Propaganda Departments had made to enhance their ability in guiding public opinions through the media and called them to "treat the media well, use the media well and manage the media well".[37] This call was absolutely necessary for the Party and government to stop officials at different levels from taking it for granted that the media is the mouthpiece of the Party. For instance, rhetoric from officials such as "are you prepared to speak for the Party or for the people" when interviewed by journalists on housing problems certainly damages the pro-people image the Party has been trying to construct.

To boost the credibility of the government with the public and to improve the relations between them, which have become vital in the creation of a confident and open-minded image of the Party and government, the news briefing and spokesperson system has been introduced to every department of the central government and at the provincial level since 2004. One the one hand, it regulates and standardises the press conferences. On the other, it introduces and promotes the system by organising the training of thousands of spokespersons at the central and local government levels. In late 2004, it was announced to the public that the first group of 80-odd spokespersons in the 70 departments under the State Council

---

[37] Zhang, Wei, 'National Conference on Propaganda Work in Beijing; Li Changchun Attended the Conference and Delivered a Speech', from the website of the Xinhua News Agency, 4 January 2010, at http://news.xinhuanet.com/politics/2010-01/04/content_12752787.htm, accessed on 15 July 2010.

would be set up. In the same period, 20 provincial governments began offering press conferences with specially designated spokespersons. Today, SCIO sponsors regular press conferences, inviting different government department heads to give presentations. For instance, the National Bureau of Statistics and General Administration of Work Safety hold four regular press conferences each year at SCIO.

THE OPERATION OF "MULTIPLE LAYERS OF CENSORSHIP"

There is no doubt that the Chinese leadership is determined to maintain control over the development of the media industry. As discussed earlier, much of the Party's control over the media comes from a combination of formal bureaucratic procedures and informal regulatory means. During Mao Zedong's era, the Propaganda Department was the foremost agency in charge of media supervision and control. It was used pervasively to effectively control the media and to launch waves of mass campaigns for political indoctrination and thought control, as well as for mobilising people to support the regime's particular economic or foreign policies. The control of the media by the CCP was pervasive, totalistic and repressive. Today, express or implied coercion is still an important element in the mix. According to the Committee to Protect Journalists based in New York, China was the world's leading jailer of journalists for the 10th consecutive year in 2008, with at least 28 journalists imprisoned as of December 1, 2008. According to People's Daily, censorship agencies closed down 338 publications in 2004 for printing "internal" information, 202 branch offices of newspapers, and punished 73 organisations for illegally "engaging in news activities".[38]

---

[38] From http://www.cpj.org/2009/02/attacks-on-the-press-in-2008-china.php; accessed on 2 January 2011; Hilton, Isabel, 'Beijing's media chill', 15 February 2006, at http://www.opendemocracy.net/democracy-china/chill_3272.jsp, accessed on 2 January 2011.

However, because of the complexity and scope of control in an increasingly commercial environment, the regime has adopted multiple layers of censorship in managing the media, some of which are discussed below.

Differentiated Control

A strategy of differentiated control across media outlets and media content has been adopted by the leaders. Preoccupied with the concern for stability, the Party-state adopts this strategy of differentiated control to minimise the reach of certain practices and ideas, by confining them to certain spaces and niche publications. This practice limits the impact of undesirable practices and ideas, i.e., those that have the potential of political organisation and social mobilisation on the one hand and ensures the growth of the media industry on the other. In that sense, communication is not simply a matter of "free" expression or not; rather, it is the perception of the leaders on the reach of the media that decides the level of control to be exercised. It means that film and television, which have the broadest audience reach, are most tightly controlled. As television gradually takes over film, television gets more attention from the censors. This is confirmed by Chen's research[39] which shows that up till 2005, television was regarded by the authorities to be the medium that has the most far-reaching influence and the broadest audience basis in China. He argues that the extensive attention given to the television industry indicates the importance the government attaches to the grass-roots level of information circulation. Compared to the print media and the Internet which either need certain level of literacy or access to the technology, television is a more convenient medium to most of the general public in China. It is far more accessible and affordable.

---

[39] Chen, 'Dynamics of News Media Regulations in China', at https://louisville.edu/asiandemocracy/conferences/links-and-images/dynamics-of-news-media-regulations-in-china.html, accessed on 14 July 2010.

Not surprisingly, influential national media outlets and leading regional media outlets are the focal targets of control. Obscure niche market journals targeting an elite academic audience, on the other hand, are given more leeway. The same happens with elite intellectual websites, with which "the process of government censorship has evolved from old totalitarian control mechanism to a new 'looser system with some room for manoeuvring', because 'as long as no one reads them, they don't care' ".[40] Therefore, in cases relating to the elite political debates and intellectual discourses, the technologies of censorship have undergone a process of refinement, and as a result, censorship is increasingly "more a matter of negotiation than negation".[41] As Lokman Tsui observes, "the government, after all, is less interested in containing the elite than in making sure that the vast majority do not get unfiltered access".[42] The control that has changed during the past two decades or so over the Internet is a good example. At its early stage, the Internet was less tightly controlled than the print media, not only because of the technical challenges of control but more importantly because of its smaller number of users. However, as the number of users increases, and as the users are part of an important demographic to the government, the attention from the government has been greatly increased during the past few years. As outlined earlier in the chapter, many mechanisms have been set up to control the undesirable effects of the Internet. Within the online sphere itself, the regime has also taken a selective approach to the exercise of control, depending on different priorities assigned to different issues, some of which are controlled more closely than others, or more closely at some times than at others, which explains the selective targeting of cyber dissidents, blocking of foreign web sites, and closing of domestic sites.

---

[40] Schell, Orville, 'A Lonely Voice in China is Critical on Rights and Reform', *New York Times*, 24 January 2004, E45.

[41] Barme, Jeremie, *In the Red: On Contemporary Chinese Culture*, (New York: Columbia University Press, 1999), p. 258.

[42] Tsui, Lokman, 'The Panopticon as the Antithesis of a Space of Freedom: Control and Regulation of the Internet in China', *China Information*, Vol. 17, (October 2003), pp. 65–82.

Self-Censorship

In the construction of hegemony, it is obvious that the general trend is a move, albeit gradual, from repressive power to disciplinary power, from hard control to soft control. In contrast to hard control, soft control is more about self-discipline, indirect guidance, efficient management, positive cues, and rule by law. That is to say, while the state continues to use coercive means to control the content of the media, it exercises indirect control through ambiguous policies, as well as its ideological and organisational power over the media workers.

Ambiguous Policies — Creating an Atmosphere of Self-Censorship

Much has been said about the lack of firm and predictable rules about what is permitted or prescribed for the media to cover in China, despite the state's recent move towards the provision of more formal regulations. This lack means different things for Chinese media organisations, journalists and the Chinese authorities. For the Chinese media organisations and journalists, this lack could result in two different scenarios: first, amidst the loosening of economic and ideological restraints, Chinese journalists face opportunities to pursue news more assertively. Those bold enough to throw caution into the wind might get away with a lot more than they would if the boundaries of behaviour were clearly defined. The elasticity of Chinese press controls was most evident during the height of the 1989 demonstrations, when journalists pressed their luck to the utmost.[43] There are also others who practise "hitting line balls", a reference to the risky and difficult table tennis strategy of aiming the ball so it barely nicks the far edge of the opponent's side,[44] meaning media organisations and journalists could be more "creative" in interpreting the ambiguous policies. However, the other scenario could be that the economic line takes command over the political line and emboldens the media

---

[43] Polumbaum, 'Striving for Predictability', pp. 113–128.
[44] *Ibid.*

to assume a more critical posture toward the government. Whenever hardliners abruptly dump cold water on the economic fervour, however, the media tend to be caught unprepared and fail to withdraw in time to avoid a full scale attack.

The Chinese media can therefore suffer from the uncertainty of the policies. For instance, "Regulations" often include such expressions as "at an appropriate moment", "among appropriate people", and "under certain circumstances", making the regulations ambiguous and difficult to interpret.[45] However for the authorities, the strategic uncertainty and ambiguity in media policies have allowed them to try by error in their reform of the media industry. In other words, the uncertainty and ambiguity allow the authorities tremendous latitude in terms of how these regulations may be defined and interpreted. Rigid concepts and practices that had withstood the Maoist era proved dysfunctional in the post-Mao period, and flexibility became essential to the maintenance of the system itself. One consequence that comes from this kind of uncertainty, although it may be unintended initially, is that media workers are forced to practice self-censorship, as Jonathan Hassid argues.[46] It often leads the media to be either over-concerned or overcautious.[47]

Because of the political and social context, all major print media outlets, broadcasting outlets and websites play important filtering and editorial roles themselves. Through allotting responsibilities to the private sector and individuals, a new mechanism for achieving the goal of maintaining economic privatisation and political control is

---

[45] Du, Junfei, 'The Road to Openness: The Communication Legacy of the Wenchuan Earthquake', in Liang (Ed.), *Convulsion: Media Reflections*, (Beijing: China Democracy and Legal System Publishing House, 2008), pp. 30–38.

[46] Hassid, Jonathan, 'Controlling the Chinese Media, an Uncertain Business', *Asian Survey*, 48(3), (2008), pp. 414–430.

[47] Zhang, Junchang, 'Major Breakthrough and Reflections Brought by Reports on Catastrophic Emergencies', in Liang, (Ed.), *Convulsion*, pp. 55–63;
Zhu, Yujun and Niu, Guangxia, 'A Study on the Humanization Process of Television Communication in the Respect of Live Broadcast of the Wenchuan Earthquake', in Liang, *Convulsion*, pp. 205–214.

achieved. For instance, according to the deputy CEO of Sina,[48] a leading online media company and mobile value-added service (MVAS) provider for China and for global Chinese communities, new members of staff are all given training sessions on what they can do and what they must not do. This understanding of what they can do and what they must not do is widely shared among Chinese media outlets, and has informed their every action. Some observers therefore argue that the indoctrination of producers, reporters and editors has made many of them keenly aware of the limits beyond which they should not venture. Some observers have voiced their concern that while state interference through coercion is a serious threat to the autonomy of media outlets, more often autonomy is constricted by media outlets' self-censorship. Self-censorship has become a main mechanism against further liberalisation of the media.

Rigorous Control Mechanism

To say that the Chinese media functions on a self-censorship basis does not necessarily paint the whole picture. To ensure that media organisations and workers adhere to the practice of self-censorship, formal bureaucratic procedures and impromptu rules on "special cases" are combined to maximise disciplinary power. Both the GAPP and the SARFT maintain rigorous implementation of three controlling mechanisms: (i) licensing, (ii) the annual review system for newspaper, broadcast, and film and television programme production license holders and (iii) the certification of journalists. The SARFT's "Stipulations on TV Drama Censorship and Management", for instance, is a subsector administrative order deriving its authority from the 1997 "Regulations on Radio and Television Management". It establishes two crucial mechanisms of state control in this important area of media and culture: pre-production topic approval and post-production censorship. So, although the government has adopted a more relaxed policy towards the production of TV dramas, its strict

---

[48] Wen, Jin, 'The Way of Sina — Internet in China', paper delivered at the China Media Festival, School of Oriental and African Studies, London, 18–19 June 2008.

control on the broadcasting of dramas decides what will be produced. The recent initiatives from the government for "strengthening of management" are pertinent here[49]:

- The TV drama production permit system: on the one hand, from December 2001, any organisation wanting to produce dramas requires a permit from the SARFT. On the other, production units that receive such permits are effectively regulated.
- Inspection before production: before production can begin, the production units must report their topic to the Chinese Television ARTS Committee for clearance. There is no transparent system or time limit for the decisions, which are often made in accordance with the political environment rather than its value for the market.
- Monitoring of broadcasting itself: the SARFT, CCTV and all other level stations, have inspection procedures. When programmes exhibit any perceived "political problems" they can be officially terminated.

These measures ensure that production and circulation of programming are in accord with the political interests of the state. For instance, in April 2004, the SARFT banned the broadcasting of crime dramas during primetime (not until after 23:00) as part of the so-called "screen cleansing project". It is worth noting that such dramas normally deal with crimes revealing the depravity of government officials. Before the implementation of the ban, crime drama was one of the most popular genres. For Shanghai Television, for example, it topped the ratings. But after the rule came into effect, many directors changed themes and started to direct other dramas such as martial arts. The royal-court "costume" drama craze is to a large extent the result of commercialisation and political control.

---

[49] Hong, Yin, 'Meaning, Production, Consumption: The History and Reality of Television Drama in China', in Stephanie Hemelryk Donald, Michael Keane and Yin Hong, (Eds.), *Media in China: Consumption, Content and Crisis*, (Routledge Curzon, 2002), pp. 28–40.

The separation of operational rights and ownership rights and the separation of routine editorial responsibility and final gate-keeping responsibility have been considered "institutional innovation".[50] That is, although private producers in the broadcasting sector have more freedom to produce programmes, the banning of private ownership of broadcast channels and private provision of news and current affairs means the state sector enjoys the right to programme purchase and sales, as well as editorial and broadcasting sales.

Personnel Control and Certification of Journalists

The government also exploits a longstanding hierarchical relationship among Chinese print and broadcast entities in seeking to maintain some control over the media. It appoints the leaders of the most powerful media institutions, and then uses these organisations to try to dominate the rest of the media countrywide. De Burgh observes that

> there has always been a close relationship between media personnel and [the] CCP and, therefore, state leadership. Journalism is a recognised road to the higher reaches of Party and state and the editor of The People's Daily and the director of the New China News Agency, for example, are officials of ministerial rank rather than simply public figures as they might be in western countries. The current President of China Central Television was, until his age required his retirement from the government post in 1997, concurrently a government Deputy Minister. The current Deputy Mayor of Shanghai, a significant national politician, is a former journalist and Dean of Fudan University's School of Journalism.[51]

A less visible but no less significant development in personnel control has been the formalisation of government certification of journalists, chief editors, and broadcast hosts, making China the only state in the world to formerly license journalists. The SPPA came to oversee issuance of press credentials as well as permissions for news organisations to operate "journalism stations", or local news bureaus.

---

[50] Zhao, *Communication in China,* p. 205.

[51] de Burgh, Hugo, *The Chinese Journalist: Mediating Information in the World's Most Populous Country,* (New York: RoutledgeCurzon, 2003), p. 24.

As of 15 November 1990, all journalists were required to have SPPA press cards. By the end of 1990, 74,254 journalists were credited, with the process not yet completed. Another 6,335 temporary credentials had been issued as well. In addition, there were 939 news bureaus registered nationwide.[52] By the early 2000s, the government had stepped up efforts to certify journalists. The Chinese state is thus subjecting journalists to a system of professional certification and self regulation in a way that has some superficial resemblance to the self-regulation of the legal, medical, and accounting professions in the west. Of course, what set China apart is the fact that the state, rather than the professional associations, issues the licenses. Ironically, this system was simultaneously a response to the corrosive impact of the market forces on news organisations and the journalistic profession.

REGULAR CAMPAIGNS AND BIG SCALE OPERATIONS

Another method to ensure orderly development of the media industry is launching regular campaigns. Take the Internet sector for example. Liu Yunshan, head of the Propaganda Department, stated that Internet pornography is "eroding people's minds and destroying the moral standard of society".[53] A one-month long campaign was therefore launched in January 2009 to clamp down on websites that spread pornography and threaten to weaken the morals of the society. This campaign was extended to cover contents of cell phone websites, chat-rooms and instant messenger groups. An equally important reason for the tightening of internet control in 2009 has to do with the need to set the right atmosphere in the run-up to a number of key anniversaries that would take place in China in the year, including the 50th Anniversary of the uprising in Tibet against Chinese rule (in March), the 20th Anniversary of the Tiananmen incident (in June),

---

[52] Polumbaum, 'Striving for Predictability', pp. 113–128.

[53] 'China Vows to Intensify Online Porn Crackdown after Shutting Down Thousands of Sites', *Xinhuawang*, 6 February 2009 at http://news.xinhuanet.com/english/2009-02/06/content_10776684.htm, accessed on 5 May 2009.

the 60th Anniversary of the founding of the Communist Party of China (in October).

Zhou[54] found a new development that the state is actively promoting for the purpose of control of the Internet — chain-style Internet café operations involving large amounts of capital and operated on a large scale. In March 2003, the Ministry of Culture proclaimed that it would issue permits for up to ten companies to operate nationwide internet café chains, which would have relatively standardised services and management and thus be more easily subject to government regulations. Zhou argued that the entrance of these companies into the operation of internet cafes could represent the beginning of a closer relationship between state and capital in which the state and state-backed capital work together to achieve the two-fold task of maintaining control for the former while making profit for the latter.

CONCLUSION

While steadfast in controlling the media, the Party-state now aims for effective domination rather than total control of media messages. The combination of traditional institutional management and control mechanisms and ongoing reorientation approach to media the management, as well as the mix of hard control and soft control by the Party-state shows the Party-state's determination to stay in control of the media. However, it also indicates Chinese society's persistent challenges against such control in the realm of communications. Eager to acquire some legitimacy but anxious to avoid democracy, the leadership has upgraded and refined its controlling management skills and administrative institutions. Various controls are in place to prevent the media outlets from becoming platforms used by subversive elements to challenge the authority of the Party and government. What is more noticeable is that rather than being

---

[54] Zhou, Yongming, 'Privatizing Control: Internet Café in China', in Li Zhang and Aihwa Ong, *Privatising China, Socialism from Afar*, (Ithaca, N.Y.: Cornell University Press, 2008), pp. 214–229.

reactive to pressures, the Chinese leadership has played a proactive role in finding ways to keep up with the rapid commercialisation of the industry and technological advances. Its extensive attention to the development of the media clearly indicates the Chinese government's interest in sustaining its influence on the guidance of public opinion in China.

Negotiation between the Party-state and Media Organisations

It is generally agreed that media policy-making has become more complex due to the rapid changes in the policy environment, including the emergence of new and varied interest groups developed out of economic liberalisation, the increased importance of international factors, and the CCP's continuing imperative of maintaining power with legitimacy. As discussed in previous chapters, despite its authoritarian nature, in the face of drastic socio-economic changes, the Party-state has had to transform itself and redefine its relations with social forces, including media organisations, in order to maintain its hegemonic position. It is true that to maintain its domination, the Party-state has to exercise control over social forces from time to time; but to reproduce its hegemonic position over other social forces, it also has to maintain equilibrium among different interest groups. Consequently, media policy has now become more susceptible than ever to interventions and prescriptions of different interest groups with different ideological stripes. Some groups will benefit more than others; some other groups might become victims of such changes.

DIFFERENT ACTORS AFFECTING MEDIA POLICY-MAKING

Actors with a stake in the media industry are many, business groups, academics, global media barons and media organisations themselves all trying to wield influence on China's media policies. Although by no means equal partners, together with the Party-state, they jointly shape the Chinese media system and broader cultural environment by trying to influence, lobby, and get channelled into media policy-making. No doubt the Party-state continues to play the dominant role in media policy changes: it has played multiple roles as media policy maker, media owner, resource distributor, controller, manager and supervisor for years. However, in the construction of hegemony and to maintain equilibrium between various interest groups and social forces, the Party-state has allowed certain space for input from different interest groups for media development:

1. Influence from academics: academia provides a viable venue for policy recommendations. Challenges from commercialisation, globalisation and new media technologies to liberalise China's media industry provide the state with an impetus to develop think-tanks within the academy as conservatories for well-trained communication scholars to serve the bourgeoning industry. These think-tanks are often commissioned by the government to perform research and make policy recommendations. For instance, the National Centre for Radio & TV Studies (NCRTS), an institute within the Communication University of China in Beijing, has conducted several projects commissioned by the SARFT on media policy, institutional transition, media development strategy and media management.[1] With the growing attention from the leadership to the development of the cultural industry including the media, many research centres sponsored by the central government have been set up to strengthen academic research on and facilitate the development of cultural industries in

---

[1] From personal communication with Prof. Hu Zhengrong. Director of the NCRTS.

China.[2] These centres include those such as the National Research Centre for the Cultural Industry established in 2004 in Tsinghua University in Beijing and in 2006 in the Ocean University of China in Shandong. In the meantime, blue books on culture industries are published annually by the Centre of Culture Research at the Chinese Academy of the Social Sciences, such as the "Blue Book of China's Media" edited by Baoguo Cui in 2009.

2. Influence from private investors: recent state policies that selectively legitimate private media activities bring in another actor onto the scene — the private investors. In television drama production for instance, private capital now accounts for 80% of the total annual investment. Advertisers, state-owned television stations, production companies and to some extent, the SARFT, share common ground in television drama commercialisation, as television stations primarily — if not entirely — depend on their drama programmes for advertising revenue, which in turn accounts for 90% of the total revenue for the stations.[3] It is not surprising that private investors try to persuade media policy makers and regulators to give them more autonomy, to make the media market more open instead of being monopolised by the government. There is a noticeable tendency that dominant political powers, though decentralised, would co-operate with less powerful, but incrementally enhancing commercial interests groups in media policy-making and regulations.

3. Transnational companies (TNCs): on the one hand, TNCs are working hard to get into the Chinese media market. On the other, they are also trying to lobby the Chinese media policy makers and regulators to be more open and responsive to their needs, especially after China's entry to WTO in 2001, when these needs have manifested themselves as a strong pressure upon the

---

[2] From the website of the National Research Centre for Cultural Industry, Tsinghua University, at http://www.rcci.org.cn:81/en/index.html, accessed on 1 August 2010.

[3] Zhu, *Television in Post-Reform China*, p. 10.

Chinese government to open up the Chinese media market to the outside world. According to Cui, although China's total production of TV programmes has increased rapidly in the last two decades, amounting to 2,553,200 hours in 2007, the total hours of broadcasting per week are 279,000,[4] making it 14,508,000 hours a year. That translates into 11,954,800 hours short per year in total. This shortage of content, largely due to the increasing number of media outlets but also to the state-owned media's incapability for production, has given domestic and overseas investors bargaining power, not only over the production of content and distribution of media products, but also some other services like digital channel operation as well.

4. Media organisations: due to their nature, their influence on media policy-making has seldom been taken into consideration. However, I argue that the media are as much a product of political changes as they are an influence on them. Because of their increasing bargaining power, they are gaining in their interaction with the state in the changing socio-political context, which will be discussed in greater detail below. Media organisations have also sought to maximise their financial and professional interests in their negotiations with the state. Although the Party's efforts at incorporating market-based media outlets have been persistent and unyielding, many of the institutional innovations have in fact been initiated by media organisations at the margins of the system in their pursuit of professional and economic interest.

In the following section, I will concentrate on the negotiation between the Party-state and the media industry for autonomy. I will first discuss the changing relationship between the Party-state and media outlets that is characterised by negotiation, the pre-condition that is making the negotiation rather than conflict possible, and the negotiation powers of different media outlets.

---

[4] Cui, Baoguo and Zhou, Kui, 'A General Report on China's Media Industry Development 2009', in Baoguo Cui, (Ed.), *Blue Book of China's Media*, pp. 3–37.

HEGEMONISATION THROUGH BARGAINING AND RECIPROCITY

Jiang Zemin said in an interview by Wallace on the 60 Minutes CBS in 2000[5]: "I think all countries and parties must have their own publications to publicise their ideas. We do have freedom of the press, but such freedom should be subordinate to and serve the interests of the nation. How can you allow such freedom to damage the national interests?" Why then should the Party-state allow different media organisations to negotiate or bargain at all, for matters ranging from preferential tax treatment to the naming of a particular TV programme, and the areas of coverage?

To answer this question, I will draw on Gramsci's concept of hegemony to examine the changing relation between the Party-state and media outlets. As Zheng rightly points out,[6] new Marxism provides us with a powerful tool to examine the dynamics of interaction among actors; it helps to interpret the nature of the domination and how the pattern of domination is reproduced and reconstructed in accordance with changing socio-economic environments. Hegemonisation as an effective mode of legitimation places its emphasis on the interaction between the Party-state and social forces. Although hegemonisation implies the process of Party-state dominating social forces, this does not mean that social forces are completely powerless since otherwise the Party-state would not be able to acquire legitimacy. Legitimation means that the Party-state solicits loyalty from citizens through non-coercive means, and citizens accept the domination of Party-state power because they believe in the wisdom of its leaders or the fairness of its policies.

In a system of hegemony, bargaining and reciprocity, compared with coercion, are often more effective forms of domination. Drawing from Gramsci, Zheng posits that power can be exercised through bargaining or power exchange. When power is exercised

---

[5] 'Jiang Zemin Talks with Wallace', at http://www.cbsnews.com/stories/2000/08/31/60minutes/main229663.shtml, accessed on 15 January 2010.
[6] Zheng, *The Chinese Communist Party as Organisational Emperor*, pp. 18–19.

through bargaining or power exchange, it means that "I will do something for you, in order to get you to do something for me". Power can also be exercised through reciprocity and persuasion. It is the ability to induce people's voluntary obedience and cooperation. To Gramsci, developed capitalist polities whose legitimacy rests on a fairly stable "equilibrium of hegemonic and coercive institutions" are directly contrasted with an older type of state that lacks this vital reciprocity with civil society.[7]

Media Organisations' Growing Negotiation Powers

The Chinese state has retained a dominant presence in the economic and social sphere. It is this basic condition that has given rise to the Chinese media's dependence on the state. In other words, media organisations are not autonomous in pursuing their own development, because they depend on their relations with the government.[8] However, as the media has undergone dramatic changes since 1978, instead of playing the traditional instrumental role only, it is now also expected to perform multi-faceted functions, which has given rise to the possibility of negotiation between the state and media organisations.

First is the need for innovation from the media for appeal: from a Gramscian perspective, the state relies on the moral, intellectual and cultural system formulated by intellectuals not only for justifying and maintaining its dominance, but also for winning the consent of those over whom it rules. The media acts as a mediator between society and the state for the achievement of stability, legitimacy, and persistence of the overall socio-political system. Because of their popular nature, media organisations are in a position to organise and lead the discussion on particular populist causes such as social justice, stability, harmony and economic development. As the state is faced with an increasingly complex and empowered society, it needs the media to be more sophisticated and more creditable in mass persuasion and

---

[7] Gramsci, *Selections from the Prison Notebooks*, p. 54.
[8] Zheng, *Technological Empowerment*, p. xvii.

mass mobilisation, to ensure the Party-state's ideology is accepted or adopted by society as its own view. Indeed, few people in China today believe that communism or Marxism-Leninism-Mao Zedong thought provide a persuasive explanation of how the world works or a useful guide to official policy. This places journalists and the media that are required to act as if the ideology remains plausible in a difficult position on the one hand, but on the other, the need for innovations to present the ruling ideology in a way that may still have some appeal to the vast majority of the population and to shape the public opinion environment lends them more bargaining power for autonomy.

Second is the media's contribution to economic growth: China's information industries grew at an annual rate of 25% in the 1990s, three times the country's GDP growth.[9] Between 1988 and 1998, the mass media industry in China was the most profitable industry with the high rate of investment return of 17–30%.[10] This suggests China's mass media industry "might be the last industry with staggering profits in the world".[11] The recent redefinition of the media as an economic product not only effectively displaces media reform as a key component of political reform but also makes the media space a new site for economic growth. The media industry is expected to continue to contribute to the economic growth of the country by making profits in the increasingly commercialised and competitive market. According to a report by the Chinese Academy of Social

---

[9] 'China's Cable TV Shake up', from BBC News, Monday, 3 December 2001, at http://news.bbc.co.uk/1/hi/business/1689097.stm, accessed on 26 July 2010.

[10] Dong, R., 'The Mass Media Engages with Capital', 2000, at ultrachina.com/english/doc.cfm?OID=405&MIDtoc=0&CIDtoc=62, quoted and accessed 6 March 2003 by Chengju Huang, 'Trace the Stones in Crossing the River: Media Structural Changes in Post-WTO China', *International Communication Gazette*, 69, pp. 413–430, October 2007.

[11] Tao, T., 'Media Stars in Its Own Investment Extravaganza', *Shanghai Star*, http://www.chinadaily.com.cn/star/2001/0614/bz10-1.html, quoted and accessed 6 March 2003 by Chengju Huang, 'Trace the Stones in Crossing the River: Media Structural Changes in Post-WTO China', *International Communication Gazette*, 69, October 2007, pp. 413–430.

Sciences, China's media industry output grew 16.3% year-on-year to 491 billion Yuan ($72 billion) in 2009, with operating revenue from newspaper advertisements increasing 8% to 37 billion Yuan despite the global economic downturn. In 2010, total output of China's media industry is expected to grow 14.5% year-on-year to 562 billion Yuan.[12] Given that the industry generates important revenue, organisations in the industry may well use the commercial imperative to bargain with propaganda officials for greater autonomy. That means the government has to deal with an increasingly commercialised media that have their own agendas to follow. As China sets in process the marketisation of the media, each level of the media (the central, the provincial, the pre-fectural and the county) becomes largely self-financed and is operated by the regional and local governments. Take the broadcasting sector for example. While continuing to serve as the mouthpiece of the Party, TV stations at all levels are profit driven. According to Hu, advertising has been the main source of revenue for the Chinese broadcasting media, and comprises almost 90% of the total income while the government subsidised only 10.7% in 2004.[13] Concerns about ratings, circulations and market shares are driving the Chinese media to follow market logic. State authorities and regulators fully understand the contribution the media industry is expected to make to the economic growth, even if they have to deliver the "right" kind of media content and operate within the hegemonic framework of maintaining social stability at the same time.

Third is the construction and projection of a rising world leader to an international media public: the Party-state's growing imperative to project China's soft power abroad and to compete with transnational media corporations for the global flow of information has stimulated it to proactively forge internationally competitive Chinese

---

[12] From China Daily, at http://www.chinadaily.com.cn/china/2010-04/22/content_9762751.htm, accessed on 2 August 2010.

[13] Hu, Zhengrong, *Towards the Public? — The Dilemma in Chinese Media Policy Change and Its Influential Factors.*

media enterprises through the coordinated efforts of government support and media enterprises. The media industry thus needs more credibility and autonomy to be able to compete with transnational media companies.

Finally, another important new role taken up by the media has enabled media institutions to include their audience as a means to bargain with the authorities for more autonomy. This new role is as the people's mouthpiece. In other words, media governance is now subject to both "the Party Principle" and "the People Principle". Not only must journalists publicise the Party line and mobilise the pubic to support government policies, they should also represent the interests of the people and express their desires and grievances. Indeed, media reports can provoke the public, including the elite and the masses. The reaction of the public, often reported in the media, in turn puts pressure on the policy makers. Although the state continues to maintain its strategic control over the media market through licensing, regulating and allocating resources to specific state media, media organisations are affecting the making of state policy by representing their own economic interests in terms of general public interests.

To summarise, media organisations in China are expected to do many things at the same time: to create an environment favourable for political and social stability, to construct a good image of the Party-state, to harness popular support for the government, to compete with transnational media corporations for the global flow of information, and to be commercially successful in a very crowded marketplace. These expectations of the media from the Party-state, sometimes conflicting but always interrelated, have become leverage for, media organisations lending the media more bargaining power with the authorities over the exercise of restraint while under their control and regulation. In other words, media organisations have been gaining increased latitude to pursue self-interested goals although they are at the same time regulated or controlled by the Party-state. Li Changchun's call to "treat the media well, use the media well and manage the media well", and speeches such as the one made by the deputy head of the Propaganda Department in Yunnan

Province in the Renmin University in Beijing in April 2010 entitled "Good Management of the Media through Treating the Media Well and Using the Media Well" indicate that the media is no longer the mouthpiece to be used at will but needs to be managed with care.

SNAPSHOT: NEGOTIATION WITH THE STATE FOR MORE AUTONOMY

Media organisations and workers have been quick to realise their new bargaining power and ready to use the power they have to negotiate for more autonomy. In May 2008, the Chinese media broke free of their reputation as propaganda instruments of the Party-state in their coverage of the Sichuan Earthquake. What makes the coverage unique is that for the first time, the Chinese media reported on a breaking news event before getting approval from the Central Government.[14] Take China Central Television as an example, according to Zhao Huayong, then president of CCTV,[15] the earthquake took place at 14:28 on May 12th and at 14:50, CCTV started to broadcast news on the earthquake by rolling captions and at 15:00, screening live reports by presenters. At 15:20, the News Channel started the special programme "Exclusive Reports on Wenchuan". Over the next few days, the CCTV News Channel, CCTV-1, CCTV-4 and CCTV-9 all suspended their regular programmes to provide live coverage of the disaster, turning the earthquake into a global media event.[16]

As a rule, Chinese state media follow the rule of "timely reporting", which means timely reporting to the authorities.[17] They do not

---

[14] Shao, Peiren and Pan, Xianghui, 'The Inherent Linkage between Crises and Media System Innovation Reviewed from the Wenchuan Earthquake', in Liang (Ed.), *Convulsion: Media Reflections,* pp. 116–125.

[15] Zhao, Huayong, 'Respect Laws Governing News and Perfect Emergency Contingency System', in Liang (Ed.), *Convulsion,* pp. I–X.

[16] Shao and Pan, 'The Inherent Linkage between Crises and Media System Innovation Reviewed from the Wenchuan Earthquake', pp. 116–125.

[17] Bao, Junhao, 'Timely Report This Time vs. Timely Report to the Above before', *Southern Weekend*, 22 May 2008, p. 30.

aim to be "the fastest, but the most correct".[18] As a result, although CCTV has set up the News Channel since 2003 as a platform for live coverage, CCTV mainly carries out live coverage of events that they can plan in advance.[19] But this time instead of "holding meetings to disseminate the instructions from the Central Government",[20] the Chinese media took advantage of the scale of the disaster and allowed their media logic to prevail over Party logic. The way the Chinese state media responded to the event was hailed by many as a milestone in the history of the media.[21] In the words of Bai Yansong, a household name for live coverage in China, "this time, it is not a simple live coverage".[22] Many observers of China also commented that the coverage of the Sichuan disaster may have wider political implications.

My examination of two sites for the discourses of media and academic professionals reveal that media scholars and professionals seized the opportunity presented by the well-received breakthrough in the coverage of the earthquake to bargain with the state for more autonomy. The first site examined is the *China Academic Journals Database* which covers more than 8,000 academic and policy journals. A search of the word "earthquake" in abstracts from June to the end of 2008 brings up 458 articles. The second is the book series entitled *Convulsion* which consists of *Convulsion: TV File*, one

---

[18] Lu, Di and Gao, Fei, 'The Power of Media and Its Inspirations', in Liang (Ed.), *Convulsion: Media Reflections*, pp. 87–91.

[19] Ye, Fengying, 'Devastating Earthquake: Rebuilding the Media Image of China Central Television', in Liang (Ed.), *Convulsion*, pp. 283–291.

[20] Shao and Pan, 'The Inherent Linkage between Crises and Media System Innovation Reviewed from the Wenchuan Earthquake', p. 120.

[21] E.g., Fang, Hanqi, 'Live Broadcast of Disaster — A Milestone in China's History of Journalism', in Liang (Ed.), *Convulsion: Media Reflections*, pp. 1–6;

Du, Junfei, 'The Road to Openness: the Communication Legacy of the Wenchuan Earthquake', in Liang (Ed.), *Convulsion: Media Reflections*, (Beijing: China Democracy and Legal System Publishing House, 2008), p. 30–38.

Shao and Pan, 'The Inherent Linkage between Crises and Media System Innovation Reviewed from the Wenchuan Earthquake', p. 118;

Zhou, Haiyan, 'The Beginning and Ending of News Power', in Liang (Ed.), *Convulsion: Media Reflections*, pp. 215–226.

[22] Shao and Pan, 'The Inherent Linkage between Crises and Media System Innovation', p. 121.

month's record of CCTV's coverage and the Central Government's response to the earthquake and to the media coverage; *Convulsion: Field Notes from Media Workers*, with 96 field notes by media professionals involved in the coverage; and *Convulsion: Media Reflections*, with 54 articles from well-known media scholars and senior editors from other media organisations, as well as a dozen from the CCTV News Centre. This series, edited by the CCTV News Centre and published on 5 July, 2008, less than two months after the earthquake, provides valuable insights into the response of the state media to the earthquake, the Central Government's response to the way the quake was covered, and above all, how media workers and scholars use the well-received breakthrough to push the state for more openness. The examination is enhanced by interviews with media practitioners and academics in the summer of 2008, which assist in providing a critical evaluation of the discourses from the examined sites.

Media Construction of the Party-state as a Competent Leader

The Chinese government has long been attentive to its image in the eyes of domestic and foreign audiences, but especially in the 21st century, in which China aspires to become a more important player in the international community. Hence "leadership image design" has become a new topic for applied communications research and everyday media management practices. As such, it is on the argument for image construction by the media that the case for information openness is first built.[23]

---

[23] See Gong, Wenxiang, 'The Build-up of National Image: An Analysis Based on China Central Television's Report on the Sichuan Earthquake', in Liang (Ed.), *Convulsion: Media Reflections*, pp. 64–70;

'Li, Datong, 'The Establishment of Disaster Reporting's Core Value and Mature Mode', in Liang (Ed.), *Convulsion: Media Reflections*, pp. 151–156;

Li, Shiquan, 'Reviewing the Breakthroughs of CCTV's Live Broadcast of "Relief and Rescue Unite as One" from the Perspective of the Changing Concept of Disaster Report in China', in Liang (Ed.), *Convulsion: Media Reflections*, pp. 175–182;

Han, Biao, 'Recording History and Creating History — Inspirations for the Future Brought by the Earthquake Report', in Liang (Ed.), *Convulsion: Media Reflections*, pp. 388–393.

Media scholars and professionals alike highlight the fact that the state's image has been greatly enhanced, thanks to the media's coverage of its rescue efforts immediately after the earthquake, especially following CCTV's live coverage. They argue that CCTV's live coverage opened a window into the workings of the powerful central leadership and the advantages of socialism that allowed the swift coordination of efforts by the Central Government, the army and the whole society.[24] They point out that instead of the negative coverage China had been receiving since the beginning of 2008, the international community started to speak very highly of the government's practice of information transparency, thus creating an international environment conducive to the subsequent Olympics.[25] In fact, they argue that the Beijing Olympics Games' mission to demonstrate to the world a contemporary China had already been achieved by the coverage of the rescue efforts.[26] If the rescue efforts by the government demonstrated the hard power of the country, then the media's coverage demonstrated its increasing soft power.[27]

Media Credibility in Image Construction

Following the argument that the disaster coverage has resulted in a very favourable image of the Party-state, media workers and scholars continue to argue that in order to better enhance the image of the

---

[24] For instance, Ba, Xiaofang, 'The Degree of News on Disaster', *News Front*, No. 6, (2008), pp. 2–5;

Zhao, 'Respect Laws Governing News and Perfect Emergency Contingency System', VI;

Fang, 'Live Broadcast of Disaster', p. 5;

Shi, Tongyu, 'The Significance and Value of CCTV's Live Coverage of the Earthquake', *China Radio and TV Academic Journal*, 7, (2008), pp. 64–66.

[25] E.g., see He, Xiaolan, 'Unprecedented Earthquake, Unprecedented Live Coverage, and Unprecedented Reception Rate', *Journalists*, No. 6, (2008), pp. 21–25.

[26] Li, 'Reviewing the Breakthrough of CCTV's Live Broadcast', p. 179.

[27] Luo, Ming, 'When TV Encounters Disasters', in Liang (Ed.), *Convulsion: Media Reflections*, pp. XI–XVIII;

China Soft Power Project Team of the University of Beijing, 'Information Disclosure in the Earthquake Relief', in Liang (Ed.), *Convulsion: Media Reflections*, p. 238.

Party, it is important that the Chinese media builds up its credibility,[28] because the media's credibility and the image of the Party rise or fall together. Unfortunately, the initial silence and later positive coverage of the outbreak of SARS in 2003, the limited or only positive coverage of the 3.14 Tibet Riot and of the Torch Relay overseas in 2008, have turned the domestic audience to other forms of media or overseas media. Media workers and scholars warn that information control comes at a cost: it could turn natural disasters into social crises and government credibility crises, such as during the government's cover up of the outbreak of SARS.[29] It was only through the coverage of the earthquake that the credibility of the media, especially the TV sector, was restored to some extent, as demonstrated by the return of the audience.[30] They argue that media restrictions not only reduce the trust of citizens in the Chinese media but also damage the image of the Party-state. They go further to argue that if media policy allows the mainstream media to report openly, accurately, and in a timely fashion on breaking news events, the credibility of both the government and the media would be restored.

Guidance of Public Opinion, Domestic and International

The guidance of public opinion has been an important political task entrusted by the state to the media. It is therefore not surprising that scholars also build their argument on the important role the media plays in the guidance of public opinion, both domestically and internationally. They point out that with the world's largest number of cell phones and internet users, and with the increasing in-bound flow of

---

[28] Gong, 'The Build-up of National Image', p. 69;
Lu and Gao, 'The Power of Media and Its Inspirations', p. 89;
Li, 'Reviewing the Breakthrough of CCTV's Live Broadcast', p. 176;
Shi, 'The Significance and Value of CCTV's Live Coverage of the Earthquake', p. 64.
[29] Du, 'The Road to Openness', p. 35.
[30] *Ibid.*, 32; Lu and Gao, 'The Power of Media and Its Inspirations', p. 90.

overseas information,[31] China's media environment has been changed forever and is still changing. If conventional media do not adapt their style and content to the new media environment, they not only lose credibility but also fail to guide public opinion. In its competition with other forms of media and overseas media, CCTV, for instance, had lost to Phoenix on several occasions, and thus its leading position in the guidance of public opinion.[32] However the coverage of the earthquake won the state-owned media a leading position in the guidance of public opinion for the first time[33]: during the coverage of the earthquake, 23 domestic satellite channels merged with CCTV's News Channel, which, together with its website, became an important platform for the public to gather information.[34] Scholars also believe that information transparency has contributed greatly to national cohesion.[35] According to Zhao Huayong, public opinion on the Internet was first "rebellious, independent and irrational", especially that of young people born in the 1980s and 1990s. But CCTV successfully guided these opinions into ones supporting the Party and government.[36] Internationally, 28 TV

---

[31] Yang, Rui, 'Transformation Complex of Chinese Media', paper presented at the conference "Post-Olympic China: Globalisation and Sustainable Development after Three Decades of Reform", 19–21 November 2008, School of Contemporary Chinese Studies, The University of Nottingham, UK.

[32] Gao, Xin and Zhang, Tao, 'China Central Station's Live Broadcast of the Wenchuan Earthquake from the Perspective of Crisis Communication', in Liang (Ed.), *Convulsion: Media Reflections*, pp. 135–142.

[33] Cheng, Zhixia, Zhou, He and Gao, Yunhong, 'Changes on the Internet Reflected on the Coverage of the Earthquake on May 15 on people.com.cn', *News Front*, No. 6, (2008), pp. 7–8;

Wang, Xu, 'To Occupy the Commanding Ground of Public Opinion', in Liang (Ed.), *Convulsion: Media Reflections*, pp. 106–115;

Li, 'Reviewing the Breakthroughs of CCTV's Live Broadcast', p. 180.

[34] Liang, Xiaotao, 'Record of History', in Liang (Ed.), *Convulsion: Media Reflections*, p. XVI.

[35] Zheng, Wenhua, Gao, Dingbo and Yan, Yue, 'Report for Life: Actively Guide International Public Opinion', *Overseas Communication*, No. 6, (2008), pp. 22–24.

[36] Zhao, 'Respect Laws Governing News and Perfect Emergency Contingency System', p. VIII.

stations in 113 countries and regions used CCTV's footage, and CCTV, Xinhua News Agency and Sichuan TV became the primary sources of information for global media companies such as BBC and CNN,[37] thus turning the construction of a positive image of the Party from "self-construction" to "construction by others" and "collective construction".[38]

Source of Information for Policy Makers as well as for the Public

Scholars and media professionals also argue that providing timely and accurate information serves two purposes: ensuring "people's right to know", and helping policy makers to understand the situation so that the right decisions are made. First, they refer to the 17th Congress in 2007 as a historical moment when "the people's right to know" was reiterated.[39] They believe that the implementation of "the Government Transparent Regulations" in May 2008. In particular, the deletion of the clause that "it is against the regulation to publicise information without approval" under the section "Response to Breaking News Events" further laid the foundation for information openness both politically and legally.

Secondly, scholars and media professionals argue that an effective government needs accurate information. However, in the Chinese context there is always a paradox: leaders are aware that a clear understanding of public opinion improves their legitimacy, and yet at the

---

[37] Zhou, Xiaopu, 'The 2008 Dialectics', in Liang (Ed.), *Convulsion: Media Reflections*, pp. 7–16;
Gong, 'The Build-up of National Image', p. 66.

[38] Han, 'Recording History and Creating History', p. 391.

[39] China Soft Power Project Team of the University of Beijing, 'Information Disclosure in the Earthquake Relief', p. 239;
Zhao, 'Respect Laws Governing News and Perfect Emergency Contingency System', p. VIII;
Zhang, Junchang, 'Major Breakthrough and Reflections Brought by Reports on Catastrophic Emergencies', in Liang (Ed.), *Convulsion: Media Reflections*, pp. 55–63;
Lu and Gao, 'The Power of Media and Its Inspirations', p. 91.

same time, their own censorship departments are manipulating or shutting out the public space for true public opinion. If this paradox is not resolved, the authorities will never really know what the public thinks. Media scholars and professionals hope that the government will resolve the paradox of primary information and censorship. They argue that the positive response to coverage of the earthquake proves that live reporting not only satisfies the public's right to know but also provides timely, accurate information and reliable evidence for policy-makers.[40] They point out that the media has proven its capacity to expand its functions from being the government's tongue and throat to becoming its "think tanks", and to helping the government set the agenda.[41]

Openness, Trust and Stability

Some also base their arguments on utilitarian grounds. They reason that press freedom is not only a right but also conducive to political stability. They emphasise that information openness during the earthquake did not cause instability or turmoil.[42] On the contrary, "the media sent out the voice of the Party and government and dispelled panic among people".[43] In that sense, it has promoted national cohesion and mutual understanding between the people and the government and among different segments of society.[44]

More importantly, they also point out, the unusual performance of the media not only stemmed from its own improvement over the

---

[40] Gong, 'The Build-up of National Image', p. 68;
Lu and Gao, 'The Power of Media and Its Inspirations', p. 91;
Bai, Yansong and Wu, Qiang, 'Love Is like Waves that Never Recede' in Liang (Ed.), *Convulsion: Field Notes from Media Workers*, (Beijing: China Democracy and Legal System Publishing House, 2008), pp. 11–17.

[41] Shao and Pan, 'The Inherent Linkage between Crises and Media System Innovation', p. 122.

[42] Du, 'The Road to Openness', p. 32;
Gong, 'The Build-up of National Image', p. 68.

[43] Zhao, 'Respect Laws Governing News and Perfect Emergency Contingency System', p. V.

[44] China Soft Power Project Team, 'Information Disclosure in the Earthquake Relief', p. 237.

years, but also from the trust of the Party and government.[45] The media has shown that it should and can be trusted in times of crisis. Its performance proves that when allowed to speak, the media did not abuse the freedom; instead it was trustworthy, lawful, and self-disciplined.[46] They hope that enough has been learned from the coverage of the Tibet Riot, the Olympic Torch Relay and the earthquake — the sky will not fall if the media's right to speak is allowed.[47] Media professionals and scholars do not forget to remind the authorities of the importance the media played during crises: CCTV's timely, accurate, detailed and continuous reports have actually become part of the country's contingency system through not only information transmission but also mass mobilisation and organisation.[48]

Towards a More Relaxed Media Policy

All these arguments lead to the conclusion that media organisations should enjoy more autonomy. Both media professionals and academics hope that the coverage of the earthquake will provide a positive example for the government to practise media reform.[49] They have tried to make links between a media working under transparency and a favourable image of the state,[50] using the coverage of the 3.14 Tibet Riot[51] as an example. They argue that information transparency helps demonstrate a country's confidence of its culture, value system,

---

[45] Lu and Gao, 'The Power of Media and Its Inspirations', p. 90.

[46] Gong, 'The Build-up of National Image', p. 68;
Lu and Gao, 'The Power of Media and Its Inspirations', p. 90.

[47] Zhou, 'The 2008 Dialectics', p. 9.

[48] Cheng, Xiumin, 'Timeliness, Depth and Width in the Coverage of the Sichuan Earthquake', *Overseas Communication*, No. 6, (2008), pp. 50–51.

[49] Du, 'The Road to Openness', p. 37.

[50] Lin, Rupeng, Wu, Fei and Feng, Shaowen, 'The Rebuilding of National Image in the Reports of Sudden Public Events', in Liang, (Ed.), *Convulsion: Media Reflections*, pp. 71–79.

[51] China Soft Power Project Team, 'Information Disclosure in the Earthquake Relief', p. 237.

development model, system and policies.[52] Media transformation has a great impact on the development of society, which also serves as a social barometer.[53]

AREAS OF NEGOTIATION

The change of social context has inevitably altered the conditions in which the media operates. As is shown above, there has never been a better moment in the history of the Chinese media since 1949 for media organisations to bargain for more autonomy. Take the production and broadcasting of TV dramas as an example. The SARFF proclaimed[54] at the beginning of 2005 that one of the major tasks of the year was to promote domestic TV dramas and to increase its competitiveness in the world. With the government's encouragement for more competitive TV dramas as part of the globalisation project ("going-out" project) — although the factor of the Party/government policies continue to play a decisive role in China's TV programme menus, and hence continue to influence the market — the country's increasing need for international political power as a result of its growing interdependence with the world will continually lead the Party to adopt a more expansive, liberal TV policies and regulations, so that TV dramas adapt to the needs of the market. There are signs that transparency, to a certain degree, is expected of the system of inspection. As mentioned in Chapter 4, one of the optimistic signs is the information provided on the website of the SARFT, which, while serving as rules and guidelines, also helps administrative departments, broadcasting, circulation and production organisations, and other related bodies, producers and investors to make more effective decisions.

However, this newly acquired bargaining power does not suggest a power-free situation. The power structure of the Party-state and

---

[52] *Ibid.*;
Gong, 'The Build-up of National Image', p. 68.
[53] Zhang, 'Major Breakthrough and Reflections', p. 61.
[54] Dou, Xiaofeng and Hou, Lu, 'The Huge Differences in the Budget of Production: The Low Price of Domestic TV Dramas', at http://news.xinhuanet.com/newmedia/2005-11/22/content_3815863.htm, accessed on 3 January 2007.

media organisations remains asymmetrical. Neither does it mean that media organisations can bargain with the state in all areas. Instead, it only implies that as media organisations have something unique to offer to the Party-state, they are in a position to bargain with the state for more autonomy in certain areas. The question then is, what are the negotiable areas? To answer the question, it is useful to imagine the media workers' world as divided into three spheres, as developed by Danial Hallin[55]: the spheres of consensus, legitimate controversy and unacceptable controversy.

The innermost circle, the Sphere of Consensus, encompasses the CCP ideology, the one-party political system, Party and government policies, etc., that the CCP brooks no challenge or opposition. Media workers' role is to serve as an advocate or celebrant of the values as dominant values of the whole society.

In the middle region is the Sphere of Legitimate Controversy, where media workers are permitted or even encouraged to exercise

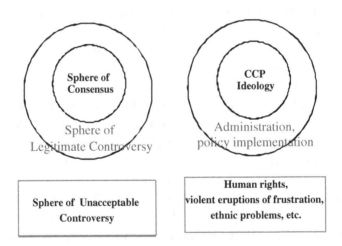

Figure 5.1. The Spheres of Consensus, Legitimate Controversy and Unacceptable Controversy

---

[55] Developed to aid our understanding of the American media's position on the Vietnam War.

criticism if the criticism is seen to help the day-to-day administration and the implementation of policies, areas which are seen to be constructive and helpful for the legitimacy of the Party.

Beyond the Sphere of Legitimate Controversy lies the Sphere of Illegitimate Controversy, which no media workers are allowed to cross. The media today is certainly more critical of the government than at any time in the past. However, it does not discuss issues that lie in the sphere of unacceptable controversy. If the media advocates Taiwan independence or religious freedom, for instance, then it would have crossed the boundaries, and its activities could be classified as illegal. Other topics such as ethnicity, human rights, the influence of NGOs, the separation of Party and government functions, and multi-party democracy also fall into this sphere. Despite the different natures of the media organisations, they all have to operate within the spheres of consensus and legitimate controversy.

However, changes in the past three decades show that the boundary between what is legitimate and what is illegitimate, or the boundary between the Sphere of Legitimate Controversy and the Sphere of Illegitimate Controversy, is in no way fixed. For instance, social problems that used to be taboo subjects such as poverty, unemployment, crime, and corruption, mundane issues that used to be unworthy of news reporting such as traffic congestion, family relationships, consumer information and entertainment programmes as well as celebrity gossip, which used to be viewed as a manifestation of unhealthy bourgeois taste and sentiment, all fell within the Sphere of Illegitimate Controversy. Yet, they are now all daily routines. This fluidity between the two spheres creates a grey zone, which is the result of many factors: first of all, over the years, the Party-state has been gradually loosening its control over reports of this kind despite intermittent attempts to crackdown on what is perceived to cause political and social instability. The shift of the Hu-Wen leadership to a more "people-centred" approach to governance has also legitimated certain forms of exposure of the wrongdoings of some officials. To maintain its power with legitimacy, the CCP has been taking a proactive approach to promote rapid socio-economic development, which has political consequences that the CCP has to cope with. For instance, the satisfaction of material needs would breed immaterial ones, such as demands for political participation and pluralisation, and lead also to social inequalities that fuel a sense of injustice.[56] For issues that lie within the grey zone between the Spheres of Legitimate Controversy and Illegitimate Controversy, the Party-state has been compelled to rule with more subtlety, and even to "negotiate" with media organisations.

Secondly, driven by market competition, media organisations need to be as innovative and independent as regulations would allow, so that they can maximise audience share by giving them what they want, while fulfilling the political role they are expected to play by the CCP. To some extent and on many occasions, Chinese media outlets test the border of the legitimate and illegitimate spheres and the tolerance of the controller. They call this a tightrope walking. When commercial demands of the market clash with political responsibility, the media is driven to follow the market logic as much as the Party logic. The best-known case is the prime-time TV programme, "Focus" on CCTV, which since its beginning has been the most popular programme of investigative journalism. Although the targets of critical reporting are problems of policy implementation rather than the government policies *per se*, and although they tend to involve low-level government agencies and officials, negative reporting certainly marks a major departure from the media's traditional role as the Party's mouthpiece. The existence of the grey zone has opened up possibilities for media workers to push the boundary and enlarge the Sphere of Legitimate Controversy. However, why do central authorities respond to media and public pressure in some cases and turn a deaf ear to other cases?

Since the Third Plenary Session of the Eleventh Central Committee of the CCP held in December 1978, Deng Xiaoping had consistently advocated stability as the foremost condition for China's economic growth. Over the past twenty odd years, along with the push for economic development, Deng's emphasis on political

---

[56] Holbig and Gilley, 'In Search of Legitimacy in Post', p. 12.

stability and unity within the Party and in the whole nation has always remained a key element of his theory of "building socialism with Chinese characteristics". The post-Deng Party-state has steadfastly adhered to Deng's line and attached great importance to political and social stability in the nation-building agenda, as is reflected in Zhu Rongji's report[57] on the government towards the end of its five years' term:

> Doing everything possible to maintain social stability and creating a favourable environment for reform and development, we steadfastly upheld the principle of attaching overriding importance to stability, and took great care to handle the relationships among reform, development and stability. While making giant strides in reform and accelerating economic development, we have made vigorous efforts to safeguard social stability.

Whether a matter is considered to cause political and social instability is usually decided at the very top with almost no input from below. It is no exaggeration to say that the role the media can play during this process of transition depends to a great extent on the perceptions of the Chinese leadership. Not every issue is considered to be political, and not every issue is resolved politically. It is true that the Chinese leadership has significantly reduced in scope the definition of what counts as political, but it continues to regard messages that would be considered innocuous in other societies as holding the potential to undermine political and social stability and Communist Party rule. Thus, media policy in China has, frequently and easily, swung between control and openness, entirely dependent on the authorities' perception of its impact on political and social stability.[58] The central authorities are likely to respond to media and public pressure when social stability and the regime's legitimacy are at risk. When the leadership perceives a situation as undermining and

---

[57] Zhu, Rongji, 'Report on the Work of the Government', at the 10th National People's Congress, March 5, at http://news.xinhuanet.com/english/2003-03/19/content_787742.htm, accessed on 2 April 2007.

[58] Hu, 'Towards the Public?';
Zheng, *Technological Empowerment*, p. 169.

threatening to the political power structure, it is likely to tighten control and even initiate a crackdown. That is, once a movement radicalises and its leaders begin to mobilise nationwide support for the cause it is perceived to have transformed itself from a loyalty option to an exit one and therefore invites a conflict strategy on the part of the state. The political crisis of 1989 induced a qualitative change in the leaders' understanding of the trade-off between economic reform and communications control, and prompted a much more thoroughgoing attempt to root spiritual pollution and bourgeois liberalisation out of the media industry.

On the other hand, however, if the leadership is convinced that certain media practices, such as reports on natural disasters, do not bring any undesirable consequences but could actually contribute to the maintenance of social stability and efficient rule, (which Shue[59] believes have kept the Party in power since 1989), then it relaxes its firm grip on such practices. It may be cooperative and even supportive of any proposals for policy reform if these are perceived to be helpful and constructive to the leadership. Working inside the system, media workers know the importance of the perception of the leaders. The way media workers convinced the state to give a more relaxed media policy by presenting their initiatives during the coverage of the earthquake in 2008 as "loyal" and lending a helping hand to the Party-state, confirms this point.

Interviews with an editor of Singapore's Lianhe Zaobao confirm that although it can be very critical of certain issues, its web presence in China is nevertheless perceived to be constructive. Thus, the leadership's perception is the key factor behind the success of any reform initiatives by media organisations. Whether the leadership perceives an initiative as "right" or "wrong" depends on its perception of political and social stability.

A close examination of CCTV's coverage of the two breaking news events in 2003 — the war in Iraq and the outbreak of

---

[59] Shue, Vivienne, 'Legitimacy Crisis in China?', in Gries, Peter Hays, and Stanley Rosen, (Eds.), *State and Society in 21st-century China: Crisis, Contention, and Legitimation*, (New York: RoutledgeCurzon, 2004).

SARS — illustrates that the Chinese media's news agenda is driven by political stability and the government's perception of a situation. The war in Iraq was taken as a unique chance to not only achieve the dream of having China's voice heard as a permanent member of the United Nations (UN),[60] but also to reconstruct the image of the Party-state and the media as being more objective, transparent, and respecting people's "right to know". It was unique because it was an international event and therefore the coverage was intended to bring international fame. It was also a safe event to cover, as it was away from China. Furthermore, it was not "breaking" in the real sense of the word, which was completely different from the sudden attacks on the Twin Towers on September 11, 2001. Media workers had plenty of time to prepare and to get approval from the government as to when, how and what to cover. CCTV, and indeed all Chinese media outlets were thoroughly absorbed in covering the progress of this international event. The coverage of the Iraq War illustrates that CCTV does not lack the capacity to honour "people's right to know". However, its response to the outbreak of SARS reveals that the government's perception of the situation decided its curve of attention on SARS. The coverage of SARS in China went through three stages: complete silence, limited coverage and saturated coverage. At the time of the first recorded case of SARS, CCTV and indeed all TV stations in China were busy with the political task of covering the 16th National Congress of the CCP which lasted from 8 to 14 November 2002. Following the central goals of TV news, which are "national unity, integration, development and political stability",[61] CCTV played a pivotal role in creating a social and psychological environment favourable for the transition of top leaders. In late February, the Propaganda Department ordered a halt to public reporting on the disease, in order to "ensure the smoothness" of the

---

[60] Yang, Gangyi, 'Focus on Iraq War special coverage-CCTV4', *TV Research*, No. 6, (2003), pp. 10–12.

[61] Zhao, Huayong, 'Greet the 16th Congress of the Chinese Communist Party with New Achievements — Report at CCTV Annual Conference 2002 (abstract)', *TV Research*, 3 (2002), pp. 8–13.

National People's Congress meetings in March.[62] As a result, although SARS was far from being controlled in March, there was hardly any report on its progress throughout the nation. Instead, all media were completely engaged in facilitating the Politburo's order to "thoroughly study and implement the spirit of the 16th National Congress of the CCP, to achieve consensus of opinion among the party and people of all ethnic groups in the spirit of the Congress".[63] Any negative report during this period was not allowed, as the exposure of too many problems was perceived to be a threat to stability and social order.[64] The "citizen's right to know" in China is thus greatly restricted by the paramount discourse of political stability.[65] Any perceived or imagined threat and any doubt from the government may stop the release of information. Indeed, maintaining political and social stability for economic development has been a consistent theme in the explanation and justifications of media control.

There are also temporary measures or regulations that primarily refer to media liberalising changes introduced by the Party or government in response to events that may happen from time to time. These measures may either be effective during the duration of the event or may continue to apply after the end of the event. Whether these measures continue to work or not also depends on the consideration of the Party and government. If these temporary measures do not cause instability or any other unwanted consequences but actually win applause domestically and internationally for being more transparent and competent, then these measures are likely to become permanent. The most recent ad hoc event that provided the impetus

---

[62] Link, Perry, 'Will SARS Transform China's Chiefs?' *TIMEasia Magazine*, 28 April 2003, at http://www.time.com/time/asia/covers/501030505/viewpoint.html, accessed on 27 July 2010.

[63] From the website of the Chinese government at http://www.china.org.cn/english/features/48992.htm, accessed 10 August 2010.

[64] Jiang, Heping, 'Increase TV Exchanges, Expand China's Impact over the World', *TV Research*, 2, (2003), pp. 27–28.

[65] For further discussion on the coverage of the two events, please see Zhang, Xiaoling, 'Breaking News, Media Coverage and "Citizen's Right to Know" in China', *Journal of Contemporary China*, 16(53), (2007), pp. 535–545.

for media liberalisation in China was the Olympic Games. As part of its overall effort to present its best face to the world, China liberalised the operating environment for foreign media organisations and foreign journalists in the country. "The Regulations on Reporting Activities in China by Foreign Journalists during the Beijing Olympic Games and the Preparatory Period" was introduced from 1st January 2007 to 17th October 2008. Thereafter, it was made permanent in Decree No. 537, effective since 17 October 2008. This is an example of how ad hoc measures eventually became a permanent fixture.

Another event that prompted the Party and government to introduce ad hoc measures in the direction of greater media liberalisation was the Sichuan earthquake in May 2008. As evidence of the quickness and decisiveness of the Chinese response, the leadership decided to grant foreign and local journalists considerable leeway in the coverage of the disaster, at least in the initial stages. The media was given a relatively free hand to report on the outpouring of support and rendering of disaster relief. The issue at the time was whether the apparent liberal approach in dealing with the local and foreign media in the Sichuan earthquake would continue. It is therefore not surprising that some media workers warn against any extreme reaction from society to the information openness seen during the coverage of the earthquake, especially the irrational behaviour of some netizens.[66] They are concerned that such reactions would only cause conservatives in the Party and government to demand information control based on fear of instability. They therefore call on the society to exercise self-restraint and to encourage the government when there are any signs of opening up.

As the previous section shows, in the process of negotiation and renegotiation with the state, media organisations have attempted to affect media policy by trying to establish common ground with the Party-state. Wang Shaoguang has talked about a new "popular pressures" model of policy making in China that has resulted in "an

---

[66] China Soft Power Project Team, 'Information Disclosure in the Earthquake Relief', pp. 238–239.

impressive congruence between the priorities of the public and the priorities of the Chinese government".[67] The same applies to media policy making. If some kind of common ground is established between the state and media organisations such as in areas of image construction and projection of soft power, then what used to fall in the Sphere of Illegitimate Controversy could move into the Sphere of Legitimate Controversy. Needless to say, there are serious implications from this practice of establishing common ground, which need to be further researched in another research project.

TRUST AND THE LEVEL OF BARGAINING POWER

Media organisations differ in their nature, preferences and interests. There are national ones, transnational ones and local ones, official ones and private ones, Party organs and commercial ones. Zheng's observation on the influence of social forces on the Party-state also applies to the bargaining power of media organisations with the Party-state:

> With the hegemonisation of Party/state power over social forces, some social forces are more autonomous, better organised and politically more influential than others. [...] Accordingly, the political behaviour and the power capabilities of social forces vary. Even for the same social group, its political action and influence are contingent on the political weight that the Party/state will assign to it at a given time.[68]

Although the Chinese media as a whole enjoys limited autonomy, some media organisations have more bargaining power with the Party-state and thus enjoy more autonomy than others. The level of

---

[67] Wang, Shaoguang, 'Changing Models of China's Policy Agenda Setting, *Modern China*, 34(1), (2008), pp. 56–87.

[68] Zheng, *The Chinese Communist Party as Organisational Emperor: Culture, Reproduction and Transformation*, p. 148.

bargaining power, and hence autonomy, is related to the level of trust that media organisations get from the Party-state. In other words, how much bargaining power a media outlet has depends on the nature of a media outlet. The nature of a media outlet refers to its relation with the CCP and the government — political capital. Political capital could be in the form of its status or personal connections.

Organ Media vs. Commercial Media

Party organ media are media outlets which are closely related to and partially financed by the Party and the government. Commercial media are media outlets which are less related to the CCP and the government and which depend entirely on the market financially. Because of their different natures, they differ in their coverage and distribution. Take the newspaper for an example. Organ papers publish a high volume of political news such as leaders' speeches and the proceedings of official meetings. Because of their political role, organ papers have various advantages, including subsidies and privileged distribution through Party channels to state-owned firms and institutions — the so-called official world. Publications such as evening and weekend papers, sports papers, book review papers and digests brought about by reform are commercial papers. In contrast to the organ papers however, the more commercial and popular papers enjoy brisk sales at kiosks and via home subscriptions and have become an important part of the media of the domestic sphere.

Of course it is simplistic to distinguish one from the other in this way as very often they are intermingled. For instance, the commercial papers are often, but not always, owned and published by the same organisations that own and publish the organ papers. Even within the Party organs, they have their different distribution channels and readership targets. According to Zhao,[69] among

---

[69] Zhao, *Communication in China*, p. 296.

the Party organs, the urban dailies make up the most resource-rich segment of the Chinese press. Indeed, because of their state-granted privilege and their relatively larger amounts of political capital as the subsidiaries of central and provincial level Party-organs, they are able to tap into the lucrative metropolitan advertising markets on the one hand, and on the other, have state-secured monopoly rights to produce original news, higher political status in accessing official sources and can claim provincial and above-level political authorities as their own base. Moreover, in contrast to the "old mainstream media" of central and provincial Party-organs — their parent papers, through both their capacity and their state-secured monopoly rights to produce original news, they are the agenda-setters of China's commercial websites, which are banned from having reporters of their own.

Wang and Tan's research[70] on the influence of the media on the judicial system is insightful. They examine and analyse randomly selected samples of reports on judicial affairs from 1985 to mid-2007 from Southern Weekend, a representative of the commercial media, and Legal Daily, a representative of the official media, as well as two websites — people.com.cn, an official website, and sina.com.cn, a commercial website. Their findings from the investigation show that the criticism themes of the commercial paper Southern Weekend have remained constant or decreased a little bit during the period of investigation while the criticism themes of the official Legal Daily have increased slightly. They discovered that the official paper was more episodic and sensational in its reporting than the commercial one. These trends, they suggest, indicate that the new Chinese leadership may prefer to give official media outlets more opportunities, albeit still limited, to engage in critical reporting while reining in commercial media outlets.

---

[70] Wang, Hongying and Tan, Honggang, 'Chinese Media and the Judicial System under Soft Authoritarianism', at http://jpm.syr.edu/pdf/fellowpdfs/1_a.pdf, accessed on 10 August 2010.

Zhao Yuezhi also finds that tabloids are often politically conservative, arguing that while they expose lurid examples of corruption, they generally present the state as benign and celebrate many hard-working and well-intentioned officials, including the police. Moreover, she finds that tabloids frequently reinforce traditional stereotypes (for example, that rural migrants are a source of crime) and pander to patriarchal norms. On the other hand, she finds that they do celebrate entrepreneurs, including women who succeed against the odds. She concludes that tabloids are a mixed bag, neither "oppositional texts" nor "new opium handed down by the Party's propaganda department.[71]

These findings are contradictory to the expectations placed on the commercial outlets which are expected to play a bigger role in this process of bargaining for autonomy. The logic is simple: their possession of independent economic resources will allow private entrepreneurs to emerge as an autonomous social class. As their fortune is tied to the market, which for healthy long-term development needs the protection of democratic political institutions, the private business class have a strong interest in promoting political reforms and will join hands with other social forces to struggle against the authoritarian state in order to bring about democratic political changes. Furthermore, policy makers and policy implementers have already been unable to be separated from commercial groups such as advertisers, and other profits engines.

However, instead of forging horizontal alliances among themselves and with other social groups, studies reveal that private entrepreneurs have sought to advance their interest by cultivating patron-client ties with government officials to increase their political capital. They rely on such ties for both commercial advantages and political protection. Because of the different amounts of political capital they have, differences are found between Party organs and the

---

[71] Zhao, Yuezhi, 'The Rich, the Laid-off, and the Criminal in Tabloid Tales: Read All About It!' in Perry Link, Richard Madsen and Pauil G. Pickwicz, (Eds.), *Popular China: Unofficial Culture in a Globalising Society,* (Lanham: Rowman & Littlefield, 2002), pp. 111–135.

commercially oriented ones in their push for autonomy. Zhao found that although Beijing Youth Daily had a power base in the powerful Beijing Municipal Party Committee,[72] and pioneered a style of journalism that fused the Party line with popular journalism by addressing popular concerns, especially the concerns of ordinary Beijing citizens in the early 1990s,[73] it left the more established China Youth News, official newspaper of the Communist Youth League of China since 1951, to publish the most poignant critique of a dominant knowledge-money-power regime in the Chinese social structure.[74] Apparently, China Youth News enjoys more trust from the Party-state and can therefore be more aggressive in its criticism since it is trusted to play a constructive role in the maintenance of the ruling power of the CCP. Furthermore, differences are also found in the strategies of the organ papers and those of commercially oriented outlets. When the earthquake erupted in May 2008, for example, CCTV knew that the coverage of the event without approval would not please the government, but it nevertheless decided to proceed with a fait accompli first and deal with the consequences later. This kind of behaviour stands in stark contrast with that of commercially oriented outlets, which tend to apply self-censorship out of the fear that if the government does not like them on political grounds, it may find fault with, say, some financial decisions they make, then punish user that as a pretext for punishment.

Wang and Tan also find from the analysis of reports on judicial affairs on people.com.cn and sina.com.cn during the same period that the commercial website has not departed from the old mouthpiece model as much as one would expect. In fact, along the state-oriented educational theme and the three criticism themes, its orientation is closer to the old model than the official website and the commercial newspaper. Wang and Tan attribute this apparent "conservative" tendency of the commercial website to self-censorship on

---

[72] *Ibid.*, p. 118.

[73] Zhao, *Media, Market, and Democracy in China*, p. 141.

[74] Zhao, *Communication in China*, p. 298.

the part of the commercial website: with profit as their main goal, commercial websites are interested in attracting eyeballs by adopting a lively style and by engaging in some critical reporting, but they are not willing to take major political risks. On the one hand, the state is more on its guard against these commercial websites. It inquires into their affairs more frequently (there is a set of mechanism for the state ones, while for the non-state ones, it is more ad hoc, and so more difficult to follow). On the other hand, there is always the fear on the side of the commercial groups that if they do anything the government does not like, they will be banned outright. Therefore before making any move, they need to guess what the government's reaction would be.

Parallel to the official paper, Wang and Tan find that the official website has strayed farther away from the old mouthpiece model than expected. Indeed, with regard to the CCP-government theme, the education theme and the three criticism themes that they identify in the analysis, the official website is either equally or more untraditional than the commercial website. They attribute this relatively "liberal" orientation to a possible deliberate tactic used by the CCP to be competitive in cyberspace.

Most interesting is Wang and Tan's interpretation of their analysis, as it agrees with my argument in Chapter 4 that the reach of a media outlet decides the level of control from the government. They find that in general, the commercial newspaper stands out as the most "liberal" among all the media outlets studied. The fact that the commercial newspaper shows a more "liberal" orientation than the commercial website may be explained by the different political space each finds itself to be in. The commercial newspaper, Southern Weekend, is mostly distributed in Guangdong and neighbouring provinces. The central government could be less relaxed about its content than it would be if the paper were distributed nationwide. In contrast, the commercial website, www.sina.com.cn is borderless. Therefore, the CCP and the government watch it with great intensity, leaving little room for the website to wander far from the politically correct line.

National vs. Local

Even within the same group, such as the organ papers, the negotiation power is different, depending on the political weight that the Party/state assigns to it in a given time. In general, China's leaders are significantly more satisfied with the mouthpiece role of the national-level media outlets such as CCTV and People's Daily than with those created and circulated by outlets lower in the administrative hierarchy, to say nothing of those originating abroad. This is perhaps not surprising, given the fact that the capital's propaganda cadres monitor the central outlets relatively easily and directly appoint the outlets' leading personnel. In the words of Liu Yunshan, head of the Propaganda Department, on CCTV's coverage of the outbreak of SARS[75]: "CCTV is a team capable of fighting in the war against SARS; it is an excellent journalist team, a reliable journalist team of the Party". Two facts speak of the political weight of CCTV: first, it was trusted by the Party-state to start the current affairs programme "Focus" in order to help the government to deal with specific problems and to combat bureaucracy and cadres' indifference, thus closing the distance with the masses. Secondly, other local stations and programmes were warned not to deal with hot topics: "the phenomena of putting on hot topics in every programme must be stopped. They are to be done by 'Focus' only".[76]

Keane has forcibly argued, based on the general acceptance that national media in China have more constraints, that "the further away from Beijing the more we find evidence of 'edge-ball' activities or creative compliance".[77] This argument led to the understanding that in the struggle between central, provincial, municipal and county-level authorities over the restructuring of the Chinese media system, local media outlets, driven by market forces, have the potential to carve out a public space that may allow critical debate around issues that are otherwise regarded as only a matter

---

[75] Liu, 'Talk on the Visit to CCTV Staff', p. 5.

[76] Ibid., 4.

[77] Keane, Michael, 'Broadcasting Policy, Creative Compliance and the Myth of Civil Society in China', *Media, Culture and Society*, 6(23), (2001), pp. 783–798.

for the Party-state.[78] I carried out an investigation in order to find out whether media outlets at the county level, the lowest of the media hierarchy, constitute more autonomy from the state, and thus become more effective channels for participation and representation. I discover that despite the fact that Chinese official media outlets at the county level enjoy a relatively more relaxed political environment, they are nevertheless tightly bound to the Party-state through different mechanisms, including the institutional and structural nature, the reporting system handed down from Mao's time, and the strong local social network. These mechanisms make it impossible for local media outlets to contribute to the development of public sphere, "where information, ideas and debates can circulate in society, and where political opinion can be formed".[79] On the contrary, they guarantee that media workers work cooperatively with the local government. The similarities with media at the national level, in particular those topics that receive *no* coverage, suggest that their potential as a counter-hegemonic force is thus far negligent. Keane's proposition that "the further away from Beijing the more we find evidence of 'edge-ball' activities or creative compliance" seems to apply only to commercial activities carried out by local media.[80]

State-Owned vs. Private Outlets

Needless to say, state-owned outlets enjoy far more trust and thus bargaining power for autonomy than the private sector. The government has brought in the private sector to the media industry only to sustain economic growth, but for the private sector to possess

---

[78] For further discussion on the topic see Zhang, Xiaoling, 'Seeking Effective Public Space', pp. 55–77.

[79] See Dahlgren, Peter, *Television and the Public Sphere: Citizenship, Democracy and the Media* (London: Sage Publications, 1995), p. ix.
See also Fraser, Nancy, 'Rethinking the Public Sphere: A Contribution to the Critique of Actually Existing Democracy', *Social Text*, No. 25/26, (1990), pp. 56–80.

[80] Keane, 'Broadcasting Policy, Creative Compliance and the Myth of Civil Society in China', pp. 783–798.

political legitimacy, it needs to conform to the official ideology and support the goals and policies of the state as the criteria of political legitimacy are set entirely by the state. Administrative legitimacy stems from association or contacts with the state bureaucracy, therefore it also derives from the state.

However, the distance between the authorities and private media outlets is not fixed. This fluidity means the trust and autonomy from the state changes. In order to gain political and administrative legitimacy, private entrepreneurs have always proactively integrated themselves with the existing political system, depending on the political resources of the Party-state to develop their business. They speak "the language of the system," and this has served them and their businesses well.[81] To use the example from Zhao again: Wang Changtian's private media company emerged from having a symbiotic relationship with the state sector to gain some legitimacy. When he first started, he had to struggle to register his operation as a proper business.[82] When the business first started and operated as an unregistered business, state television's economic interests and demands for his popular programme provided him with a power base. Wang used this relationship to not only expand his reach in television markets across the country but also for policy support and editorial gatekeeping. As an independent producer, he does not have direct access to official propaganda guidelines, including the latest Propaganda Department orders that ban certain stars or content. These guidelines are instrumental in producing politically safe programming that ensures broadcast. Indeed, partial reform has left private business to operate in an environment with many uncertainties, such as the state's constraint on private property rights, administrative interference in commercial activities, and the constancy of government policies. Bureaucratic patronage is therefore needed in order to reduce these uncertainties. As the state moves from tolerating private television content producers to officially encouraging private capital

---

[81] Zhao, Yuezhi, *Communication in China: Political Economy, Power and Conflict*, p. 229.
[82] *Ibid.*, p. 221.

participation and espousing the separation of broadcasting and production, it has also started to incorporate private producers into its own administrative orbit. Consequently, Wang's company has gained more legitimacy. In other words, his status within the state policy establishment has improved. Wang became a business partner of the SARFT in 2003 when he contracted with the SARFT-affiliated China Radio and Television Journal to publish "Big Star". In December 2004, Wang, together with two other private television producers, was for the first time invited to participate in the annual national meeting of the broadcasting bureaus, the most important annual meeting of the broadcasting administration in which policy issues concerning the entire broadcasting industry are discussed and formulated.

Private business's dependence on the state bureaucracy for legitimacy, however, means that they can do only two things: those things which the government wants to do but does not have a chance to do it itself; and those things which the government has not thought of doing, but would not object to if private businesses were to do them first.

Transnational vs. Domestic and Private

Compared with domestic private capital, transnational capital has something unique to offer to the Chinese state. There is no doubt that transnational media organisations hold strong bargaining chips, such as allowing Chinese state media to gain access to foreign audiences through their cable networks or other promotional venues. They also have management expertise that is deemed essential in modernising China's national media industry and content favoured by a domestic elite audience eager to constitute themselves as the Chinese segment of the transnational consumer strata. Nevertheless, overseas media companies that wish to set up business in China have learned the importance of political capital or "government support" as the first condition that must be met before anyÿinitiative can succeed in China, as is shown in the following example.

A UK company makes an investment proposal[83] to accept an offer of a minority stake of up to 40% as a partner to develop the company (currently based in Macau) in Mainland China, via direct broadcasting from Macau via satellite and via a network of local CCTV provincial stations. Special emphasis is made about the great benefit the partnership will receive from the very strong connections established by the owners of the company in Mainland China: the chairman and founder of the company is the daughter of a former top general of Mao Zedong, who was also a vice premier of China. As the chairman of China National Heritage Foundation, she recently set-up a nationally recognised fund sponsored by some 100 top mainland companies, a great source of advertising revenues for the company. Close connections have been secured with members of China State Council as well as with the Chairman of the SARFT, China's regulatory body for all media, who are supporting the project.

CONCLUSION

As China becomes a major player in the global economy, the Party-state is trying to balance the need for more information with its goal of controlling content as a means to maintain power. One thing we should remember is that one major force that has and will continue to shape China's media policies is the imperative of the CCP to maintain its political power with legitimacy. Understanding this major force is crucial in order to comprehend the tensions between political stability and economic growth, mirrored in the constant swings of the Chinese media policy between control and openness. This vacillation is the result of conflicts between different interest groups wanting to exert influence on media policies. The interplay — the continuous and dynamic contention and negotiation between different interest groups and factors maximising their own interests and powers — has resulted in the dynamic dilemma of the co-existence of control and

---

[83] I am very grateful to one of my former part-time students who showed me the proposal. For reasons of security, I am unable to disclose names and further details.

openness, which characterises Chinese media policy and system change.

The authorities in China know the need for press freedom but are worried about opening the door to the type of freedom that could lead to the regime's downfall. For the Chinese media sector, they need trust from the Party-state first of all, because to take advantage of any economic opportunities and to develop their businesses at a meaningful scale, they need to maintain their political loyalty to Party bosses. But the Chinese media also needs credibility in the eyes of the public, which gives media organisations the leverage to bargain for more autonomy. However, when the credibility in the eyes of the public and the central authorities are in conflict, there are uncertainties as to the reactions of the government to any initiatives by media organisations for reform. It appears that the less political capital a media outlet has, the more likely it is to fear incurring the displeasure of the state. The private sector appears to be the least able to maintain autonomy owing to the fear of punishment from the state for disregarding its rules. The most effective way to success is to make use of the State's needs to further their own interests, be they commercial, professional or political. This kind of negotiation between the state and media organisations has expanded the grey area between the Sphere of Illegitimate Controversy and Sphere of Legitimate Controversy, giving the media more autonomy in their activities.

"Occupying the Commanding Heights"

The media in China has undoubtedly demonstrated increased autonomy and diversity in the reform era as a result of the liberalisation in all facets of Chinese society. However, this in no way means that the media has become free from political supervision. On the contrary, the Party-state has been very active in using the media to reconstitute its moral leadership and build consensus, to resolve the tension between political control and economic openness, especially after 1992. This chapter serves to illustrate by examples, how the Party-state has used different innovative forms, ranging from current affairs programmes to cultural products that emerged at different stages, to occupy the commanding heights of the changed media sphere after Deng launched the economic reform.

THE SPRING FESTIVAL GALA PARTY SINCE 1983

"The more our cultural products conquer the market, the more fortified our ideological front will be, the better the social benefits".

— Li Changchun[1]

---

[1] Sun, Zhengyi and Liu, Tingting, '2004: A Retrospective View of China's News Media in 2004, Part I', at http://www.people.com.cn/GB/14677/40606/3038055.html., accessed on 20 June 2010.

In its effort for effective domination rather than total control of media messages, the Party-state has become proactive in rearticulating the terms of its ideological hegemony and in proactively managing the symbolic environment. Two of the most noticeable things it has been doing since late 1980s are first, elaborating on its ruling ideology in a way that may still have some appeal to the vast majority of the population, secondly, packaging it in a more attractive way.

With regard to the first task, there has been, from the late 1980s not only an intensified rearticulation of the official discourse on socialism, but also growing sophistication in the traditionally orthodox ideology of politics, characterised by Chinese-context oriented pragmatism. Holbig and Gilley observed that Jiang Zemin and Hu Jintao, heeding the words of Deng Xiaoping who, after the Tiananmen Massacre of 1989, reflected that "our biggest mistake was in the area of education, in particular ideological and political education",[2] have invested much conceptual energy and large sums of money into modernising the Party's ideology. The leadership under Jiang Zemin came forward with an explicit strategy to adapt its dominant ideology to a changing environment. Jiang Zemin's controversial "Three Represents" concept signalled that the CCP was redefining its formerly proletarian social base and casting its lot with the newly affluent segments of society.[3] When Hu Jintao took over from Jiang Zemin as Party chief in late 2002, he came forward with two more theoretical concepts of his own. The first was the "Scientific Outlook on Development", introduced in early 2004 as a grand strategy of "comprehensive, coordinated, and sustainable development". With this concept, the new leadership distanced itself from the growth-only mentality of the first two decades of economic reforms and instead promised to balance economic development with

---

[2] Deng, Xiaoping, *Speech to Cadres and Soldiers of the Beijing Martial Law Corps*, 9 June 1989 in Beijing, at http://web.peopledaily.com.cn/deng/, accessed on 26 March 2008.

[3] Lewis, John W., and Xue, Litai, 'Social Change and Political Reform in China: Meeting the Challenge of Success', *China Quarterly*, 176, (December 2003), pp. 926–942.

social and ecological aspects. This concept was followed closely by another, the "Harmonious Socialist Society", which was innovative in explicitly acknowledging the existence of social tensions and claiming to tackle their root causes, increasingly perceived as a risk to social stability and to the political legitimacy of CCP rule. Hu stated that a "Harmonious Socialist Society" was "essential for consolidating the Party's social foundation to govern and achieving the Party's historical governing mission".[4]

For better packaging of the ruling ideology, the Party-state has tried many means, including the colonisation of CCTV's Spring Festival Gala Party. Since its first appearance in 1983, the CCTV's Spring Festival Gala Party, a continuous four- to five-hour TV variety show, has been institutionalised as part of the ritual of the Chinese New Year celebration. On Lunar New Year's Eve, the televised Gala Party starts at 8:00 pm to the eager anticipation of people all over the country and overseas Chinese worldwide, thanks to satellite transmission. It has been taken as the highest mode of celebration for the Chinese New Year in the country. As a show targeting at a wide audience, spectrum it tries to offer something for everybody, young or old, male or female, providing an atmosphere of fun and rejoicing together.

However, this joy does not come without strings attached. The CCP was quick to recognise its huge popularity and to realise that this form of cultural production had great potential as an effective vehicle for the maintenance of hegemony and as a political and ideological vehicle for its reform agenda. Viewed by an audience of more than one billion people each year, a unique situation in which families are wired via television to the central state, CCTV's Gala Party over the years has played a role in integrating members of the society, affirming common values, legitimating institutions and reconciling different sectional elements in an era when China is experiencing rapid cultural and ideological changes in values and beliefs, and when the market economy is deeply taking root in the society. Many of the

---

[4] 'Hu Jintao on the Construction of Harmonious Socialist Society on February 19, 2005', 26 June 2006, at http://www.china.com.cn/chinese/news/899546.htm, accessed on 2 January 2011.

programmes aim to evoke a sense of togetherness, the quickening of hope, the celebration of a shared sense of purpose or common values. One important function of the Gala is to remind the Chinese people of the material achievements the Party-state has made through reform, to instil in people, hope and confidence in the government.

The Gala has evolved over the years to meet the changing needs of social conditions as well as the need of the authorities to establish control. Indeed, although the audience does not have the final say in what should and should not be put on stage, nobody can really stop them from turning away from the show. Since 2003, a large audience has been invited to the studio every year to provide suggestions and comments. The feedback plays an important part in the composition of the programmes. From tender for ideas and directors for the Gala in July to the time it is shown, for more than half a year every year, great effort is put into the preparations. However, regardless of the different venues (from performing halls of different sizes to huge stadiums), actors/actresses, often the most famous in the country as only CCTV has the resources to do that, or presenters, as the highest mode of celebration in the country, the form itself has not undergone too much change. It invariably consists of the following:

1. Singing and dancing.
2. Cross-talks (xiang sheng 相声), mini-dramas (xiao pin 小品).
3. Traditional operas.
4. Acrobatic shows, conjuring, etc.

Among them singing and dancing and mini-dramas have been the most popular. For that very reason, they have been used to show more effectively, the achievements of the Party-state. It shows that the CCP has learned to package and market its ideologies in ever more popular forms to reach the audience.

Cross Talks and Mini-Dramas

Of all the programmes, cross talks and mini-dramas are the two main "language" programmes. While the cross-talk is a traditional performance of more than a hundred years old, with two performers using exaggeration and irony in dialogue to make the audience laugh, the mini-drama is a newly emerged genre. It utilises simple stage property, and several performers act out an interesting and instructive story. It contains many side-splitting jokes and the laughter is meant to fill audience with joy so that everyone forgets the troubles and cares of the past year. As the contents of these mini-dramas are very close to real life, praising the "good" and speaking "ill" of the bad, they have been welcomed by the audience. As mini-dramas can also be readily turned into effective social propaganda conveying clear-cut messages and inducing predictable emotional responses with little risk of formal subversion, they engage the audience as well as please the Party. The increase of mini-dramas in numbers from only one in 1984 and 1985 to two in 1986 and the stabilised number of five or seven since 1991 speaks of their popularity and success as a product of the marriage between market-derived imperatives for entertainment value and state ideological indoctrination. The genre ensures that satisfying audiences' desire and titillating their fantasies is no less important than meeting the political standards of the state. Mini-dramas are therefore considered the most appropriate form of performance to "educate the masses through entertaining them". They have become so successful that even traditional operas have borrowed the form and started to have their own "mini-operas". Because of their popularity, mini-dramas have been used to reflect the important events of the year: for instance, in 1996 there was a story in relation to the handover of Hong Kong. With the return of Macau was a story in relation to Macau in 1999. In year 2000 when there was an earthquake in Taiwan, there was a story entitled "Story that Happened at a Small Station", and of course in the year 2010, a few months after the 60th anniversary of the Founding of the People's Republic of China, there was a mini-drama on female pilots practising for the anniversary show.

Songs and Dances

Whether sung solo, in a duet, group, or chorus, apart from creating a festive and happy atmosphere, songs play an important role in expressing the "mainstream melody". They are often accompanied by dancing. As a variation from "language programmes", "folk dance", dance of a certain region with local flavour, or modern dance performances are common. The boisterous and joyful dances performed by China's different ethnic groups tend to appear either at the beginning or towards the end of the Gala to provide a picture of unity of the whole nation. Unlike mini-dramas that can be satirical against social ills, singing has been used as the most appropriate form for eulogising the positive side of things, arousing nationalism and patriotism, and praising the achievements of the Party. Typically, the song "Oh, Party, My Dear Mother" (1984), compares the Party to China's mother.

In the late 1970s and early 1980s when China started to open its door to the outside world, popular songs were officially rejected as the music of "bourgeois spiritual dejection" when they were first smuggled in from Hong Kong and Taiwan. The Spring Festival Gala Party broke with tradition and started to use pop stars from Hong Kong and Taiwan. The impact of a Hong Kong singer singing patriotic songs is of course different from anyone from the Mainland doing the same. It not only stirs up patriotic sentiments among the audience, but also serves to forge a united front between Mainland, Hong Kong and Taiwan. A minor singer from Hong Kong, for instance, became a household name overnight for singing "My Chinese Heart" in the 1984 Gala. On the Eve of the Chinese New Year in 1990, shortly after the Tiananmen Incident, the same singer was brought back onto the scene, hoping he would again stir up nationalistic sentiments as he had done in 1984.

Very often, old tunes are now dubbed using words of popular propaganda, as is well demonstrated by the theme songs laden with overt moral and ideological messages. In 2004, the song "Heart to Heart with People", eulogised the Party as the saviour during the outbreak of SARS. 2009 saw ethnic riots in Xinjiang that killed almost 200 people in July. In order to provide a more convincing picture of Uyghur in Xinjiang enjoying the Party's good policies in the area, at the 2010 Spring Festival Gala Party, a group of Uyghur sang and danced to a tune entitled "CCP's Policies, Yakexi", "yakexi" being the Uyghur word for good.

Everlasting Themes vs. Changing Events with the Times

There is an official statement of the theme for the show each year to reflect first and foremost, Party policies, lines and directions. Over the years, "unity", "unification", "one country, two systems" and "world peace" have been the themes. "Building a harmonious society and harmonious world" has been the main official slogan of the country from 2004, whereas building a harmonious family, society and world has been the theme adopted for the Gala since.

Although the themes remain more or less the same, the Gala Party highlights different important political events of the past year annually, just as Zhong (2002: 23) puts it: "[the] Spring Festival Gala is [meant] to give artistic expression to important events of the year". In the 1980s, the programmes reflected the lives and tastes of small entrepreneurs, who were just appearing in China at that time. In 1984, the central government proposed "one country, two systems" which caused much reverberation both at home and abroad. In complete compliance with the intention of the government, a show was successfully put on with the theme "patriotism, unification and unity". In the mid-1980s, the Party called on the whole nation "to learn from the soldiers fighting in Vietnam". Thus, the 1986 and 1987 Spring Festival Galas were dedicated to the propaganda guidelines of the year. Songs such as "Blood-stained Style" (xue ran de fengcai 血染的风采) were performed to mourn the soldiers who had lost their lives during the Sino-Vietnamese border war. However, in comparison with the 1990s, especially the early years, the programmes before 1989 were marked by liveliness, relaxation, laughter, and an atmosphere of gradual de-politicisation. On the other hand, the early years of the 1990s were marked by measured control and seriousness. In 1990, "stability and unity" was the paramount theme of the year after the chaos in 1989. Since 1992, the atmosphere again changed dramatically. With Deng's watershed speech early that year granting wider, faster, and deeper economic reform, people seemed to wake up from a long, depressing slumber and suddenly become aware of the whole world of opportunities opened up to them. Some were confused, some panicked, but many sprang into action. This change was reflected in the programme of the Gala Party after 1992, when individual entrepreneurs were in the Party's spotlight; the East Asian Games were highlighted in 1993. The disappointment and frustration at the failure in the bid to host the Olympics in 1993 was channelled into passionate patriotism, which permeated the Spring Festival Gala of 1994, with the theme of "Unity, Self-respect, Vigorous Progress and Expectation". 1997 of course provided a rare historical opportunity for instilling national pride in the whole nation with the handover of Hong Kong — naturally the theme of the year was "United, Proud and Hardworking Chinese". At the Spring Festival Gala Party of 2000, Beijing's bid to host the 2008 Olympics Games was the primary focus. 2002 was a year for celebration: accession to WTO and success in the bid to host the Olympics in 2008. 2004 celebrated the successful manned space mission and the control of SARS; 2009, the successful hosting of the Olympic Games and 2010, the 60th anniversary of the founding of the PRC.

New Values and Concepts

The Party-state has over the years, attempted to devise a new set of values and concepts in line with the changed and changing social circumstances under reform, in order to maintain its power with legitimacy. Indeed, the Party faced great challenges in the early 1990s to remobilise its people to support it: the first half of the 1990s was marked by a deep sense of ideological apathy in the aftermath of the 1989 Tiananmen Incident. It was marked by despair over political reform and the rising social craze of money worship. At the same time, the young generation in the 1990s presented a real problem for Party propaganda. These young people, in their late teens and early 20s, could not relate to the experiences and memories of the elder generation of revolutionaries. So the problem was not that they were resistant but that they were indifferent to ideological indoctrination, be it socialism or Marxism. They were sceptical of any ideological propaganda and less eager to jump on an extremist bandwagon. In other words, this new generation of Chinese were more interested in lifestyle than revolution. In a desperate search for new unifying ideologies preserve the status quo in the early 1990s, the Party turned to patriotism/nationalism as a rather obvious option. Indeed, modern China by no means lacks the cultural and historical resources for mobilising popular patriotic sentiments. No other nation has suffered the same degree of humiliation, pain and loss as China did in the hands of western powers in the hundred years following the Opium War with Britain in 1841. As the communist ideology gradually became an empty shell, patriotism/nationalism became increasingly used by Chinese officials to hold the country together. It became one of the only legitimate banners that could be summoned to remobilise the Chinese people. To give the people something to believe in that could prove more compelling than the threadbare official ideology, CCP leaders stressed patriotism. The Chinese were required "to love the socialist system and road chosen by all nationalities in China under the leadership of the Communist Party, which is not only the choice of history, but also the choice of people". As a result, patriotism/ nationalism by and large replaced the political and class struggle messages that dominated government propaganda before.

This effort to restore confidence in the CCP by promoting patriotism and nationalism is reflected in such cultural products as the Spring Festival Gala Party. Since 1984, when China announced its "one country, two systems" proposal, efforts to promote patriotism and nationalism in Hong Kong gradually stepped up through the years. The Spring Festival which belongs only to the Chinese is certainly the best opportunity to stir up patriotic and nationalist sentiments. For the Hong Kong and Taiwan audience, nationalistic motifs such as the image of China as the motherland of Hong Kong, or message that Hong Kongers, Taiwanese and Mainlanders are members of one big Chinese family has permeated the Gala Parties. Apart from having pop stars and popular presenters from these places, songs, dances and mini-dramas are all part of the apparatus to promote the two sentiments.

Revamped Confucianism

In Confucianism, the nature of a nation is the same as a family. In other words, family is the basic unit of a nation, and the nation is the extension of the family. An individual's relationship with the state is the extension of the relationship of the individual with the family. Therefore to be a good son, one should be filial to parents at home and to be a good subject, one should be loyal to the emperor.

The Spring Festival Gala Party emphasises the unity and warmth of a family — kindly father and dutiful son, amicable brothers and gentle couples. Extending from the family are the good relationships between relatives, neighbours, and extending further is the unity of the 56 nationalities of the whole nation. This age-old tradition of the Spring Festival as the most celebrated time of the year also provides the Chinese government with a good opportunity to address Chinese emigrants all over the world. Propaganda that promotes patriotism or state ideology may need to be more inclusive as the targets of propaganda increase. Therefore, this special occasion has over the years been used to establish a "united front" with Chinese people overseas. Although these expatriates, particularly the political dissidents among them, remain critical of the Chinese government, they have by no means stopped identifying with China. From 2006, the Spring Festival Gala Party has also been broadcast on English, Spanish, French and Arabic channels, linking audiences from different national backgrounds throughout the world as one harmonious family.

More importantly, in 1990, a few months after the Tiananmen Incident, Jiang Zemin, then General Party Secretary, and Li Peng, then Premier, appeared on the programme with the help of modern technology (in the form of a short video clip). They addressed the whole nation with good wishes for the coming year and wished the nation "stability and unity". Their appearance on the screen reflected Jiang' and Li's better understanding of the usefulness to which the media, especially television, could be put to increase their popularity. It created an atmosphere conducive for officials and the masses to celebrate the festival together, and emphasised the solidarity and unity between the masses and the CCP as a big happy family. Since then, at each year's Gala, a video clip of the top leaders is shown, reminding everyone of the leadership under which China has made progress. The

Spring Festival Gala on CCTV has therefore also become a platform for the Party and government to show concern for the people. Since 1990, the camera has dutifully followed the Party officials' activities on Chinese New Year's Eves, which are shown on the Gala Party.

In summary, the Spring Festival Gala fits in easily with the family-centred Chinese way of life and is naturally favoured by the Party-state as the most effective and powerful propaganda tool.

CURRENT AFFAIRS PROGRAMME AS A BETTER VEHICLE SINCE 1994

The Party's proactive reform of the media is best illustrated by its encouragement for the TV current affairs programme "Focus" to be put on by CCTV, which has been used as a far more effective force for control than crudely made propaganda to strengthen political and social stability. This section examines the emergence of "Focus" and its response to the extraordinary event in 2003 — the outbreak of SARS — to reveal how the Party-state has pushed for the emergence of "Focus" and exploited it to play a key role in shaping public discourse and creating a social or psychological climate favourable for political stability.

The Emergence of "Focus" and Its Coverage of SARS

In the spring of 2003, the world was introduced to a new word and a new cause of anxiety — SARS. Media reaction throughout the world was instant, following an alert from the World Health Organisation (WHO). The Chinese media, however, followed its own agenda and reacted to this epidemic in its own way: although the first recorded case of SARS appeared on November 16, 2002 in Foshan in China's southern province of Guangdong,[5] the first reports on SARS from the state media did not appear till the mid of February.[6] On February 17, the CCTV

---

[5] From the website of China Central Television, 23 April 2004, at http://www.cctv.com/program/dysj/20040423/100897.shtml, accessed on November 12, 2009.

[6] E.g., on February 10, 11 and 13 in *Yangchen Evening Post*, *Nanfang Daily* and *Southern Weekend* respectively, in Guangdong Province which is generally considered to be more liberal. The pioneering bi weekly magazine *Finance & Business* (Caijing) first reported on SARS on February 20, and in *People's Daily*, it did not appear till April 12.

current affairs programme "Focus" made its first coverage of the deadly virus. These first reports on SARS were followed by a complete media silence for a number of weeks.[7] The second programme by "Focus" at the beginning of April was again followed by weeks of limited coverage. But from 18th April onwards, the world saw a significant increase in the state media's coverage of SARS. On 21st April, news of the dismissal of Beijing Mayor Meng Xuenong and China's Health Minister Zhang Wenkang was reported in state newspapers, one day after they were charged with mishandling the outbreak of the disease. That followed an announcement by the Health Ministry that the number of SARS cases in Beijing had jumped from 37 to 339 — nine times as many cases as previously reported. From that day on, SARS dominated the content of the Chinese state media. Daily reports on SARS were provided till August 17, 2003, when the last two SARS patients were discharged from hospital. Although China's image, both domestically and externally, was battered by its initial lacklustre reaction to the outbreak of SARS in the country, the change from limited to an overwhelmingly all-out coverage of SARS was taken by many observers, both Chinese and overseas, as a turning point (U-turn) in media reform in China.[8] They believed that though China's pre-reform style for secrecy would hardly vanish overnight, a new trend was emerging.

---

[7] With the exception of *Finance & Business*, which carried a related article on March 5. Its next report on SARS was on 5th April.

[8] For instance, the *China Daily* on 22 August 2003 claimed that "the order issued by the Political Bureau of the Central Committee of the Communist Party of China to openly disseminate information on the spread of SARS and the warning that any officials found to be withholding or distorting information would be severely punished, led to a real turning point in the Chinese media coverage of SARS". Also see deLisle, Jacques 'SARS, Greater China, and the Pathologies of Globalization and Transition', *Orbis*, (2003), p. 597;

Pomfret, John, 'SARS, a Political Issue in China', 23 May 2003, *The Washington Post*;

Cheng, Qian and Zhu, Tian, 'Changes and Development of China's TV News Concept 2003', *TV Studies*, No. 2 (2004), pp. 25–27.

As "Focus" had become a famous vehicle of investigative journalism in China, it is natural that at times of crisis such as SARS, audiences would expect "Focus" to scrutinise the system for its failure to curb the disease. Indeed, among all the changes and developments in the media in the early 1990s, the rise of CCTV's current affairs programme "Focus" became the most noticeable. Launched on April 1, 1994, it is a 13-minute programme that starts at 7:38 pm on the primary national television channel, CCTV-1, immediately after the 7 o'clock evening news and the national weather forecast, and is broadcast on several other CCTV channels at different time slots. The programme produces news features with a special in-depth or investigative aspect and adopts the format of discussion on topical issues rather than merely echoing official political slogans. The most important aspect of the programme is that it breaks the convention of covering good news and avoiding the bad, marking for the first time that television in China has come out to openly criticise bureaucracy, corruption, pollution and other social problems. The public warmly welcomed this intervention into the fraught relationship between the state and the people after the Tiananmen Incident in 1989. Around 30% of the audience, the equivalent of 300 million people, watched this programme every night in the mid-1990s. Its impact was unprecedented. Stories from "Focus", for example, were often carried in the print media and transcripts of "Focus" appeared in many books. As "Focus" gained popularity throughout the country, almost every provincial and local television station started their own current affairs programme. As a result, over sixty similar programmes[9] emerged throughout the country, making criticism of wrongdoings a common practice.[10] Soon other media — radio

---

[9] From the website of CCTV, at http://www.cctv.com/programme/jdft/20040520/102170.shtml, accessed on 16 June 2005.

[10] However, in 1996, for better control, other local stations and programmes besides *Focus* from CCTV were directed not to deal with hot topics. Yang Weiguang, the president of the CCTV then, directed that "the phenomena of putting on hot topics in every programme must be stopped. They are to be done by *Focus* only. *Focus* is, after all, one of the Party's strategies to do theoretical propaganda".

stations, newspapers and magazines — started to report investigations and revelations of corruption as well.

Some scholars were encouraged by the phenomenon to believe that the programme was an attempt by CCTV to test whether the government and the public were truly prepared to accept exposures of truth and criticism.[11] Others expressed their optimism that the multi-media cross-promotions had significantly amplified the "supervision" of government officials by the media[12] and that eventually this open atmosphere for public discussion on real life cases would be conducive to the development of a more open, tolerant and democratic society in the long run.

However, a reading of the speeches by the head of the Propaganda Department, the head of the SARFT and the president of CCTV over the years shows that the emergence of CCTV's "Focus" is the result of the Party-state pushing the news media hard for new strategies for more effective propaganda. As it lost much of its public credibility and authority due to the 1989 Tiananmen Incident, and as it was faced with the globalisation of information, the Party-state found it crucial that the news media came up with new and appealing strategies to construct a good image of the Party-state as showing concern and care for the people and to disperse social frustration. In 1992, Ding Guangen, then head of the Propaganda Department, gave explicit instructions on the content and form of propaganda[13]:

> The effectiveness of propaganda should be paid attention to. The democratic form of discussion and interaction should be adopted so that the programmes are lively and convincing.

---

[11] Li, "'Focus' (Jiaodian Fangtan 焦点访谈) and the Changes in the Chinese Television Industry", p. 22.

[12] For instance, Guo Zhenzhi, 'Supervision by Public Opinion and the Western Concept of Journalistic Professionalism', *International News Festival*, 5, (1999), pp. 32–38.

[13] Xin, Wen, 'Ten Years' Exploration and Pursuit: Review on CCTV's Reform', *TV Research*, No. 4, (1996), 10–21.

At a later meeting specifically held for TV work, he emphasised again[14]:

> TV stations can add current affairs programmes, invite leaders to explain policies and answer questions, or invite both experts and ordinary people to hold discussions on hot topics and puzzling issues, so that people can inspire each other and draw the correct conclusion. In this way, the programmes will become more attractive and convincing.

Despite the encouraging rhetoric by leaders however, news programmes remained the same in form and content, a phenomenon that could only be explained by the dubious attitude of the people working at all levels in TV stations. At the beginning of 1993, Ding pushed harder:

> This year, programmes should try to make greater changes. There should be new programmes which must relate to the needs of the people. The forms must be original.[15]

It is therefore in answer to the requirements, specifications and directions from the Propaganda Department that CCTV, among other reforms, put on "Focus" in 1994. In other words, although "Focus" adopted the democratic approach of interaction and discussion, with experts and ordinary people talking on the programme, this cannot simply be interpreted as a sign that previously closed domains are opening up. Rather, it serves to act as a more effective mask for the exercise of power. The formal application of democracy — investigative reports, interaction between presenters and audience, discussions on hot topics — should therefore be seen to have been adopted under the direct interference of the top leaders with two faces in mind to show, one towards the domestic and the other towards the international audience. To the domestic audience, it is a sign of the Party and the people sharing the same interest in order to secure its legitimacy. To the international community, it is a

---

[14] *Ibid.*, p. 11.
[15] *Ibid.*

sign of the Chinese government's firm control, growing confidence, stability, prosperity and openness.

In order to reveal whether CCTV's "Focus" experienced a real "breakthrough" in the coverage of SARS after two decades of reform, which has greatly increased the power of market relative to the old political imperatives, I examined the way "Focus" responded to the emergence, rise and fall of SARS. Both content analysis and critical discourse analysis were employed to examine the coverage of SARS by "Focus" from February 17, 2003 when the first report on SARS appeared, till the World Health Organisation gave Beijing an all-clear in late June (forty-five programmes on SARS out of 116 days).[16] The analysis was enhanced by the examination of the programme from April 20, 2001 to January 31, 2003,[17] the study of official rhetoric on TV work during the last decade[18] and interviews with media practitioners during the investigator's field trip in February and March 2004.

Findings[19] from the study show that far from some observers' optimistic belief, the change in the coverage of SARS lies in frequency rather than in content. This frequency is characterised by the singing of "main stream melodies" rather than critical reports. Furthermore, analysis also shows that the change in frequency is in absolute conformity with the agenda set by the Party, suggesting that the Party had complete control of the propaganda apparatus throughout. From the first programme on February 17 to April 17, 2003, only seven programmes were found on SARS. Apparently, this limited coverage was the result of following strict

---

[16] The content analysed from *Focus* comes from the transcripts of the programme on the website of the CCTV: http://www.cctv.com/program/jdft/01/index.shtml, accessed on 17 June 2005.

[17] The starting date chosen for the analysis of the programme is based on the availability of the transcripts of the programme on the web-site of CCTV.

[18] The decision to examine official rhetoric from the early 1990s is based on the time of the appearance of *Focus* (1 April 1994).

[19] For detailed analysis of the programme, see Zhang, Xiaoling, 'Reading between the Headlines: SARS, *Focus* and TV Current Affairs Programmes in China', *Media, Culture and Society*, 28(5), (2006), pp. 715–738.

guidelines: in late February, the Propaganda Department ordered a halt to public reporting on the disease in order to "ensure the smoothness" of the National People's Congress meetings in March.[20] As a result, although SARS was far from being under control in March, there was hardly any report on it throughout the nation.[21] The few programmes that were made during that period by "Focus" relied on positive self-representation and countered the charge of China being the place of origin of SARS (April 2, 4 and 6). On April 17, at a meeting of the Politburo's Standing Committee, it was ordered that "government organisations at all levels must know accurately the development of the disease and report honestly. The condition should be released to the public at regular intervals and there should be no delaying and hiding in reports".[22] That explains the significant increase on the coverage of SARS including by "Focus" from 18th April. The programmes appealing to patriotism and national unity in fighting against SARS were apparently in answer to the calls of the Propaganda Department, which held a meeting on April 25, presided over by Li Changchun, the Politburo member in charge of propaganda.[23] Drawing on the line used by President Hu Jintao, Li emphasised that "the strongest motif of our times" was "uniting the will of the masses into a fortress".

Analysis of the programmes also shows that despite the superficial resemblance to the western practice of relying on experts' opinions, the journalistic convention of "balance" — that is, citing experts who hold opposing views on an issue, was hardly practiced.

---

[20] Link, 'Will SARS Transform China's Chiefs?', at http://www.time.com/time/asia/covers/501030505/viewpoint.html, accessed on 27 July 2010.

[21] Of the few voices on SARS, the bi weekly magazine *Finance and Trade* (Caijing) reported on SARS on 5th March after it first reported on it on February 20. The next one was on April 5.

[22] Dai, Yuanguang *et al.*, 'Report on SARS and the Objectivity of Journalism', in Weizhi Deng, (Ed.), *SARS and the Chinese Society*, (Shanghai: Shanghai University Press, 2003), pp. 312–325.

[23] Fewsmith, Joseph, 'China and the Politics of SARS', *Current History*, 102(665), (2003), pp. 250–255.

The narrow range of expert sources and their non-contested perspectives mean that these experts were utilised to help explain and interpret government policies. The analysis shows that this kind of democratisation concerns merely the approach rather than the content.

From the examination of the programme "Focus" and from the response it got from the audience (through letters)[24] and the authorities, it is certain that "Focus" in its early stages was bolder in its exposure and criticism. To a certain extent, it is not wrong to claim that "by publicising cases of wrongdoings, the media have put pressure on the government to take note of the problem and to respond".[25] But one must not forget that it was the government that initiated this programme to help deal with in a controlled manner, specific problems and to combat bureaucracy and cadres' indifference, thus closing the distance between the Party-state and society. The exposure of too many problems was therefore seen as a threat to the stability and social order or even as an attempt to "misguide the public" into thinking that there were too many problems within the Party. In his speech, Sun Jiazhen, then Minister of the Radio, Film and Television Ministry, warned at the 1995 Radio and TV Current Affairs Programme Conference[26]:

> Although we have spent considerable time preparing for the appearance of the programme, we must know that it has not been long enough for us to put it on widely. Some programmes put on by other stations are just a few months old. There are many problems that require time to study and investigate. Some programmes have made mistakes to different extents. We must draw lessons from these experiences.

---

[24] See, for instance, a letter from Heilong Jiang, at http://www.cctv.com/news/focus/focus.html, accessed on 20 December 2005.

[25] Li, '"Focus" (Jiaodian Fangtan 焦点访谈) and the Changes in the Chinese Television Industry', p. 27.

[26] Sun, Jiazheng, 'Make Efforts to Run Well the News Commentary Programme; Enhance the Level of the Guidance of Public Opinion', *TV Research*, No. 10, (1995), pp. 4–10.

Yang Weiguang, then president of CCTV and deputy director of the Radio, Film and TV Ministry, made a similar speech in 1996:

> It appears that some departments have not been communicating widely and in a timely fashion, the Central Government's intentions and propaganda specifications. Some programmes that are not in accordance with the propaganda specifications are still being made or run.[27]

On another occasion in the same year, Yang pointed out that the most important purpose for propaganda work was to correctly guide the public opinion. Media supervision and the guidance of public opinion are therefore understood by TV workers to be the two sides of the same coin, with the ultimate aim of propaganda for the Party-state.[28] In order to shape public discourse, propaganda officials exhorted the news programmes to play up the positive side of things to boost people's confidence, foster stability and unity[29] and to take greater care with the negative.[30] To Yang Weiguang, "If a state TV station reports problems here and there every day, how can it be called the tongue and throat of the Party?" For better control, with the exception of "Focus" from CCTV, other local stations and programmes are warned not to deal with hot topics: "the phenomena of putting on hot topics in every programme must be stopped. They are to be done by 'Focus' only".[31]

---

[27] Yang, Weiguang, 'Emancipate the Mind, Seek Truth from Facts, and Deepen Reform and Promote All Work at CCTV to a Higher Level', *TV Research*, No. 9, (1996), pp. 4–9.

[28] Ying, Yungong, 'Correctly Understand and Grasp the Relationship between Media Supervision, Reform, Development and Stability', *TV Research*, No. 10, (1997), pp. 16–19.

[29] Yang, Weiguang, 'Be Worthy of the Great Trust from the Party and the People, Offer More and Better Programmes', *TV Research*, No. 10, (1996), pp. 4–7.

[30] E.g., Yan, Shi, 'Follow the Basic Lines, Be Dauntless in Reform', *TV Research*, No. 8, (1995), p. 7.

[31] Yang, 'Be Worthy of the Great Trust from the Party and the People, Offer More and Better Programmes', p. 4.

Under strict control and discipline,[32] and by carrying out firm policies and following directions from the Central Committee, "Focus" exercises great caution in relation to the following: selection of topics, timing, level and degree of criticism.

Selection of Topics

A very strict editorial control system is exercised for "Focus". Journalists are required to submit the topics they have selected to the producer of the programme, who then passes them on to the head of the News Centre if approved. The final decision rests with the president of the TV station.[33] In selecting topics, journalists and producers closely follow the "two don'ts": "Do not report anything that cannot be solved at the moment, otherwise it can only bring panic. Do not arouse the attention of the audience to issues that cannot be solved under the present conditions in the immediate future".[34] The selection of topics also follows the rule that the topics chosen should "avoid triggering instability at home and providing subjects to be attacked from abroad".[35] Under such an editorial system, it is not strange that "Focus" was slow in covering the outbreak of SARS.

It is also understood that in different periods, different topics should be selected to facilitate the appearance and implementation of government policies.[36] For instance, around the 20th anniversary of the Land Contracted Responsibility, "Focus" broadcast a timely

---

[32] See Ding, Guangeng, 'Six Requirements for Propaganda Work', *Xinhua News Agency*, 10 May 1998.

[33] See Sun, 'Make Efforts to Run Well the News Commentary Programme; Enhance the Level of The Guidance of Public Opinion', p. 8;

Yan, Shi, 'Follow the Basic Lines, Be Dauntless in Reform', *TV Research*, No. 8 (1995), pp. 7–11.

[34] Yan, Lianjun, 'Positive Reports and Media Supervision', *TV Research*, No. 10, (1996), pp. 20–22.

[35] For instance in Li, Zhen, 'Exert Positive Influence of Media Supervision', *TV Research*, No. 11, (2001), pp. 9–10.

[36] Guan, Hongxin, 'Tentative Discussion on the Characteristics of "Focus"', *China TV*, No. 10, (1998), pp. 19–20.

series of programmes targeting the problems involved. These programmes helped prepare the way for the appearance of the government's new policies. The programmes on SARS on April 27 and May 12 are such programmes as well.

Timing

Chan has noted[37] that "Focus" did not broadcast on such occasions as the Lunar New Year holiday, the National Day and the period when the National People's Congress and the Chinese People's Consultative Conference were held in 1999, when stability is considered paramount. Similarly, my examination of the programmes on SARS finds that there were no reports from 7th–15th November 2002, during which the 16th Party's Congress was held. Neither was there any report around the National Day from 30th September–2nd October 2001, nor from 4th–18th March during which the first session of the 10th People's Congress was held. When there were reports, they were non-negative ones. The best example to illustrate the great sensitivity to timing the programme exhibits is the series on the education of children around June 4 in 1994, which started on 28th May and lasted till after 5th June. This kind of timing has often been cited as good practice as the series fits naturally with the time (June 1 as International Children's Day is celebrated every year in China) on the one hand, and avoids sensitive topics around that period on the other[38] (June 4 being the anniversary of the June Fourth Massacre at the Tiananmen Square). The absence of reports on SARS during the National People's Congress meetings in March 2003 is another example.

---

[37] Chan, Alex, 'From Propaganda to Hegemony: Jiaodian Fangtan and China's Media Policy', *Journal of Contemporary China*, 11(30), (2002), pp. 35–51.

[38] See, for instance, Wang, Xudong, 'Perspectives on the Selection of Topics by "Focus"', *TV Research*, No. 9, (1994), pp. 13–16;

Xin, 'Ten Years' Exploration and Pursuit: Review on CCTV's Reform', p. 19.

Level and Degree of Criticism

Because of the nature of the media in China, critique of major state policies or open media monitoring of policy-making processes at the top is not possible. It has been noted that the criticism from "Focus" is limited to policy implementation by local cadres. Power abuse, violation or "distortion" of policies by local bureaucracies can be reported, but must be reported with the "proper degree" and right timing. It is not surprising then that during the sensitive period of the National People's Congress meetings in March 2003, reports on the outbreak of SARS and the level of criticism were below the normal practice.

When reporting on the wrongdoing of local cadres, there have been urges[39] to give these wrongdoers a chance to correct their mistakes and errors, so that the image of the Party to clean itself of any mistakes is conveyed to the audience. From April 1998,[40] a follow-up for the problems exposed is generally required, so that "negative reports achieve positive effect". As a result, critical investigative reports in "Focus" follow more or less the same format: the programme either exposes an outrageous instance of injustice, after which the Party leadership becomes concerned and instructs that justice be served, or a social ill is exposed, followed by what has been done by related governmental organisations, and how the criminals or wrongdoers have been punished.[41]

To conclude, contrary to some scholars' belief that "Focus" was a test for the Party, it is actually a political response from CCTV to the call of the Propaganda Department of the Chinese Communist Party, to engage actively with issues of public concern and to provide an official frame on controversial topics. It is the result of the Party's urge to produce a programme that is "innovative and democratic in form" to achieve greater propaganda effectiveness. The response of "Focus" to SARS is only one of the many examples of the Party

---

[39] For instance in Li, 'Exert Positive Influence of Media Supervision', p. 10.

[40] Liang, Jianhui, 'Degree, the Critical Point for the Success of "Focus"', *TV Research*, No. 1, (2000), pp. 50–52.

[41] For instance, the programme 'Strike Hard on Ticket Mongers during the Spring Festival Holidays', on 19 February 2003.

leveraging on TV programmes for its own purpose. Analysis of "Focus" during the outbreak of SARS shows that although the effects of reform in China have gradually altered media production beyond recognition, its attempt at containing the outbreak of the disease, minimising economic consequences, and avoiding losses of confidence in the regime at home and abroad means TV current affairs programmes with their massive audience and thus their immense potential power and influence have far less freedom than ever to violate the guidelines set down by the state during times of crisis. The nature of "Focus" in China determines its discourse, which has been manifested in various ways, including selection of topics, timing, level and degree of criticism. The inspection visits from the three generations of premiers signal the continuous attention from Chinese top leaders, and CCTV's decision to increase its critical programmes from twice a week to 50% in 2004 illustrates the Party's determination to keep the programme as an example in shaping public discourse for other TV current affairs programmes in China and a symbol of media supervision for the outside world.

TECHNOLOGICAL INNOVATIONS FOR THE PROMOTION OF SOFT POWER IN THE 21ST CENTURY

While many are debating the political effects of the development of ICT on the authoritarian system, the Party-state has been actively exploiting the innovations in information and communication technologies as vehicles for the promotion of its soft power — from the use of individualised computers to the more mass-directed satellite television, as China's public diplomacy activities have moved gradually from passive (in line with Deng Xiaoping's low-profile foreign policy) to pro-active as China adopts a more active foreign policy under the leadership of Hu.[42]

---

[42] Zhao, Suisheng, 'Chinese Foreign Policy in Hu's Second Term: Coping with Political Transition Abroad', paper presented at the FPRI Asia Program's conference on Elections, Political Transitions and Foreign Policy in East Asia, Philadelphia, 14 April 2008.

Building Up Technological Capacities

As is discussed in Chapter 3, China has drastically increased its investment in its international media with the goals of airing its views, enhancing the country's global influence, and showcasing its rise as a great power in a non-threatening and non-confrontational manner. National level media organisations such as China Central Television, Xinhua News Agency and People's Daily can receive great financial support from the state for ambitious schemes geared toward enhancing China's international influence.[43] The Internet, which "simultaneously shares all the traits of television, newspapers, radio, books, and a countless number of other media",[44] was inaugurated in China in late 1994 and has brought a whole new dimension to public diplomacy. From 1995, all news media, publications, radio and TV stations started to run their own websites.[45] In 2001, government-controlled news websites were developed and launched on a massive scale, with the aim of adding new channels for propaganda and the ideological work of the Party on the one hand and taking over the new platform for public opinion supervision on the other.[46] This new platform for propaganda and ideological work consists of national and provincial key news websites, many of which originated from traditional media and business gateway sites. Naturally, many of them have become key public diplomacy outlets to project China's voice in mainstream Western society and to break the Western media blockade. Some of the leading ones include the websites of the Xinhua News Agency, People's Daily, China Radio International, China

---

[43] Lam, 'Chinese State Media Goes Global', at http://www.jamestown.org/single/?no_cache=1&tx_ttnews%5Btt_news%5D=34387, accessed on 18 March 2010.

[44] Geidner, Nicholas, W., 'Looking Toward 2008: The Effects of New Media on the Political Process', *The Review of Communication*. No. 6, (2006), pp. 93–100.

[45] Zeng, Jianhui, *Melting the Ice, Building a Bridge and Breaking through*, (Beijing: Wuzhou Publishing House, 2006), p. 12.

[46] Zhan, Xinhui and Yang, Chunlan, 'News Websites between Traditional Functions and Changes', *Media*, No. 10, (2006), at http://big5.xinhuanet.com/gate/big5/news.xinhuanet.com/newmedia/2006-10/10/content_5184606.htm, accessed on 10 August 2008.

Central Television and the Information Office of the State Council. In addition, sites designed for overseas publicity were also created. For instance, The China National Network[47] was created in 1997 as the key national overseas publicity website. All these websites are multi-lingual with specific topics and different layouts for the target regions, giving China a new medium for publicising itself to the world.

Television, which has been instrumental in constructing the political and cultural discourse to create and reproduce national identity, loyalty and pride, is seen by the Party-state as the most effective way to reconstruct China's image and to broadcast China's voice to the world. In 1991, the "Overseas Broadcasting Centre" was set up by CCTV, the only national-level TV station that has always enjoyed a special status in China.[48] In 1992, CCTV-4, China's first international channel in Mandarin Chinese, began its broadcasting service for overseas Chinese, especially those in Taiwan, Hong Kong and Macau. As a response to the government's "go-out" (or "go global") project launched in 1998 for the international expansion and multi-language coverage of China's TV satellite channels, CCTV expanded further and professionalised its international broadcasting, launching the 24-hour satellite English Channel CCTV News (also known as CCTV-9 and CCTV International) in 2000, the E&F channel (Spanish and French) in 2004, which started to run separately from 2008, the CCTV-Arabic and CCTV-Russian in 2009 and it is expected to run the Portuguese channel in 2010.

The Great Wall TV Platform (GWTV), which was set up in 2004, is another of China's centrally managed and coordinated endeavours "to enlarge and enhance its penetration into the world media market" for the promotion of China's soft power, according to the website of GWTV.[49] It is a TV package under CCTV with government-approved

---

[47] Its website address: www.china.com.cn.

[48] See Zhang, 'Breaking News, Media Coverage and "Citizen's Right to Know" in China', p. 537.

[49] 'About Us' from the website of The Great Wall TV Platform (GWTV), at http://wcm.gw-tv.cn/aboutus/, accessed 2 March 2008.

satellite channels mostly from mainland China (i.e., CCTV and provincial satellite channels). It provides Chinese movies, TV drama series, sports, news, children's programmes, music videos, documentaries and travelogues. The GWTV has so far launched its direct-to-home (DTH) satellite service in the US, Europe, Canada, Asia, Africa and Latin America.

The latest to join the existing overseas broadcasting channels is the Xinhua News Agency, which launched an English–language television news programme in July 2009 to be broadcast in supermarkets and outside Chinese embassies across Europe.

CCTV News: Winning the Hearts and Minds of Foreign Publics

CCTV News has become an essential tool of China to "improve the international opinion environment".[50] It targets a global English–speaking audience, including foreign expatriates working in China, such as embassy workers in Beijing.[51] The Chinese government has helped CCTV News to move from coverage to gaining access to foreign media markets. It opened up some southern Chinese TV markets to foreign media in exchange for cable access in the United States. For instance, "News Corp agreed that its United States network, Fox, would carry the English–language channel of Chinese state broadcaster, CCTV-9", according to a report from BBC.[52] According to John Jirik,[53] on

---

[50] Zhang, Lin, 'On the Strategies of News Report on CCTV International Channels', *Modern Communication*, 124(5), (2003), pp. 31–34.

[51] From the author's interview with one of the assistant chiefs of CCTV International in 2008.

[52] 'Murdoch wins China cable TV deal', BBC News, 20 December 2001, at http://news.bbc.co.uk/1/hi/entertainment/1721160.stm, accessed on 21 March 2010.

[53] Jirik, John, 'The AOL Time Warner CCTV (China) Television Exchange: Guanxi in Globalization Theory', paper presented at the annual meeting of the International Communication Association, Marriott Hotel, San Diego, CA, 27 May 2003, at http://www.allacademic.com/meta/p111969_index.html, accessed on 3 June 2008.

October 22, 2001, CCTV and AOL Time Warner (AOL) signed an agreement. While giving AOL Time Warner access to cable distribution in Southern China, CCTV asked AOL–TW to put its English–language channel, CCTV–9, on cable in New York, Los Angeles and Houston in exchange. A 2003 deal with Viacom-owned MTV "assisted in promoting CCTV programmes in the United States" by enabling CCTV–9 to broadcast to "30 top–class hotels in 10 major cities in the United States, including Washington D.C., New York, Los Angeles, San Francisco, Chicago, Philadelphia, and Atlanta".[54] Thanks to the efforts, CCTV News could claim to cover 98% of the world within a few years after its launch. CCTV News also claimed to have forty-five million subscribers outside China.[55]

CCTV, "representing the images of the Party and government domestically and the images of the country and nation internationally", as defined by Ding Guangen in 1994, then head of the Propaganda Department,[56] has become pro-active in providing its views as an insider from Asia and China, in an effort to break the Anglo-American monopoly. The information supplied is not limited to politics but also highlights China's achievements in all other areas, especially on cultural and economic developments. On the one hand, CCTV News shows an active defence on sensitive issues for which China is often criticised,[57] giving much prominence to China's environmental protection, political and social stability, national cohesion (especially on the issue of Taiwan and Tibet), anti-corruption, human rights, and reduction of poverty. On the other, the notions of "peaceful development", "mutual benefits of China's rise" and "harmonious society" are priorities on the overseas publicity agenda. The target audiences of CCTV News have also shifted from the peripheral group

---

[54] See 'CCTV English Channel Landing in United States', at http://english.people daily.com.cn/200305/01/eng20030501_116101.shtml, accessed on 10 February 2010.
[55] 'About CCTV International', at http://english.cctv.com/english/about/index. shtml, accessed on 10 February 2010.
[56] Chin, *From the Local to the Global: Chinese Television from 1996 to 2003*, p. 124.
[57] For example, the special series on "Made in China" in September 2007, which included such episodes as "More Attention on Toy Safety", "Haier Hammers out High Quality".

(overseas Chinese) to the mainstream, especially the elites. As a state-owned international broadcaster, it tries to increase its international competitiveness by asserting its brand and by increasing its reporting to affairs related not only to China, Asia and other developing countries but also other global affairs.

Being centrally managed and coordinated, the public diplomacy activities are more easily aligned with the government's policy and diplomacy. Undoubtedly, the Chinese political system has helped: wielding soft power resources is easier for China than for democracies where, as Nye pointed out,[58] many soft-power resources are separate from the government.

The advantages[59] of China using satellite channels to improve its attractiveness and enhance its global influence are obvious: Chinese TV stations at all levels can be centrally coordinated, by command or coercion, to work together for the expansion of activities abroad. The efforts the Party-state has made in harnessing the far-reaching changes in the technologies of international communications for the projection of China's soft power — "sending out information that is attractive to foreign publics",[60] — is remarkable.

CONCLUSION

Commercialisation, globalisation and technological advancement have brought unwanted challenges for the Party. But as the examples show here, the Party-state is by no means willing to abandon whole-sale attempts to exert influence over the media sphere. On the contrary, it has been trying to retain and at times tighten its grip over public channels of communication. But more noticeable is its

---

[58] Nye, Joseph, *Soft Power, The Means to Success in World Politics,* (New York: Public Affairs, 2004), p. 16.

[59] For the limitation of China's international communication, see Zhang, Xiaoling, 'China's International Broadcasting: The Case of CCTV International', in Jay, Wang (Ed.), *Soft Power in China: Public Diplomacy through Communication,* (Palgrave MacMillan, 2010), pp. 57–71.

[60] Li, Xiguang and Zhou, Qingan, *Soft Power and Global Communication,* (Beijing: Tsinghua University Press, 2005), p. 242.

proactive effort in taking advantage of the most popular and innovative forms and the most advanced media technologies to achieve its own purpose. CCTV's current affairs programme "Focus" has been used within the boundaries of control as an effective tool to mediate social relations amidst rapid social transformation. In the Spring Festival TV Galas, endorsed by the Cultural Ministry and censored in person by top leaders in charge of propaganda and ideology, the Party has simply found the best opportunity to convey social and ideological messages to the widest audience possible. In the face of marketisation of the media which has required more attention to the needs of the audience, the Party-state has successfully turned the Galas, one of the most popular cultural products in China, into a key player helping to re-establish the ideological hegemony of the post-1989 Chinese state. The latest development of ICT, especially the use of satellite channels and the Internet, while allowing exiled and diasporic audiences to access images and sentiments from their motherland, proves to be equally enabling to the Chinese government in packaging and moving its propaganda project offshore.

However, one should not get the wrong impression that as the Chinese Party is proactive in refining its strategies, it has complete control of the media. In fact the very fact that it has to repeatedly refine its tactics is a sign that there is strong resistance from the public. As the Party-state improves its management techniques, the public also grows more discerning of these skills.

Throughout the 1990s, television gradually replaced and marginalised other media — the press and radio — to become the most powerful influence on Chinese society. The little magic box was found to fit in easily with the family-centred Chinese way of life in the 1980s and 1990s, and was naturally favoured by the party as the most effective and powerful propaganda tool. The Party-state found in the Spring Festival TV Gala, an "electronic bridge" connecting families to the central state. Nevertheless, as the novelty value of the Gala has waned, the audience is becoming increasingly difficult to please. If subjected to the strict law of the market, the institution would probably have either petered out or taken on a very different form. The imperative of the Party-state, however, has kept it going. The audience may very well still have the TV switched on on Chinese New Year's Eve, but they have changed from gazing at the screen to glancing — from treating the Gala as the centrepiece of celebration to something supplementary.

Take the programme "Focus" as another example. Because of so many constraints on the programme in spite of some journalists' open protest about the restraints on media supervision,[61] the viewing rate for "Focus" has been steadily dropping. According to Liu Haibei, the viewing rate from 1995 to 1996 dropped by 5%, and the viewing rate from January 1998 to December 2000 were 29.57%, 27% and 23.86% respectively.[62] The survey conducted by TV Research in October 2001 shows that the viewing rate dropped to 21.35%. In the year 2002, the viewing rate dropped further to below 16%. There was a slight increase during the outbreak of SARS in 2003. However, it dropped again soon after, the lowest point being 13.84% in October. Two reasons may be suggested for the decline: first of all, the audience was getting used to the fixed format of the critical reports. Secondly, and certainly the main reason that accounts for the drop is that the audience was getting disappointed as the reports had stepped back from their early stronger critical stance when the Party first instigated the appearance of the programme.

Whether the regime's latest effort in taking advantage of the advancement in technologies, especially the Internet and satellite channels, will succeed or not is a matter that only time can tell, but one thing is certain: neither the Party-state nor the society will give up the media, conventional and new, as an arena in which they interact while pursuing their interests.

---

[61] Zhou Hong from Yiyang TV Station in Hunan for instance, wrote that all leaders only paid lip services to media supervision. When it comes to reality it is often different. 'On the Effectiveness of Media Supervision', *TV Research*, No. 9 (1999), p. 16.
[62] Liu, Haibei, 'How Will Focus Come out of Plateau', *TV Research*, No. 4, (2002), pp. 32–34.

VII

Conclusion: Chinese Media Reform between Control, Resistance and Negotiation

Since China's economic reform and its opening up to the rest of the world in 1978, the CCP's priorities have shifted from class struggle and ideological campaigns to economic development and social reconstruction. The country's unprecedented, profound political and social transition is mirrored in the transformation of the media industry as it transforms from an isolated system to one that aspires to become one of the major players in the world.

This book has examined different dynamics such as marketisation, globalisation and new media technologies that have contributed to the transformation of China's media industry, against the backdrop of the Party-state's attempt to stay in control of the reform process. I have moved beyond a negative and static control argument to show how the Party-state has tried to remain in power with legitimacy by making continuous efforts to adjust the existing structure to stay relevant to the socio-economic circumstances, in contrast to monolithic representations of censorship, protectionism, and authoritarian control, and how this adjustment affects the relationship between the Party-state and the media. This move is a tricky one because it may give the impression that I am either ignoring the counter-hegemonic forces or unreasonably pessimistic about the media reform in China. That is certainly not my intention. The reason for adopting this approach is that I believe the conventional sweeping generalisation that the Chinese communication system is still very much under the rigid control of the Communist Party gives us a partial perspective on the ongoing transformation of the political system in general and the media sphere in particular; it tells us very little about why the Chinese political system has so far withstood the challenges of the transformation.

With its significant critical insight, a hegemonic analysis of the changes in China is helpful in improving our understanding of the transformation of Chinese politics since the reform and open-door policy. There are enough signs to show that the Party-state is moving towards hegemonic rule, which requires a combination of coercion and consensus, with the latter as the driving force in social and political relations. As hegemony is based on leadership and consent, the state must be seen to continually adapt to the demands of the people so that the state is able to maintain power with legitimacy. It must also undertake political reform in order to lead morally and intellectually. A hegemonic analysis not only leads us to seek out the rationale behind all these changes, but more importantly, to examine how the Chinese Party-state interacts and uses the much commercialised media as one of the most important powers to shape public opinion. Furthermore it serves as a reminder of the existence of counter-hegemonic forces in China, since resistance, defiance and counter-official ideologies are integral parts of the production and reproduction of hegemony, which this book could only touch upon briefly due to space constraints.

As this book has demonstrated, the media has undergone a process of commercialisation, leading to growing competition, diversified content and sources. It has shifted in its function from being an exclusively ideological organ to an instrument for both political and economic purposes. At the same time, the Party-state still maintains that the media is an ideological enterprise for which it must provide political guidance, management and supervision, especially after the pro-democracy movement in 1989. It expects the media to play multiple roles, especially in the construction of a good image of the Party-state both domestically and internationally; in contributing to the economic growth; in such tasks as "disseminating the socialist core value system" and "creating healthy, rich and lively mainstream public opinion"; and more importantly in continuing to reform, renew, and enhance the effectiveness of public opinion guidance.[1] The instrumental use of the media, however, poses challenges for the Party-state. The first challenge is how to manage the much commercialised media which has developed its own agenda alongside the agenda set by the Party-state, with the support of a transformed public that demands information openness. In other words, it can no longer take the media for granted and is pressurised to "treat the media well, use the media well and manage the media well". As this book has shown, the Party-state has been proactive in finding ways to cope with the challenges, some more successful than others. Secondly, the multi-faceted expectations from the Party-state render the media more bargaining power for autonomy, which will be discussed in greater detail below. As a result, a new relationship marked by negotiation has developed between the Party-state and media organisations, albeit a asymmetrical one. It is too early to conclude if this recent development will bring any fundamental institutional changes, especially because the field is in constant flux. Nonetheless, considering negotiation as an important dynamic force driving media reform forward should help us to understand better the transformational nature of Chinese media and Chinese politics.

This concluding chapter first summarises my arguments based on the discussions in previous chapters. It then ends with a proposal of a few open-ended scenarios based on the potential effect of such transformation on the political system and the flow of global information over the next decade and beyond.

---

[1] From the speech by Chinese President Hu Jintao on his inspection visit to the People's Daily on its 60th anniversary in June 2008, http://politics.people.com.cn/GB/1024/7408514.html.

The Media, a Causal Factor and an Outcome of Political Changes

Since Deng Xiaoping opened up China's economy in the late 1970s, inaugurating an era of explosive economic growth, many China scholars and observers from different parts of the world have predicted that economic liberalisation would lead to political liberalisation and, eventually, democracy. The fact that almost all of the richest countries in the world are democratic was long taken as iron-clad evidence of this trajectory. And yet the development in China — extensive economic development under one-Party rule — has become "more than a historical curiosity".[2]

Other arguments have been made in an attempt to understand the China phenomenon. For instance, providing empirical data, Bueno de Mesquita and Downs have supported the argument that an enlightened, forward-looking authoritarian regime can effectively prolong its existence through a selective combination of growth-inducing economic liberalisation and dissent-inhibiting denial of "coordination goods" (i.e., political rights, more general human rights, press freedom, and accessible higher education).[3] They analysed data from 150 historical cases and concluded that by combining the restriction of coordination goods with economic liberalism, an authoritarian regime can extend its life-expectancy by 10–15%, thereby delaying the onset of democratisation (or, alternatively, of political collapse) by a maximum of about ten years.

Although the gist of the argument of Bueno de Mesquita and Downs is that China is only living on "borrowed time", their argument underscores the fact that if the CCP wants to hold on to power with legitimacy, it would have to proactively deal with the increasing pressures for institutional reform — including the opening up to democratic elements. Failure to adapt to the socio-political changes will lead to failure to reproduce and sustain the existing system.

---

[2] De Mesquita, Bruce Bueno and Downs, George W., 'Development and Democracy', *Foreign Affairs*, (September–October 2005), pp. 77–86.
[3] *Ibid.*

Yang has argued strongly that in the past few decades since the CCP launched economic reform, Chinese leaders have demonstrated an impressive learning curve, designing effective administrative fixes to deal with emergent problems; they have thereby succeeded in narrowing the "yawning gap" between state and society that characterised China in the 1980s and early 1990s. Consequently, China's "state capacity" has grown substantially — albeit non-democratically.[4] Indeed, the CCP has managed, since the Tiananmen incident, to stay ahead of challenges to the existing political system, by incrementally incorporating democratic elements such as the rule of law and elections at the village and township levels into the existing system; it has over the years, refined and sophisticated its management strategies in consensus-building and avoidance of clashes due to conflicting interests. The inauguration of the encompassing national project — building a harmonious society — and the popularly invigorating spectacle of China's rapidly increasing global prominence have won wide support from the Chinese public.

Examining the reform of the media in this context is important as Zheng has argued that as the largest and one of the most powerful political organisations in the world today, the CCP has played a crucial role in initiating most of the major reforms of the past three decades in China,[5] including the media reform itself. Zheng examines the CCP's transformation in the reform era and concludes that the CCP has itself experienced drastic changes on the one hand and managed these changes as a proactive player throughout. However, the nature of the CCP implies that while the Party is transforming itself in accordance with socio-economic changes, the structure of Party dominion over the state and society will not be allowed to change.

The most important change in the Chinese communications system has been its commercialisation and the Party-state has guided its transformation away from political reform into a platform for

---

[4] Yang, *Remaking the Chinese Leviathan*.
[5] Zheng, *The Chinese Communist Party as Organisational Emperor*.

capital accumulation. Jing Wang has observed that the Chinese state has not only "not fallen out of the picture, but it has rejuvenated its capacity, via the market, to affect the agenda of political culture". In this view, "the state's rediscovery of culture including the media as a site where new ruling technologies can be deployed and converted simultaneously into economic capital constitutes one of its most innovative strategies of statecraft since the founding of the People's Republic".[6] As part of the step-by-step efforts of the government to revive the industry and gear it up to compete with the international media equally in the global market, different forms of capitals have been allowed to enter the media sector as long as the state-owned capital is no less than 51%. Furthermore, practices like the separation of production of media content from delivery and separation of management from ownership have also been promoted nationwide to speed up the transformation of the media from state institutions to an industry.

At the height of political liberation in the late 1980s, the reformist Hu Jiwei, former editor-in-chief of the People's Daily, led the drive to formulate a press law that would spell out journalists' rights, enhance the transparency of government policy processes and legally ensure a certain degree of press autonomy. Reformist journalists, educators, and researchers hoped the passage of such a law would carve out explicit safeguards beyond the vague "freedom of the press" provision in article 35 of the Chinese constitution, as well as clearly spell out the limits of press freedom. The effort was however aborted by the Tiananmen crackdown.[7] Since then, the call for a press law has been dropped in Chinese communications policy discourse. As of 2006, the only communications related legislation approved by the National People's Congress is the "Advertising Code of the People's Republic of China", which is non-controversial. Instead of a press law which would give rise to debates on the meaning of press freedom, the Party has instead

---

[6] Wang, Jing, '"Culture" as Leisure and "Culture" as Capital', *Positions: East Asia Cultures Critique*, 9(1), (Spring 2001), pp. 69–104.

[7] Lee, 'Ambiguities and Contradictions', p. 7.

authorised relevant government departments to legitimate its preferred media structure by administrative "regulations", which only requires approval by the State Council. It also gives the government the flexibility to abolish former regulations when they are not considered appropriate any more. On the one hand, these regulations reflect the evident tendency towards more management-based and less prescriptive regulations, as a result of the interplay of various interests, including business interests, political interests and public interests. On the other hand, they also show the government's determination and efforts to further strengthen the supervision and management of the industry: they explicitly set the political boundary for the media industry and help to sustain the propaganda and mouthpiece role of the Chinese media, against the background of the fast developing market economy in China, which is constantly pulling all sectors of Chinese society, including the media, to the opposite direction. At the same time, these regulations regarding the management, financing, industrialisation and also foreign investment and involvement in the industry reinforce the tendency towards industrialisation, multiple-ownership and management.

That the government is making serious efforts to promote the industrialisation of the media in China guarantees the CCP's legitimacy under the new social and economic conditions. These efforts should also be seen as a response to and a preparation for the rising global competition in the field. The very action of supporting the industrialisation of the mass media industry is not evidence that the government intends to relinquish its control over the industry. Rather, it demonstrates the government's decision to upgrade its former control mechanism. Once the industrialisation of the field is realised, the control will be practised in more invisible and indirect ways. Instead of imposing political pressure, the control will be conducted more in the form of managerial and professional requirements. This is the reason that some of the former content of political control has been incorporated into the moral codes for media practitioners in recent years. For instance, in March 2006, Hu Jintao released the "Eight Do's and Don'ts" (also known as eight virtues and eight shames),[8] which has been promulgated as the moral code for Communist Party cadres and all Chinese, including media practitioners.

Obviously, the control of the media has moved from coercive measures only to a range of measures combining coercion with other methods: ranging from ownership restrictions, licensing and post-production inspection to post-distribution supervisions and self-censorship, reflecting the shift from a repressive mode of domination to a hegemonic one for political dominance of the whole society. However, focusing on the Party-state's effort to control the process of the media reform tells us part of the story only. The examination should also be placed in the context of a changed media environment which forms part of the movement towards media reform, even though it was slow and protracted. As the Party-state initiates the media reform and tries to control the process, the media environment has changed for ever: the ruling Party has changed, in its effort to adapt to the new circumstances, the unleashed market forces has catalysed further change and the changing society has itself changed its tastes. The Party-state is therefore faced with the dilemma that comes with economic growth. Take the development of ICT as an example: the rapid growth will contribute to GDP growth, but it will also reach a wider public that may contribute to popular agitation for political change, something the CCP has always kept an eye on.

In the mid-1980s, economic reforms and the open-door policy introduced market logic to the state-owned media and led to a fledgling journalism reform movement and the emergence of discourse on democratisation, which threatened to challenge the Party's monopolistic control.[9] Since the 1989 crackdown, even though media press

---

[8] According to Hu, the very acts of loving the motherland, serving the people, upholding science, working hard, being united and helpful to each other, being disciplined and law-biding, being appreciative of plain living and hard work should be considered as honours. In contrast, harming the motherland, dividing the people, being ignorant and unenlightened, being lazy, taking advantage of others, being profit-mongering, disrespecting law and wallowing in excessive luxuries should be condemned as disgraces.

[9] Zhao, *Media, Market and Democracy in China*, p. 165.

reform has taken a sharp turn toward commercialisation after the Party's unreserved embrace of a market economy in 1992, the struggle for reform in the political realm has not been abandoned. As Zhao wrote more than ten years ago, "whenever there is a chance, press reform resurfaces as a political issue".[10] Let's consider the most recent example. Since the Regulations on Open Government Information took effect on May 1st 2008, the Chinese media has taken to the topic of information openness in a big way. No sooner had the legislation taken effect than the media began questioning its inadequacies, particularly on how to ensure compliance by local governments, and how to standardise the information release process. In the aftermath of the earthquake, media practitioners have been remarkably vocal in negotiating publicly with the state over the breadth of autonomy issue. After 32 days of live coverage, for instance, CCTV organised a symposium[11] inviting scholars and professionals to review the Chinese media's coverage of the earthquake in general but with a focus on its own coverage. A book series was out within less than two months, and according to Brice Pedroletti[12] there were more than 800 articles addressing "information openness" in China's press in June 2008 alone. The significance of those discussions lies in their push for information openness in future coverage of breaking news events. In the second half of 2008, the repercussion of the earthquake continued to reverberate through the media long after the tremors had eased. The media was central in questioning the performance of the government in responding to the problems caused by the earthquake: re-housing, welfare, and unemployment, amongst others.

However, there is a distinction between the fight for media reform in the 1980s and the push in the past decade. From the late 1990s,

---

[10] *Ibid.*

[11] The symposium entitled "When TV Encounters Disasters" was held on 5 July 2008.

[12] *Quand La Chine Déblogue,* Le Monde, 3 July 2008, at http://chinedesblogs. blog.lemonde.fr/2008/07/03/emeutesdewengan20-quand-la-chine-supgrade/, accessed on 30 March 2009.

rather than confronting the state for a speedy reform of the media, media practitioners and scholars have more often taken to negotiation with the state. Media practitioners also understand that the best results from negotiation occur when their interests are seen to converge with the regime's interests, as is reflected in the areas over which they negotiate with the state. The negotiable areas include the so-called "citizen's rights", which are not perceived to be politically sensitive like human rights or to threaten the CCP's legitimacy or the political system. While the lasting effects of the breakthrough in the coverage of the earthquake remain to be seen, there is little doubt that the media has used the very fact of the government's initial acquiescence and subsequent encouragement to advance the discussion of the value of timely information sharing. The earthquake opened up a new horizon for the Chinese media, which will undoubtedly bring about positive changes to communications in China and to Chinese politics. Whether the changes are minimal, incremental and superficial, or large-scale and significant, they have raised the general public's expectations of the media. It is not impossible the government will reverse its policy, but it will be at the cost of losing its credibility and the general public's trust. Both media practitioners and scholars realise that as the Party-state needs them to help obtain popular support, this is the best moment to negotiate with the state for greater autonomy. As a result, although the central Party-state still dominates the initiation and circulation of sensitive political information, its control over every other kind of communication has eroded significantly, as is seen in the range of topics that can be discussed and the increasing variety of opinions that can be expressed in public. It may be that the Party can successfully manage the media to avoid immediate instability, but the new form of relationship marked by negotiation with the media may nonetheless gradually entail changes in the relationship between state, citizens, and information, resulting in critical long-term consequences.

As the intertwining logics of state, domestic, and international market forces negotiate the terms of domination over the Chinese media, the CCP faces challenges in furthering the development of the media: the dilemma of how to keep the balance between control, autonomy and credibility.

Balance between Control, Autonomy and Credibility

As discussed in Chapter 2, the development of the media at different stages shows that as the Party introduces reform to the media sector, gradualism has been the key that has enabled the Party and the political system to evolve and to adapt to new political and social realities. So far, the Party has stayed in control of the reform.

However, over the long run, a nation's media can influence popular attitudes only to the extent that the media is believed and trusted. Therefore the CCP faces the intertwined dilemma of control, autonomy and credibility in furthering the development of the media industry. The media is expected to perform multi-faceted functions, i.e., to create an environment favourable for political and social stability, to construct a good image of the Party-state, to harness popular support for the government, to compete with transnational media corporations for the global flow of information, and to be commercially successful in a very crowded marketplace. But these expectations of the media from the Party-state, sometimes conflicting but always interrelated, cannot be fulfilled unless China's media becomes more autonomous from the state. The authorities in China know the need for press freedom but they worry about opening the door to the type of freedom that could lead to the regime's downfall. The nature of the political system in China therefore decides that complete media autonomy from the State is highly unlikely to materialise in China in the near future: such autonomy would require the removal of the Communist Party's authority to supervise the media. Moreover, constitutional guarantees of press freedom, individual political expression and a thoroughgoing overhaul of the government-controlled judiciary would be required for a genuinely independent media sector to emerge in China.

And yet without autonomy, the Chinese media will continue to lack wide spread credibility, and popular trust of the media would not rise. How to balance control, autonomy and credibility is therefore a dilemma the Party-state faces in furthering the development of the media. In fact, this dilemma affects its endeavour to influence the global flow of information.

IMPACT OF CHINESE MEDIA REFORM ON THE GLOBAL FLOW OF INFORMATION

The last example given in Chapter 5 shows that the Chinese Party-state has been investing heavily in external communication initiatives, with a view to competing with transnational media companies. Indeed, on 13th November 2008, Li Changchun visited CCTV again and asked it to increase reports on international affairs and quicken its steps in "going global" (or "going out"). However, just as the Party-state faces the dilemma of having to keep the balance between media control, autonomy and credibility in order to further the development of the media, the state-owned media similarly faces challenges in getting across to international media publics. The following section considers the challenges that CCTV News, an English Channel targeting overseas audience, has to face, challenges that come from both within and without China.

Credibility and Timeliness in Winning over Foreign Publics

Attraction depends on credibility, a quality that a state-owned media outlet would clearly lack. As many observers have noted, all governments today are suffering to some extent from a credibility problem in communicating with foreign audiences.[13] With low official credibility, many nations' most effective public diplomacy activities are often independent of their governments. For instance, many commercial media companies and other actors such as NGOs have been successful in playing the "attractive power" games as they are considered good forces, unencumbered by the trappings of sovereignty and untainted by real politics.[14] There are signs that China is aware that its lack of NGOs is impeding its progress on this task. For instance,

---

[13] Lord, Carnes, *Losing Hearts and Minds? Public Diplomacy and Strategic Influence in the Age of Terror*, (London: Praeger Security International, 2006), p.111.

[14] Hocking, Brian, 'Rethinking the "New" Public Diplomacy', in Jan Melisen, (Ed.), *The New Public Diplomacy: Soft Power in International Relations*, (Palgrave Macmillan, 2005), pp. 28–46.

the Office of the Chinese Language Council International (known for Hanban for short), claims that it is "a non-governmental and non-profit organisation affiliated to the Ministry of Education of China",[15] although at the same time, it also asserts that "the Council is composed of members from 12 state ministries and commissions". Although the claim is contradictory, one thing is certain: the Chinese government is starting to realise the importance of non-governmental actors to achieve its goals.

Due to the politically sensitive nature of TV stations in China, they are all state-owned. The roles and missions of CCTV News are therefore obvious: basically they are to tell China's story to foreign audiences. Its nature has decided that it is neither a platform for criticism nor a channel whereby "balanced" views can be presented. In other words, CCTV News is not playing the role of a neutral observer.

The nature of the Chinese media also goes against the nature of real-time global communications via satellite television which requires accuracy, objectivity and above all, timeliness. Although reports on the earthquake in Sichuan in May 2008 have shown signs of improvement in terms of timeliness and merits further study, the process is in general organised and managed by the Information Office of the State Council. As a routine, it first drafts the press reportage and then seeks approval from the Central Government and the State Council before disseminating the news to the outside world.[16] The late and little coverage of the Tibetan Riots in March 2008 and then the turmoil over the Olympic torch relay outside China caused much dissatisfaction and controversy both domestically and in the world. This is one of the reasons that there are more feature programmes on CCTV News than news programmes, as one journalist working for CCTV pointed out. Although both Chinese media scholars and professionals know that "news reporting rather than the communication of culture plays the leading role on the world arena",[17] with such restrictive conditions, it is difficult for the Chinese media to win over

---

[15] See http://www.hanban.ca/hanban.php?lang=en, accessed on 28 February 2009.

[16] Zeng, *Melting the Ice, Building a Bridge and Breaking through*, p. 27.

[17] Li and Zhou, *Soft Power and Global Communication*, p. 34.

foreign audiences in a timely fashion, especially on perceived sensitive issues by the government.

When Party Logic and Market Logic Clash

Another challenge comes from the contradictions of the state-centric model and the marketisation of the media in China. On the one hand, CCTV News must follow the political imperatives, but on the other, it needs to live with the market forces unleashed by the state itself. China's reach for the international audience is primarily a government undertaking, driven by the Party-state's political imperatives rather than the economic benefits of the cultural and media industries. Interviews with media practitioners for CCTV News reveal that the channel set up to influence foreign public opinion was to be a non-profit making one from the outset. That is, unlike other CCTV channels and indeed all other TV stations in China, which generate much advertising revenues by offering popular programmes such as TV dramas to the domestic audience, CCTV News needs to be more selective in its programmes for the construction of the Party-state's image. For instance, it could not show foreign films, which is seen by CCTV News professionals to be the only way to increase the viewership and to attract advertisers.[18] Interviews show that as the aim of the channel is not for commercial profit, there is little incentive among staff members to improve the programmes.

While the national level CCTV News has low commercial incentive to improve its programmes, provincial satellite channels are prohibited from taking initiatives to expand overseas. Undoubtedly, provincial level TV stations which do not enjoy the same political status and government support as CCTV are keen to get outside China for commercial profit. However, the SARFT issued a notice in 2004 which stipulates that the "going-out" project should be planned and managed by the SARFT only and that without its approval, no radio or TV stations are allowed to rent or buy radio and television channels (frequency), time or to establish radio and television stations

---

[18] Author interview with the assistant controller of *CCTV International*.

outside China.[19] This regulation effectively prevents any TV or radio stations from expanding outside China on their own. It is therefore safe to say that although the Chinese government can centrally control and manage satellite channels at all levels, as public diplomacy outlets by regulations and command, it is getting more difficult to manage and coordinate the outputs of these channels, an issue that was discussed at the coordination conference for overseas publicity hosted by the SARFT in 2006.[20] In other words, it has to deal with an increasingly commercialised media that has its own agenda to follow. As China sets in process the marketisation of the media, each level of the media (the central, the provincial, the prefectural and the county) becomes largely self-financed and is operated by the regional and local governments. While continuing to serve as the mouthpiece of the Party, TV stations at all levels are all profit driven. Advertising has been the main source of revenue for the Chinese media and comprises almost 90% of its total income while the government subsidised only 10.7% in 2004. This means that although the DOP requires all local TV stations to provide programmes to CCTV News, and an annual conference is held to make sure this happens, local stations lack commercial incentives to invest resources in producing programmes for overseas publicity.[21] On the contrary, concerns about ratings, circulations and market shares are driving the Chinese media to produce more sensational programmes, that are sometimes even pornographic in order to maximise economic returns.[22]

---

[19] 'Notice on Further Strengthening the Radio, Film and Television Going-out Project Management', at http://www.chinasarft.gov.cn/articles/2004/10/26/20070919141825580844.html, accessed on 13 March 2008.

[20] See 'National TV Foreign Propaganda Co-operation Conference 2006 in Yunnan', at http://www.cctv.com/tvguide/special/wyh/20060713/103251.shtml, accessed on 16 January 2009.

[21] *Ibid.*

[22] For instance, the first three months of 2008 witnessed three broadcasting stations at the provincial level being severely criticised by the SARFT for putting on pornographic programmes. See "Publicity", at http://www.chinasarft.gov.cn/catalogs/gldt/20070903170530620224.html, accessed on 30 June 2008.

Professionalism vs. the Party-Line

Very often, interesting situations arise when the views of those working in the media industry conflict with those of the government. Another effect of media commercialisation and the further opening up of China is enhanced journalistic professionalism among media workers. For instance, a new crop of young professionals now populate CCTV, especially CCTV News, the majority of whom have received training in the West. Interviews show that they tend to adhere to journalistic professionalism and view interference with their professional judgement as illegitimate. The remarks of a journalist summarise the way many of them felt about working for CCTV: "it is difficult and different (from the West) to work for CCTV, as it is under strict censorship, and we all know about it". Another journalist expressed his doubt as to whether restrictions on media reportage will relax during and after the Olympics, since it is "the golden opportunity for the Party to propagate good images in the world, and I don't see that expected changes could happen this year". One journalist also commented that without a reform of the political system in China, it would be difficult to see fundamental changes in the media industry.

An analysis of "Dialogue", a daily 30-minute interview programme on current affairs, over a 2-month period in late 2007 and early 2008, also shows that occasionally, the two hosts pushed the boundaries by asking guest speakers sensitive questions. For instance, China is greatly concerned with its international image, which is reflected in the frequency of the topic being discussed: three times within one and a half months (on 24th December 2007, 1st January and 31st January 2008 respectively). The western-trained host, Yang Rui, challenged the guest speakers a few times on what constitutes a nation's image on 24 December 2008. He asked if it is values or ideological institutions which constitute a nation's image. My interviews with guests on the programme also reveal that they were encouraged to become more confrontational. What is interesting is that some guests chose not to answer some of the questions directly as they considered them too "ideological". The behaviour of the guests during such programmes deserves another study but it is apparent that the hosts are trying to achieve better viewership by pushing the limits, meeting the standards of professional journalism while not deviating too far from the Party's principles. Interviews with practitioners for CCTV prove that it is the case. It is difficult to anticipate the consequences of discrepancies between the journalists' way of thinking and their daily observance of government regulations. However it is certain that within the state-centric model, there are discordant notes that are not harmonious with the aims of the government.

To conclude, within just a few years, CCTV News has claimed its stake in the global communication landscape. However, unless the above mentioned contradictions are dealt with, it is difficult for China to achieve its desired goals. While state-based public diplomacy is by no means unimportant in the promotion of soft power, the efficiency of its international broadcaster will remain small in the global flow of information. This is decided by the nature of the Chinese media which makes it difficult to offer news coverage in a timely and effective manner, since media professionals work under political constraints. In the era of the proliferation of satellite TV channels and websites, when information increases exponentially with every passing minute and when "information is demand-driven rather than supply driven",[23] credibility and timeliness are the keys to getting the attention of audiences. Finally, the increasingly professionalised media workers and the market forces which drive media workers to follow their professional aspirations as well as the logic of markets will make the Party-state's centralised public diplomacy operations less easy. China may have been successful in other public diplomacy activities, but the outcome of relying on its own mouthpiece to attract and influence foreign publics remains speculative. What China needs is to develop a more independent media whose programmes can reinforce messages generated by the government.

---

[23] Seib, Phillip, 'New Media and Prospects for Democratisation', in Phillip Seib, (Ed.), *New Media and the New Middle East*, (Palgrave Macmillan: 2007), pp. 1–18.

CONCLUSION

Economic reform in China is distinct from that of other transitional countries: it is gradual and selective, following its own roadmap and timetable. It first started in the rural areas in a radical way, was followed by a quick opening of the economy to trade, and continued with only gradual reform of the state-owned enterprises. As the existing political system has become more adaptable to the changing circumstances, and thus more resilient, it started the reform of the media sector in the late 1970s, certain aspects only but beginning with expanding more substantially in scope from 2003.

The last three decades have seen more relaxed media policies, especially in such areas as infotainment, natural disasters and accidents, that were all formerly banned. However, one thing that we must bear in mind while assessing the changes taking place in China is that the Party-state will want to stay in power, but with legitimacy in the eyes of the ruled. Therefore, the media today has not only become a platform where interaction between the state and society and the struggle for their different interests take place, but has become an ideological force in its own right. In interacting with the Party-state, it is transformed, while transforming the latter to some extent at the same time. Because of the new relationship characterised by negotiation, media reform in China is marked by gradualism.

References

'2007 Market Research Report on China's Blog Development', from the website of the China Internet Network Information Centre (CNNIC), at http://www.cnnic.cn/uploadfiles/doc/2007/12/26/113707.doc.

'About CCTV International', at http://english.cctv.com/english/about/index.shtml, accessed on 10 February 2010.

Alagappa, Muthiah, 'Part I. Legitimacy: Explanation and Elaboration', in Muthiah Alagappa (Ed.), *Political Legitimacy in Southeast Asia: The Quest for Moral Authority*, (Stanford: Stanford University Press, 1995), pp. 1–58.

'Appendix 1: Journalist Fellows 2007–2008', in *Annual Report 2007–08*, Reuters Institute for the Study of Journalism, (University of Oxford, 2009).

Ba, Xiaofang, 'The Degree of News on Disaster', *News Front*, 6, (2008), pp. 2–5.

Bai, Yansong and Wu, Qiang, 'Love is like Waves that Never Recede' in Xiaotao Liang (Ed.), *Convulsion: Field Notes from Media Workers*, (Beijing: China Democracy and Legal System Publishing House, 2008), pp. 11–17.

Bandurski, David, 'China's Guerrilla War for the Web', *Far East Economic Review*, 7 July 2008.

Bao, Junhao, 'Timely Report This Time vs. Timely Report to the Above before', *Southern Weekend*, 22 May 2008.

Barme, Jeremie, *In the Red: On Contemporary Chinese Culture*, (New York: Columbia University Press, 1999).

Baum, Richard, 'The Limits of Consultative Leninism', in Mark Mohr (Ed.), *China and Democracy: A Contradiction in Terms?* Asia Program, Woodrow Wilson International Center for Scholars, Special Report, No. 131, June 2006, pp. 13–20.

'Beijing Discovers SARS Case', 23 April 2004, at http://www.cctv.com/program/dysj/20040423/100897.shtml, accessed on November 12 2009.

Bhattacharji, Preeti, Zissis, Carin and Baldwin, Corinne, *Media Censorship in China*, from Council on Foreign Relations, New York, 2010, at http://www.cfr.org/about/, accessed on 15 July 2010.

Brady, Anne-Marie, 'The Beijing Olympics as a Campaign of Mass Distraction', *The China Quarterly*, 197, (2009), pp. 1–24.

Cao, Jianwen, 'The Significance of Premier Wen's "Do not Wait for My Approval"', at http://politics.people.com.cn/GB/30178/9038416.html, accessed on 10 July 2010.

Castells, Manuel, *End of Millennium*, (Malden, MA: Blackwell, 1998).

'CCTV English Channel Landing in United States', at http://english.peopledaily.com.cn/200305/01/eng20030501_116101.shtml, accessed on 10 February 2010.

Central Department of Propaganda, at http://www.wenming.cn.

Chan, Alex, 'From Propaganda to Hegemony: Jiaodian Fangtan and China's Media Policy', *Journal of Contemporary China*, 11(30), (2002), pp. 35–51.

Chang, Won Ho, *Mass Media in China: The History and the Future*, (Ames: Iowa State University Press, 1989).

Chen, M. and Chu, J., 'People's Republic of China', in G. Kurian (Ed.), *World Express Encyclopaedia*, (New York: Facts on File, 1982), pp. 219–231.

Chen, Xi, 'Dynamics of News Media Regulations in China: Explanations and Implications', *The Journal of Comparative Asian Development*, 5(1), (Fall 2006), at https://louisville.edu/asiandemocracy/conferences/links-and-images/dynamicsof-news-media-regulations-in-china.html, accessed on 14 July 2010.

Cheng, Qian and Zhu, Tian, 'Changes and Development of China's TV News Concept 2003', *TV Studies*, 2, (2004), pp. 25–27.

Cheng, Xiumin, 'Timeliness, Depth and Width in the Coverage of the Sichuan Earthquake', *Overseas Communication*, 6, (2008), pp. 50–51.

Cheng, Zhixia, Zhou, He and Gao, Yunhong, 'Changes on the Internet Reflected on the Coverage of the Earthquake on May 15 on people.com.cn', *News Front*, 6, (2008), pp. 7–8.

Chin, Yik-chan, *From the Local to the Global: Chinese Television from 1996 to 2003*, PhD thesis, (London, University of Westminster, 2005).

'China's Cable TV Shake up', from BBC News, 3 December 2001, at http://news.bbc.co.uk/1/hi/business/1689097.stm, accessed on 26 July 2010.

'China Postpones Mandatory Installation of Controversial Filtering Software', *Xinhuawang*, 30 June 2009, at http://news.xinhuanet.com/english/2009-06/30/content_11628335.htm, accessed on 8 August 2009.

China Soft Power Project Team of the University of Beijing, 'Information Disclosure in the Earthquake Relief', in Xiaotao Liang (Ed.), *Convulsion: Media Reflections*, (Beijing: China Democracy and Legal System Publishing House, 2008), p. 238.

'China Vows to Intensify Online Porn Crackdown after Shutting Down Thousands of Sites', *Xinhuawang*, 6 February 2009, at http://news.xinhuanet.com/english/2009-02/06/content_10776684.htm, accessed on 5 May 2009.

'China's Wen makes Internet debut', section of 'Breaking news technology', *The Sunday Age*, 1 March 2009, at http://news.theage.com.au/breaking news-technology/chinas-wen-makes-internet-debut-20090301-8l5r. html.

'Chinese News Media Will Not Accept Foreign and Private Investment', *News Front*, 2, (2002), at http://peopledaily.com.cn/GB/paper79/5498/566029.html, accessed 20 July 2010.

'Chinese Premier to Talk Online with the Public', *Xinhuawang*, 28 February 2009, at http://news.xinhuanet.com/english/2009-02/28/content_10916529.htm, accessed on 20 July 2010.

Chu, Leonard, 'Continuity and Change in China's Media Reform', *Journal of Communication*, 44(3), (1994), pp. 4–21.

Chu, Leonard, 'Mass Communication Theory: The Chinese Perspective', *Media Asia*, 13(1), (1986), pp. 14–19.

Chu, Leonard, 'Press Criticism and Self-Criticism in Communist China: An Analysis of Its Ideology, Structure, and Operation', *Gazette*, 31(1), (1983), pp. 47–61.

Comaroff, Jean and Comaroff, John, *Ethnography and the Historical Imagination*, (Boulder: Westview Press, 1992).

'CPC Political Bureau Arranges for Study of 16th Congress Spirit, Xinhua News Agency, 7 November 2002, available at http://www.china.org.cn/english/features/48992.htm, accessed 10 August 2010.

Cui, Baoguo and Zhou, Kui, 'A General Report on China's Media Industry Development 2009', in Baoguo Cui, (Ed.), *Blue Book of China's Media*, (China: Social Sciences Academic Press, 2009), pp. 3–37.

Dahlgren, Peter, *Television and the Public Sphere: Citizenship, Democracy and the Media*, (London: Sage Publications, 1995).

Dai, Yuanguang *et al.*, 'Report on SARS and the Objectivity of Journalism', in Weizhi Deng, (Ed.), *SARS and the Chinese Society*, (Shanghai: Shanghai University Press, 2003), pp. 312–325.

Davidson, Alastair, 'Hegemony, Language and Popular Wisdom in the Asia Pacific', in Richard Howson and Kylie Smith, (Eds.), *Hegemony: Studies in Consensus and Coercion*, (New York: Routledge, 2008), pp. 63–79.

De Burgh, Hugo, *The Chinese Journalist: Mediating Information in the World's Most Populous Country*, (London: RoutledgeCurzon, 2003).

deLisle, Jacques 'SARS, Greater China, and the Pathologies of Globalization and Transition', *Orbis*, (2003).

De Mesquita, Bruce Bueno and Downs, George W., 'Development and Democracy', *Foreign Affairs*, (September–October 2005), pp. 77–86.

Deng, Xiaoping, *Speech to Cadres and Soldiers of the Beijing Martial Law Corps*, 9 June 1989 in Beijing, at http://web.peopledaily.com.cn/deng/ accessed on 26 March 2008.

Dickson, Bruce, *Red Capitalists in China: The Party, Private Entrepreneurs, and Prospects for Political Change*, (New York: Cambridge University Press, 2003).

Dickson, Bruce, *Democratization in China and Taiwan: The Adaptability of Leninist Parties*, (Oxford: Clarendon, 1997).

Ding, Guangeng, 'Six Requirements for Propaganda Work', *Xinhua News Agency*, 10 May 1998.

Dong, R., 'The Mass Media Engages with Capital', 2000, at ultrachina. com/english/doc.cfm?OID=405&MIDtoc=0&CIDtoc=62, quoted and accessed 6 March 2003 by Chengju Huang, 'Trace the Stones in Crossing the River: Media Structural Changes in Post-WTO China', *International Communication Gazette*, 69, (October 2007), pp. 413–430.

Dou, Xiaofeng and Hou, Lu, 'The Huge Differences in the Budget of Production: The Low Price of Domestic TV Dramas', at http://news.xinhuanet.com/newmedia/2005-11/22/content_3815863.htm, accessed on 3 January 2007.

Du, Junfei, 'The Road to Openness: The Communication Legacy of the Wenchuan Earthquake', in Xiaotao Liang (Ed.), *Convulsion: Media Reflections*, (Beijing: China Democracy and Legal System Publishing House, 2008), pp. 30–38.

Dudek, Mitch and Xu, L. Lucy, 'Market Access Report: Media & Publishing', *China Law & Practice*, May 2002, at http://www.chinalawandpractice. com/Article/1693674/Channel/7576/Market-Access-Report-Media-and-Publishing.html, accessed on 25 June 2010.

Eley, Geoff and Nield, Keith, 'Why Does Social History Ignore Politics?', *Social History*, 5(2), (1980), pp. 249–271.

Fang, Hanqi, 'Live Broadcast of Disaster — A Milestone in China's History of Journalism', in Xiaotao Liang (Ed.), *Convulsion: Media Reflections*, (Beijing: China Democracy and Legal System Publishing House, 2008), pp. 1–6.

Fang, Hanqi, Chen, Yeshao and Zhang, Zihua, *A Brief History of Chinese Journalism*, (Beijing: People's University Press, 1982).

Fewsmith, Joseph, 'China and the Politics of SARS', *Current History*, 102(665), (2003), pp. 250–255.

Fontana, Benedetto, 'Hegemony and Power in Gramsci', in Richard Howson and Kylie Smith, (Eds.), *Hegemony: Studies in Consensus and Coercion*, (New York: Routledge, 2008), pp. 81–105.

'For China, A Costly Lesson in Engaging Its Netizens', *Straits Times*, 2 March 2009.

'Foreign Magazines Facing China's Newsstand Fever', *Business Week Magazine*, 5 November 2003, at http://www.chinadaily.com.cn/en/doc/2003-11/05/content_278774.htm, accessed on 25 June 2010.

Fraser, Nancy, 'Rethinking the Public Sphere: A Contribution to the Critique of Actually Existing Democracy', *Social Text*, 25/26, (1990), pp. 56–80.

Fukuyama, Francis, *State Building: Governance and World Order in the Twenty First Century*, (London: Profile Books, 2004).

Fung, Anthony, 'Think Globally, Act Locally: China's rendezvous with MTV', *Global Media and Communication*, 2(1), (2006), pp. 71–88.

Gao, Xin and Zhang, Tao, 'China Central Station's Live Broadcast of the Wenchuan Earthquake from the Perspective of Crisis Communication', in Xiaotao Liang (Ed.), *Convulsion: Media Reflections*, (Beijing: China Democracy and Legal System Publishing House, 2008), pp. 135–142.

Geidner, Nicholas, W., 'Looking Toward 2008: The Effects of New Media on the Political Process', *The Review of Communication*, 6, (2006), pp. 93–100.

Gilley, Bruce, *China's Democratic Future: How It Will Happen and Where It Will Lead*, (New York: Columbia University, 2004).

Gong, Wenxiang, 'The Build-up of National Image: An Analysis Based on China Central Television's Report on the Sichuan Earthquake', in Xiaotao Liang (Ed.), *Convulsion: Media Reflections*, (Beijing: China Democracy and Legal System Publishing House, 2008), pp. 64–70.

'Governor of Qinghai Song Xiuyan Answered Messages Delivered by Netizens', *People's Daily*, 11 February 2009.

Gramsci, Antonio, *Selections from the Prison Notebooks*, in Q. Hoare and G. Nowell Smith (Eds. and trans.) (New York: International Publishers, 1971).

Gros, Jean-Germain, 'Toward a Taxonomy of Failed States in the New World Order: Decaying Somalia, Liberia, Rwanda and Haiti', *Third World Quarterly*, 17(3), (1996), pp. 458–461.

Guan, Hongxin, 'Tentative Discussion on the Characteristics of "Focus"', *China TV*, 10, (1998), pp. 19–20.

Guo Zhenzhi, 'Supervision by Public Opinion and the Western Concept of Journalistic Professionalism', *International News Festival*, 5, (1999), pp. 32–38.

Han, Biao, 'Recording History and Creating History — Inspirations for the Future Brought by the Earthquake Report', in Xiaotao Liang (Ed.), *Convulsion: Media Reflections*, (Beijing: China Democracy and Legal System Publishing House, 2008), pp. 388–393.

Harada, Yoko, 'Hegemony, Japan, and the Victor's Memory of War', in Richard Howson and Kylie Smith, (Eds.), *Hegemony: Studies in Consensus and Coercion*, (New York: Routledge, 2008), pp. 219–236.

Hassid, Jonathan, 'Controlling the Chinese Media, an Uncertain Business', *Asian Survey*, 48(3), (2008), pp. 414–430.

Hazelbarth, Todd, *The Chinese Media: More Autonomous and Diverse — Within Limits: An Intelligence Monograph*, (Central Intelligence Agency: Center for the Study of Intelligence, 1997).

He, Xiaolan, 'Unprecedented Earthquake, Unprecedented Live Coverage, and Unprecedented Reception Rate', *Journalists*, 6, (2008), pp. 21–25.

Hilton, Isabel, 'Beijing's media chill', 15 February 2006, at http://www.open democracy.net/democracy-china/chill_3272.jsp, accessed on 2 January 2011.

Hocking, Brian, 'Rethinking the "New" Public Diplomacy', in Jan Melisen, (Ed.), *The New Public Diplomacy: Soft Power in International Relations*, (Palgrave Macmillan, 2005), pp. 28–46.

Holbig, Heike and Gilley, Bruce, 'In Search of Legitimacy in Post-revolutionary China: Bringing Ideology and Governance Back In', German Institute of Global and Area Studies (GIGA) Working Paper 127, (2010), at http://www.gigahamburg.de/dl/download.php?d=/conent/publikationen/pdf/wp127_holbig-gilley.pdf, accessed on 29 July 2010.

Hong, Yin, 'Meaning, Production, Consumption: The History and Reality of Television Drama in China', in Stephanie Hemelryk Donald, Michael Keane and Yin Hong, (Eds.), *Media in China: Consumption, Content and Crisis*, (RoutledgeCurzon, 2002), pp. 28–40.

Hood, Marlow, 'The Use and Abuse of Mass Media by Chinese Leaders during the 1980s', in Chin-Chuan Lee (Ed.), *China's Media, Media's China*, (Boulder, Colorado: Westview Press, 1994), pp. 37–57.

'Hu Jintao on the Construction of Harmonious Socialist Society on February 19, 2005', 26 June 2006, at http://www.china.com.cn/chinese/news/899546.htm, accessed on 2 January 2011.

Hu, Yaobang, 'On the Party's Journalism Work', speech delivered to the CCP Central Committee Secretariat, 8 February 1985, published in the People's Daily on 14 April 1985.

Hu, Zhengrong, 'Towards the Public? The Dilemma in Chinese Media Policy Change and Its Influential Factors', Joan Shorenstein Center on the Press, Politics and Public Policy: Harvard University (2005), at http://www.global.asc.upenn.edu/docs/anox06/secure/july21/zhen grong/21_zhengrong_reading1.pdf, accessed on 25 June 2009.

Hughes, Lyric, 'Written Testimony of China Online', Public Hearings on WTO Compliance and Sectional Issues before the U.S.-China Economic & Security Review Commission, 18 January 2002, at http://www.uscc. gov/textonly/transcriptstx/teshug.htm, accessed on 15 July 2010.

Huntington, Samuel, *The Third Wave: Democratization in the Late Twentieth Century*, (Oklahoma: University of Oklahoma Press, 1992).

Jiang, Heping, 'Increase TV Exchanges, Expand China's Impact over the World', *TV Research*, 2, (2003), pp. 27–28.

Jiang, Jianguo *et al.*, "Cadres Must Enhance the Capacity to Work with the Media", in *Forum for Chinese Party and Government Cadres*, 17 November 2008, at http://theory.people.com.cn/GB/49150/49152/8352146.html, accessed on 20 July 2009.

'Jiang Zemin Talks with Wallace', *CBS News*, 31 August 2000, at http://www.cbsnews.com/stories/2000/08/31/60minutes/main229 663.shtml, accessed on 15 January 2010.

Jirik, John, 'The AOL Time Warner CCTV (China) Television Exchange: Guanxi in Globalization Theory', paper presented at the annual meeting of the International Communication Association, Marriott Hotel, San Diego, CA, 27 May 2003, at http://www.allacademic.com/meta/p111969_index.html, accessed on 3 June 2008.

Kalathil, Shanthi, 'China's New Media Sector: Keeping the State In', *The Pacific Review*, 16(4), (2003), pp. 489–501.

Kaplan, Robert, 'The Coming Anarchy', in Phil Williams, Donald M. Goldstein and Jay M. Shafritz, (Eds.), *Class Readings and Contemporary Debates in International Relations*, 3rd Edition, (Belmont, California: Thomson Wadsworth, 2006).

Kaufmann, Daniel, Kraay, Aart and Mastruzzi, Massimo, 'Governance Matters VI: Governance Indicators for 1996–2006', *World Bank Policy Research Working Paper* 4280 (July 2007), at http://ssrn.com/abstract=999979, accessed on 20 February 2009.

Keane, Michael, 'Broadcasting Policy, Creative Compliance and the Myth of Civil Society in China', *Media, Culture and Society*, 6(23), (2001), pp. 783–798.

Laclau, Ernesto, *Politics and Ideology in Marxist Theory*, (London: New Left Books, 1977).

Lam, Willy, 'Chinese State Media Goes Global: A Great Leap Outward for Chinese Soft Power?' *China Brief*, 9(2), (2009), at http://www.jamestown.org/single/?no_cache=1&tx_ttnews%5Btt_news%5D=34387, accessed on 18 March 2010.

Lee, Chin-Chuan, 'Mass Media: Of China, About China', in Chin-Chuan, Lee, (Ed.), *Voices of China, the Interplay of Politics and Journalism*, (New York: The Guildford Press, 1990), pp. 3–29.

Lent, John, 'First the Cultural Revolution, Now the Media Revolution', *Media Development*, 1, (1986), pp. 23–25.

Leow, Jason, 'China's Media Shake-up', *The Straits Times* (Reprinted in *Asia Pacific Media: The Asia Pacific Media Network*), at http://www.asiamedia.ucla.edu/article.asp?parentid=10080, accessed on 14 June 2009.

Letter from Heilong Jiang, at http://www.cctv.com/news/focus/focus.html, accessed on 20 December 2005.

Lewis, John W. and Xue, Litai, 'Social Change and Political Reform in China: Meeting the Challenge of Success', *China Quarterly*, 176, (December 2003), pp. 926–942.

Li, Benjamin, 'Shanghai Media Group Restructure Puts Focus on Content Production', 23 October 2009, at http://www.media.asia/newsarticle/2009_10/Shanghai-Media-Group-restructure-puts-focus-on-content-production/37638?src=mostpop, accessed on 10 January 2010.

Li, Datong, 'The Establishment of Disaster Reporting's Core Value and Mature Mode', in Xiaotao Liang (Ed.), *Convulsion: Media Reflections*, (Beijing: China Democracy and Legal System Publishing House, 2008), pp. 151–156.

Li, Shiquan, 'Reviewing the Breakthroughs of CCTV's Live Broadcast of "Relief and Rescue Unite as One" from the Perspective of the Changing Concept of Disaster Report in China', in Xiaotao Liang (Ed.), *Convulsion: Media Reflections*, (Beijing: China Democracy and Legal System Publishing House, 2008), pp. 175–182.

Li, Xiaoping, '"Focus" (Jiaodian Fangtan) and the Changes in the Chinese Television Industry', *Journal of Contemporary China*, 11(30), (2002), pp. 17–34.

Li, Xiguang and Zhou, Qingan, *Soft Power and Global Communication*, (Beijing: Tsinghua University Press, 2005).

Li, Zhen, 'Exert Positive Influence of Media Supervision', *TV Research*, 11, (2001), pp. 9–10.

Liang, Jianhui, 'Degree, the Critical Point for the Success of "Focus"', *TV Research*, 1, (2000), pp. 50–52.

Liang, Xiaotao, 'Record of History', in Xiaotao Liang (Ed.), *Convulsion: Media Reflections*, (Beijing: China Democracy and Legal System Publishing House, 2008), p. XVI.

Lin, Rupeng, Wu, Fei and Feng, Shaowen, 'The Rebuilding of National Image in the Reports of Sudden Public Events', in Xiaotao Liang, (Ed.), *Convulsion: Media Reflections*, (Beijing: China Democracy and Legal System Publishing House, 2008), pp. 71–79.

Link, Perry, 'Will SARS Transform China's Chiefs?' *TIMEasia Magazine*, 28 April 2003, at http://www.time.com/time/asia/covers/501030505/viewpoint.html, accessed on 27 July 2010.

Liu, Bo, 'An Overview of Chinese Press Development in 1996', in *China Journalism Yearbook 1997*, (Beijing: China Journalism Yearbook Press, 1997), pp. 37–40.

Liu, Haibei, 'How Will Focus Come out of Plateau', *TV Research*, 4, (2002), pp. 32–34.

Liu, Yunshan, 'Talk on the Visit to CCTV Staff ', *TV Research*, 5, (2003), p. 6.

Lord, Carnes, *Losing Hearts and Minds? Public Diplomacy and Strategic Influence in the Age of Terror*, (London: Praeger Security International, 2006).

Lu, Di and Gao, Fei, 'The Power of Media and Its Inspirations', in Xiaotao Liang (Ed.), *Convulsion: Media Reflections*, (Beijing: China Democracy and Legal System Publishing House, 2008), pp. 87–91.

Lu, Keng, 'Press Control in "New China" and "Old China"', in Lee, Chin-Chuan, (Ed.), *China's Media, Media's China*, (Boulder, Colorado: Westview Press, 1994), pp. 147–161.

Lu, Yiyi, *Non-Governmental Organisations in China*, (Oxford: Routledge, 2008).

Luo, Ming, 'When TV Encounters Disasters', in Xiaotao Liang (Ed.), *Convulsion: Media Reflections*, (Beijing: China Democracy and Legal System Publishing House, 2008), pp. XI–XVIII.

Lye, Liang Fook and Yang, Yi, 'The Chinese Leadership and the Internet', *EAI Background Brief No. 467*, (2009), at http://www.eai.nus.edu.sg/BB467.pdf, accessed on 20 July 2010.

McCormick, Barrat L., 'Recent Trends in Mainland China's Media: Political Implications of Commercialisation', *Issues and Studies*, 39(1)/38(4), (2003/2002), pp. 175–215.

Mott, Glenn, 'A New Media in China: More Information, More Control', *The American Society of News Editors*, (2010), at http://asne.org/article_view/articleid/779/a-new-media-in-china-more-information-more-control.aspx, accessed on 21 July 2010.

'Murdoch wins China cable TV deal', BBC News, 20 December 2001, at http://news.bbc.co.uk/1/hi/entertainment/1721160.stm, accessed on 21 March 2010.

'National TV Foreign Propaganda Co-operation Conference 2006 in Yunnan', at http://www.cctv.com/tvguide/special/wyh/20060713/103251.shtml, accessed on 16 January 2009.

'Notice on Further Strengthening the Radio, Film and Television "Going out Project Management', at http://www.chinasarft.gov.cn/articles/2004/10/26/20070919141825580844.html, accessed on 13 March 2008.

Nye, Joseph, *Soft Power, The Means to Success in World Politics*, (New York: Public Affairs, 2004).

'Official Sacked for Costly Lifestyle', *China Daily*, 21 January 2009.

'Online Supervision Offers Fresh Dynamic Mechanism for the Fight against Corruption and the Construction of Social Harmony', *People's Daily*, 3 February 2009.

'Online Video Exposes Corrupt Officials', *Straits Times*, 24 February 2009.

Pan, Philip P., 'Making Waves, Carefully, on the Air in China', *Washington Post*, 19 September, 2005, A01.

Pei, Minxin, 'The Political Impact of the Economic Crisis on China', 29 May 2009, at http://www.carnegieendowment.org/publications/index.cfm?fa=view&id=23185, accessed on 14 July 2010.

Pei, Minxin, *China's Trapped Transition*, (Cambridge, MA: Harvard University Press, 2006).

Polumbaum, Judy, 'Striving for Predictability: The Bureaucratization of Media Management in China', in Chin-Chuan Lee (Ed.), *China's*

Media, Media's China, (Boulder, Colorado: Westview Press, 1994), pp. 113–128.

Pomfret, John, 'SARS, a Political Issue in China', *Washington Post*, 23 May 2003.

'Premier Wen Talks Online with the Public', *China Daily*, 20 February 2009.

'President Hu Jintao Asks Officials to Better Cope with the Internet', *Xinhuawang*, 24 January 2007, at http://news.xinhuanet.com/english/2007-01/24/content_5648674.htm, accessed on 20 July 2010.

"Publicity", at http://www.chinasarft.gov.cn/catalogs/gldt/20070903170530620224.html, accessed on 30 June 2008.

Quand La Chine Déblogue, Le Monde, 3 July 2008, at http://chinedesblogs.blog.lemonde.fr/2008/07/03/emeutesdewengan20-quand-la-chine-supgrade/, accessed on 30 March 2009.

Rotberg, Robert I., 'Failed States, Civil Wars and Nation Building', in Robert J. Art and Robert Jarvis, (Eds.), *International Politics: Enduring Concepts and Contemporary Issues*, 7th Edition, (New York: Pearson Longman, 2005).

Schell, Orville, 'A Lonely Voice in China is Critical on Rights and Reform', *New York Times*, 24 January 2004, E45.

Schramm, W., *Men, Messages, and Media: A Look at Human Communication*, (New York: Harper and Row, 1973).

Seib, Phillip, 'New Media and Prospects for Democratisation', in Phillip Seib, (Ed.), *New Media and the New Middle East*, (Palgrave Macmillan: 2007), pp. 1–18.

Shambaugh, David, 'The Road to Prosperity', *Time*, 28 September 2009, at http://www.time.com/time/magazine/article/0,9171,1924366-3,00.html, accessed on 22 October 2009.

Shambaugh, David, *China's Communist Party: Atrophy and Adaptation*, (Washington, DC and Berkeley: Woodrow Wilson Center Press and University of California Press, 2008).

Shao, Peiren and Pan, Xianghui, 'The Inherent Linkage between Crises and Media System Innovation Reviewed from the Wenchuan Earthquake', in Xiaotao Liang (Ed.), *Convulsion: Media Reflections*, (Beijing: China Democracy and Legal System Publishing House, 2008), pp. 116–125.

Shi, Tongyu, 'The Significance and Value of CCTV's Live Coverage of the Earthquake', *China Radio and TV Academic Journal*, 7, (2008), pp. 64–66.

Shirk, Susan L., *China: Fragile Superpower*, (New York: Oxford University Press, 2007).

Shue, Vivienne, 'Legitimacy Crisis in China?' in Peter Hays, Gries and Stanley Rosen (Eds.), *State and Society in 21st-Century China: Crisis, Contention, and Legitimation*, (New York: RoutledgeCurzon, 2004), pp. 24–49.

Simon, Roger, *Gramsci's Political Thought: An Introduction*, (London: Lawrence & Wishart Ltd., 1991).

Sparks, Colin and Reading, Anna, 'Understanding Media Change in East Central Europe', *Media, Culture and Society*, 16(2), (1994), pp. 243–270.

'Speech Delivered While on a Visit to the People's Daily', *People's Daily*, June 2009 at http://media.people.com.cn/GB/40606/7409348. html, accessed on 3 July 2009.

Starck, Kenneth and Xu, Yu, 'Loud Thunder, Small Raindrops: The Reform Movement and the Press in China', *International Communication Gazette*, 42, (December 1988), pp. 143–159.

'Statistical Survey Report on Internet Development in China', from the website of the China Internet Network Information Centre (CNNIC) at http://www.cnnic.cn/uploadfiles/pdf/2010/3/15/142705.pdf, accessed 10 July 2010.

Sun, Jiazheng, 'Make Efforts to Run Well the News Commentary Programme; Enhance the Level of the Guidance of Public Opinion', *TV Research*, 10, (1995), pp. 4–10.

Sun, Zhengyi and Liu, Tingting, '2004: A Retrospective View of China's News Media in 2004, Part I', at http://www.people.com.cn/GB/14677/40606/3038055.html, accessed on 20 June 2010.

Tao, T., 'Media Stars in Its Own Investment Extravaganza', *Shanghai Star*, http://www.chinadaily.com.cn/star/2001/0614/bz10-1.html, quoted and accessed 6 March 2003 by Chengju Huang, 'Trace the Stones in Crossing the River: Media Structural Changes in Post-WTO China', *International Communication Gazette*, 69, (October 2007), pp. 413–430.

The Blue Book Research Team, 'Survey of the Development of Press in China', in Cui, Baoguo, (Ed.), *Blue Book of China's Media*, (China: Social Sciences Academic Press, 2009), pp. 89–96.

'The Chinese Media: More Autonomous and Diverse — Within Limits', from the website of the Central Intelligence Agency, USA, at https://www.cia.gov/library/center-for-the-study-of-intelligence/csi-publications/books-and-monographs/thechinese-media-more-autono mous-and-diverse-within-limits/copy_of_1.htm#rft21, accessed on 15 July 2010.

Tsang, Steve, 'Consultative Leninism: China's New Political Framework?' The China Policy Discussion Paper 58, 2010, School of Contemporary Chinese Studies, University of Nottingham, at http://nottingham.ac.uk/cpi/documents/discussionpapers/discussion-paper-58-consultative-leninism.pdf, accessed 10 April 2010.

Tsui, Lokman, 'The Panopticon as the Antithesis of a Space of Freedom: Control and Regulation of the Internet in China', *China Information*, 17, (October 2003), pp. 65–82.

Wang, Hongying and Tan, Honggang, 'Chinese Media and the Judicial System under Soft Authoritarianism', at http://jpm.syr.edu/pdf/fellowpdfs/1_a.pdf, accessed on 10 August 2010.

Wang, Jing, '"Culture" as Leisure and "Culture" as Capital', *Positions: East Asia Cultures Critique*, 9(1), (2001), pp. 69–104.

Wang, Lianhe, 'The Logic of Publication Regulations under Authoritarianism', *Research on Publication and Distribution*, (3), (2005).

Wang, Ping and Shen Zhi Rui, 'Comrade Li Changchun Visited CCTV Staff', *TV Research*, 5 (2003), p. 4.

Wang, Shaoguang, 'Changing Models of China's Policy Agenda Setting, *Modern China*, 34(1), (2008), pp. 56–87.

Wang, Xu, 'To Occupy the Commanding Ground of Public Opinion', in Xiaotao Liang (Ed.), *Convulsion: Media Reflections*, (Beijing: China Democracy and Legal System Publishing House, 2008), pp. 106–115.

Wang, Xudong, 'Perspectives on the Selection of Topics by "Focus"', *TV Research*, 9, (1994), pp. 13–16.

'Wang Yang and Huang Huahua again Send Their Wishes to Netizens', *Southern Metropolitan Daily*, 20 January 2009.

Wang, Zhengxu, 'Political Trust in China: Forms and Causes', in Lynn T. White (Ed.), *Legitimacy: Ambiguities of Political Success or Failure in East and Southeast Asia*, (Singapore: World Scientific, 2005), pp. 113–139.

Weber, Max, *The Theory of Social and Economic Organization*, Talcott Parsons (Ed.), (New York: The Free Press, 1964).

Wen, Jin, 'The Way of Sina — Internet in China', paper delivered at the China Media Festival, School of Oriental and African Studies, London, 18–19 June 2008.

White, Lynn T., 'Introduction — Dimensions of Legitimacy', in Lynn T. White (Ed.), *Legitimacy: Ambiguities of Political Success or Failure in East and Southeast Asia*, (Singapore: World Scientific, 2005), pp. 1–28.

White, Lynn T., 'All the News: Structure and Politics in Shanghai's Reform Media', in Chin-Chuan Lee, (Ed.), *Voices of China: The Interplay of Politics and Journalism*, (New York: The Guildford Press, 1990), pp. 88–110.

Womack, Brantly, 'Editor's Introduction: Media and the Chinese Public', *Chinese Sociology and Anthropology*, 18, (1986), pp. 6–53.

Xin, Wen, 'Ten Years' Exploration and Pursuit: Review on CCTV's Reform', *TV Research*, 4, (1996), 10–21.

Yan, Lianjun, 'Positive Reports and Media Supervision', *TV Research*, 10, (1996), pp. 20–22.

Yan, Shi, 'Follow the Basic Lines, Be Dauntless in Reform', *TV Research*, 8, (1995), p. 7–11.

Yang, Dali, *Remaking the Chinese Leviathan: Market Transition and the Politics of Governance in China*, (Palo Alto: Stanford University Press, 2004).

Yang, Fei, "China Readjusts the Press Market; Many Papers are to be Stopped", 2003, at http://www.people.com.cn/GB/14677/14737/22036/1997395.html, accessed on 15 March 2008.

Yang, Gangyi, 'Focus on Iraq War special coverage-CCTV4', *TV Research*, 6, (2003), pp. 10–12.

Yang, Guobin, *The Power of the Internet in China: Citizen Activism Online*, (New York: Columbia University, 2009).

Yang, Rui, 'Transformation Complex of Chinese Media', paper presented at the conference "Post-Olympic China: Globalisation and Sustainable Development after Three Decades of Reform", 19–21 November 2008, School of Contemporary Chinese Studies, The University of Nottingham, UK.

Yang, Weiguang, 'Be Worthy of the Great Trust from the Party and the People, Offer More and Better Programmes', *TV Research*, 10, (1996), pp. 4–7.

Ye, Fengying, 'Devastating Earthquake: Rebuilding the Media Image of China Central Television', in Xiaotao Liang (Ed.), *Convulsion*, (Beijing: China Democracy and Legal System Publishing House, 2008), pp. 283–291.

Ying, Yungong, 'Correctly Understand and Grasp the Relationship between Media Supervision, Reform, Development and Stability', *TV Research*, 10, (1997), pp. 16–19.

Yu, Keping, 'Let Democracy Serve China; Economic Crisis can also be Political Opportunities', at http://npc.people.com.cn/GB/28320/160692/166630/9897870.html, accessed on 18 September 2009.

Yuan, Yan, 'Dilemma and the Way Out for County-level TV Stations during the Reform Era', *Journalism University*, 80(2), (2004), pp. 56–62.

Zeng, Jianhui, *Melting the Ice, Building a Bridge and Breaking through*, (Beijing: Wuzhou Publishing House, 2006).

Zhan, Xinhui and Yang, Chunlan, 'News Websites between Traditional Functions and Changes', *Media*, 10, (2006), at http://big5.xinhuanet.com/gate/big5/news.xinhuanet.com/newmedia/2006-10/10/content_5184606.htm, accessed on 10 August 2008.

Zhang, Junchang, 'Major Breakthrough and Reflections Brought by Reports on Catastrophic Emergencies', in Xiaotao Liang, (Ed.), *Convulsion*, (Beijing: China Democracy and Legal System Publishing House, 2008), pp. 55–63.

Zhang, Lin, 'On the Strategies of News Report on CCTV International Channels', *Modern Communication*, 124(5), (2003), pp. 31–34.

Zhang, Xiaoling, 'From Totalitarianism to Hegemony: The Reconfiguration of the Party-State and the Transform of Chinese Communication', *Journal of Contemporary China*, 20(68), (2011), pp. 103–115.

Zhang, Xiaoling, 'China's International Broadcasting: The Case of CCTV International', in Jay Wang (Ed.), *Soft Power in China: Public Diplomacy through Communication*, (Palgrave MacMillan, 2010), pp. 57–71.

Zhang, Xiaoling, 'Seeking Effective Public Space: Chinese Media at the Local Level', *China: An International Journal*, 5(1), (2007), pp. 55–77.

Zhang, Xiaoling, 'Breaking News, Media Coverage and "Citizen's Right to Know" in China', *Journal of Contemporary China*, 16(53), (2007), pp. 535–545.

Zhang, Xiaoling, 'Reading between the Headlines: SARS, *Focus* and TV Current Affairs Programmes in China', *Media, Culture and Society*, 28(5), (2006), pp. 715–738.

Zhang, Wei, 'National Conference on Propaganda Work in Beijing; Li Changchun Attended the Conference and Delivered a Speech', from the website of the Xinhua News Agency, 4 January 2010, at http://news.xinhuanet.com/politics/2010-01/04/content_12752787.htm, accessed on 15 July 2010.

Zhang, Zhixin, 'Reflections on Comrade Jiang Zemin's Work on Journalism', *TV Research*, (5), (2001), p. 20.

Zhao, Huayong, 'Respect Laws Governing News and Perfect Emergency Contingency System', in Xiaotao Liang (Ed.), *Convulsion*, (Beijing: ChinaDemocracy and Legal System Publishing House, 2008), pp. I–X.

Zhao Huayong, 'Stick to the Right Orientation and Go All out to Ensure High Quality in News Channel', *TV Research*, 5, (2003), pp. 9–10.

Zhao, Huayong, 'Greet the 16th Congress of the Chinese Communist Party with New Achievements — Report at CCTV Annual Conference 2002 (abstract)', *TV Research*, 3 (2002), pp. 8–13.

Zhao, Suisheng, 'Chinese Foreign Policy in Hu's Second Term: Coping with Political Transition Abroad', paper presented at the FPRI Asia Program's conference on *Elections, Political Transitions and Foreign Policy in East Asia*, Philadelphia, 14 April 2008.

Zhao, Yuezhi, *Communication in China: Political Economy, Power and Conflict*, (Lanham: Rowman & Littlefield Publishers Inc., 2008).

Zhao, Yuezhi, 'From Commercialisation to Conglomeration: The Transformation of the Chinese Press within the Orbit of the Party State', *Journal of Communication*, 50(2), (Spring 2000), pp. 3–26.

Zhao, Yuezhi, 'The Rich, the Laid-off, and the Criminal in Tabloid Tales: Read All About It!' in Perry Link, Richard Madsen and Pauil G. Pickwicz, (Eds.), *Popular China: Unofficial Culture in a Globalising Society*, (Lanham: Rowman & Littlefield, 2002), pp. 111–135.

Zhao, Yuezhi, *Media, Market, and Democracy in China: Between the Party Line and the Bottom Line*, (Champaign: University of Illinois Press, 1998).

Zhao, Yuezhi and Guo, Zhenzhi, 'Television in China: History, Political Economy, and Ideology', in Janet Wasco, (Ed.), *A Companion to Television*, (Blackwell, 2005), pp. 521–539.

Zheng, Wenhua, Gao, Dingbo and Yan, Yue, 'Report for Life: Actively Guide International Public Opinion', *Overseas Communication*, 6, (2008), pp. 22–24.

Zheng, Yongnian, *The Chinese Communist Party as Organisational Emperor: Culture, Reproduction and Transformation*, (Oxford, New York: Routledge, 2010).

Zheng, Yongnian, *Technological Empowerment: The Internet, State, and Society in China*, (Palo Alto: Stanford University Press, 2007).

Zheng, Yongnian and Lye, Liang Fook, 'Political Legitimacy in Reform China', in Lynn T. White, (Ed.), *Legitimacy: Ambiguities of Political Success or Failure in East and Southeast Asia*, (Singapore: World Scientific, 2005), pp. 183–214.

Zhou, Hong, 'On the Effectiveness of Media Supervision', *TV Research*, 9 (1999), p. 16.

Zhou, Yongming, 'Privatizing Control: Internet Café in China', in Li Zhang and Aihwa Ong, *Privatising China, Socialism from Afar*, (Ithaca, N.Y.: Cornell University Press, 2008), pp. 214–229.

Zhou, Xiaopu, 'The 2008 Dialectics', in Xiaotao Liang (Ed.), *Convulsion: Media Reflections*, (Beijing: China Democracy and Legal System Publishing House, 2008), pp. 7–16.

Zhu, Hong, 'Experiences from the 30 Years of Reform in TV Industry', in Cui, Baoguo, (Ed.), *Blue Book of China's Media*, (China: Social Sciences Academic Press, 2009), pp. 203–207.

Zhu, Rongji, 'Report on the Work of the Government', at the 10th National People's Congress, March 5, at http://news.xinhuanet.com/english/2003-03/19/content_787742.htm, accessed on 2 April 2007.

Zhu, Ying, *Television in Post-Reform China: Serial Dramas, Confucian Leadership and Global Television Market*, (London: Routledge, 2008).

Zhu, Yujun and Niu, Guangxia, 'A Study on the Humanization Process of Television Communication in the Respect of Live Broadcast of the Wenchuan Earthquake', in Xiaotao Liang (Ed.), *Convulsion*, (Beijing: China Democracy and Legal System Publishing House, 2008), pp. 205–214.

Index